HOW POPULAR MUSICIANS LEARN

For

Bernie Holland, Terry Ollis, Rob Burns, Nanette Welmans,
Brent Keefe, Peter Williams, Will Cragg, Steve Popplewell,
Andy Brooks, Simon Bourke, Michael Whiteman, Emily Dicks,
Richard Dowdall and Leo Hardt

How Popular Musicians Learn

A Way Ahead for Music Education

LUCY GREEN
London University, Institute of Education

Ashgate

Aldershot • Burlington USA • Singapore • Sydney

Published by
Ashgate Publishing Limited
Gower House
Croft Road
Aldershot
Hants GU11 3HR
England

Ashgate Publishing Company
131 Main Street
Burlington, VT 05401–5600 USA

Ashgate website: http://www.ashgate.com

British Library Cataloguing in Publication Data
Green, Lucy
   How popular musicians learn : a way ahead for music
   education. - (Ashgate popular and folk music series)
   1. Popular music - Instruction and study
   I. Title
   781.6'3'071

Library of Congress Cataloging-in-Publication Data
Green, Lucy.
      How popular musicians learn : a way ahead for music education / Lucy Green, London
   University, Institute of Education.
         p. cm. -- (Ashgate popular and folk music series)
      Includes bibliographical references (p.) and index.
      ISBN 0-7546-0338-5
      1. Music--Instruction and study--England. 2. Popular music--Instruction and
   study--England. I. Title. II. Series.

   MT3.E5 G74 2001
   781.64'071--dc21

                                                                        2001033362

ISBN 0 7546 0338 5

Typeset by PCS Mapping & DTP, Newcastle upon Tyne
Printed in Great Britain by MPG Books Ltd., Bodmin, Cornwall

Contents

General Editor's preface

The upheaval that occurred in musicology during the last two decades of the twentieth century has created a new urgency for the study of popular music alongside the development of new critical and theoretical models. A relativistic outlook has replaced the universal perspective of modernism (the international ambitions of the 12-note style); the grand narrative of the evolution and dissolution of tonality has been challenged, and emphasis has shifted to cultural context, reception and subject position. Together, these have conspired to eat away at the status of canonical composers and categories of high and low in music. A need has arisen, also, to recognize and address the emergence of crossovers, mixed and new genres, to engage in debates concerning the vexed problem of what constitutes authenticity in music and to offer a critique of musical practice as the product of free, individual expression.

Popular musicology is now a vital and exciting area of scholarship, and the Ashgate Popular and Folk Music series aims to present the best research in the field. Authors will be concerned with locating musical practices, values and meanings in cultural context, and may draw upon methodologies and theories developed in cultural studies, semiotics, poststructuralism, psychology and sociology. The series will focus on popular musics of the twentieth and twenty-first centuries. It is designed to embrace the world's popular musics from Acid Jazz to Zydeco, whether high tech or low tech, commercial or non-commercial, contemporary or traditional.

Professor Derek B. Scott
Chair of Music
University of Salford

Visit Project Pop: http://www.salford.ac.uk/FDTLpop/welcome.htm

General Editor's preface

Foreword

May we trust the inexpressible benevolence of the creative impulse.

The formal musical education available to one of my generation (born 1946) was clear: the music of Old (preferably Dead) White Guys From Europe was the only music to be taken seriously. In the 1960s, to wear long hair signified proof of delinquent musical talent, aberrant moral values and an implicit threat to society; the electric guitar was not quite a proper musical instrument; and improvisation – or 'making it up as you go along' – not quite an intentional musical act.

Today, the world of music is a world of musics, each with their own traditions in the transmission of musical discipline, performance conventions, repertoire and usages of music, both sacred and secular. Customarily, the aspirant player seeks an 'elder' in their tradition for instruction, whether formal or informal. The European conservatory is only one form of response, at a particular time in a particular culture, to addressing this need.

Dr Lucy Green's work deserves a wider readership than academics and music educators. Her first two books are directed primarily towards an academic readership, but they are also valuable to a working player willing to engage with the vocabulary of academe. I read *Music On Deaf Ears* in the Starbucks opposite the Beverley Center, Los Angeles, while on tour with King Crimson in June 1995; and *Music, Gender, Education* in the coffee shop of the University Hotel in Seattle during May 1998, while recording Bill Rieflin's 'Birth Of A Giant' and Rieflin-Fripp-Gunn's 'The Repercussions Of Angelic Behaviour'.

Dr Green's arguments on fetishization in those books have since moved into Crimspeak. On the US G3 tour of 1997, in the staff restaurant of the Las Vegas Hard Rock Hotel, engineer and producer R. Chris Murphy learnt this wonderful phrase: 'Why do you feel the need to radically fetishize the inherent and delineated meanings of Robert's music?' Chris would, on occasion, approach fans who were more interested in autography than music, and present his question. This present book is more immediately inviting, available and of direct practical interest to the working player in popular music, particularly those who also instruct students.

Music is a quality organized in sound and in time. The musicness of music is eternal, the forms of musical organization evolve within a culture. How we acquire a taste for music is largely determined by our cultural environment, including our educational institutions. But fundamentally, we are called by the music that calls to us. Music works where it will, where it can, where it is welcomed. The musician, with discipline, creates a bridge for music to enter our world. Some of the bridges are funky, some constructed from the vernacular, some are superb statements of form which persist through time, some are commentaries directed to the narrow moment. Sometimes music leans over and takes a musician into its confidence. Then, music directly instructs its representative in that time and place as to what is required, and a tradition is born, renewed or restored.

Within any culture, music speaks through many voices, in many dialects. In popular culture, the musician calls on the highest part in all of us. In mass culture, the musician addresses the lower parts of what we are. In mass culture, our singers shout what we want to hear. In popular culture, our musicians sing to us in our own voice. May that voice be true.

Robert Fripp
2001

Acknowledgements

Charlie Ford, who was with me every step of the way. His input to the book is extensive, and amounts to much more than reading and commenting upon two complete drafts, for that was preceded by over twenty years of talking about music, listening to music and making music together. His experiences as a young popular musician in the past, and as a classically trained musicologist have by those means entered the core of my discussions.

The series editor Derek Scott, who carefully and critically read the penultimate draft, and provided encouragement from start to finish of the project.

Rock guitarist Robert Fripp who unfailingly expressed his support during an email conversation over a lengthy period, when he read no less than three drafts of the book, and then took time away from his demanding touring schedule to provide the Foreword.

My colleagues and friends at the London University Institute of Education, Keith Swanwick, Charles Plummeridge, Robert Kwami, Anton Franks and Pauline Adams; those at other universities, Sarah Hennessy, Sara Cohen, Vic Gammon and Kyoko Koizumi; my brother Tim Green; and my friend Jen Moseley, all of whom read and commented upon all or part of the text with care, encouraged me and generously gave me many kinds of ideas, information and materials.

Dave Laing who gave me a variety of materials, information and references, and discussed the project on many occasions with his customary acumen and vast knowledge of popular music; Donald Ellman who constructively brought the perspectives of an experienced classical piano teacher and lecturer to bear on an early proposal; and Jan Banks who helped me to understand more than I can say.

Jilly Dolphin who carefully transcribed hours of interviews with musicians and questionnaire responses from teachers, as well as providing administrative and moral support in a host of other ways.

Rachel Lynch, who was consistently courteous and efficient in seeing the book through all its publication rites of passage, and everyone else who made things run so smoothly at Ashgate.

Chris Atton, Julian Costello, Anton Franks, Jane Kirby, Allan Moore and Sarah Moore for kindly putting me in touch with musicians.

The teachers who responded to a questionnaire many years ago in 1982, and those who responded to another one in 1998, often giving far more help and information than requested, in the spirit of commitment to their work, which is typical of teachers.

A number of people for generously making available photocopies of articles, dissertations and other useful materials, including Anna Barnett, Charlie Beale, Mary Ann Clawson, Maria Efpatridou, Heloisa Feichas, John Finney, Simon

Frith, Eva Georgii-Hemmingway, Alex Lamont, Pete Martin, Louise Morgan, Keith Negus, John O'Flynn and Norton York.

Others who were kind enough to provide references and information, including Barbara Bradby, Pam Burnard, Zoe Dionyssiou, Katy Gainham, Jo Glover, David Hargreaves, Adrian North, Suzie O'Neill, Dave Russell and Jason Toynbee.

The London University Institute of Education which met the costs of the empirical work and enabled me to have a term's study leave in the autumn of 1999; not to mention the colleagues, already named above, who covered my teaching and administration duties during that time.

A number of students and colleagues who made insightful and constructive comments on this work when I presented it, in various stages of development, at seminars and conferences in the UK and elsewhere.

Most importantly, the fourteen musicians who talked to me about their learning experiences, sent me tapes of their music, welcomed me to their gigs, responded to a draft of the book and sent me letters and updates on their musical involvement. Their experiences, ideas and values, their music, form the backbone of this book, which I humbly dedicate to them and their future music-making.

Chapter 1

What is it to be musically educated?

Without suggesting any romantic visions of 'Merrie England', in *Tudor Music* Wulstan (1985) depicts a sixteenth-century land where music-making was a normal part of everyday life. Hired musicians played and sang for the wealthy, travelling minstrels did so for the poor, and City Waits made music for everyone within earshot on every hour or even every quarter-hour of the day and night (pp. 41–3). Monasteries and convents placed music high in their rites, and towards the end of the century music was heard even in the change-ringing of church bells. Streets resounded with cries that were echoed in both the art music and the 'small and popular musickes' of the day (p. 40). Rich and poor made music for themselves in the home, catches and rounds were sung in catch clubs and later glee clubs, and folk songs abounded in all sorts of situations. During the seventeenth century, as A.L. Lloyd describes it,

> in country inns song-sheets were pasted up on fireplace surrounds and high bench-ends for the benefit of carters, ploughmen and others ... Milkmaids would paper the walls of byres and dairies with broadsides, and learn off the ballads as they milked and churned ... The sailor ocean-bound would paste underside the lid of his sea-chest new songs to try out on his shipmates ... In very poor districts it was not unusual for two families to club together to buy a penny ballad-sheet.
>
> (1967, p. 30)

Ehrlich (1985) reveals the bustle of music-making and music teaching that went on in eighteenth and nineteenth-century middle- and upper-class homes. Meanwhile in rural churches, gallery bands of artisans and farm workers provided music for the services on winds and strings (Gammon 1981). At the end of the nineteenth century, when educated folklorists imagined they were saving folksong by collecting its remnants on paper, the urban industrial song and 'that "most repulsive and most insidious" of enemies, music-hall song', as it was described by the composer Hubert Parry, were in full sway (Harker 1985, p. 170). Dave Russell (1997) depicts a society that resonated with music-making, from the working-class brass bands of the north, to the working- and middle-class choral societies who performed popular classics such as Handel's *Messiah*, which even the audience might join in:

> Britain in the Victorian and Edwardian periods was an extraordinarily musical place. The home, the street, the public house and the public park were almost as

much musical centres as the concert hall and the music hall. A communal or civic event was a poor affair indeed if not dignified by music. An Italian government official visiting Britain in 1897 reported that 'there are few countries in the world where music is made the object of such enthusiastic worship. It might almost be said that music is a vital and indispensable element of English life'.

(Russell 1997, p. 1)

At the end of the twentieth century Finnegan (1989) took the lid off the vast array of music-making that was occurring, from the country and western club to the local symphony orchestra, in the English town of Milton Keynes.

Communal participation in music-making is perhaps least renowned in many European and other so-called Western parts of the world. Ethnomusicologists and anthropologists of music have observed societies and communities in which virtually the entire population is, from early childhood, habitually involved in music-making. Blacking's *How Musical Is Man?* (1976) provides a classic and impassioned discussion of this phenomenon, which is succinctly illustrated by Messenger's account of the Anang Ibibo people of Nigeria:

We were constantly amazed at the musical abilities displayed by these people, especially by the children who, before the age of five, can sing hundreds of songs, both individually and in choral groups and, in addition, are able to play several percussion instruments and have learned dozens of intricate dance movements calling for incredible muscular control. We searched in vain for the 'non-musical' person.

(Messenger 1958, pp. 20–21, cited in Sloboda *et al.* 1994, pp. 349–51)

In spite of all this activity, past and present, musicians, music teachers and lecturers in the West and many other parts of the world, who are themselves deeply immersed in social networks where regular music-making takes place, will find it hard to believe that the overall proportion of people actively involved in music-making today is tiny. The evidence suggests that self-entertainment through vernacular music-making, as well as amateur performance of classical or 'art' music, were more common in the past than at the beginning of the twenty-first century, although we do not know exactly how extensive the involvement was. But we do know that, for example, in Britain today only around 1 per cent of the adult population is reckoned to be an active amateur musician, and even fewer to be a professional musician (Everitt 1997, p. 37; NMC 1996, p. 2).[1] Much larger proportions of children have the opportunity to make music as a regular part of their school work or by taking part in concerts organized by schools and youth music organizations, and many have the benefit of specialist instrumental or vocal tuition. However, as children get older, more and more of them drop out of such activities, and the vast majority give them up altogether. Many other nations and regions of the world are in similar positions, and even in areas where relatively strong music-making practices survive, participation is beginning to undergo a gradual decline (Nwezi 1999, p. 77; also see Oehrle 1991, p. 164).

As distinct from making music, a huge proportion of today's global population *listens* to music. Differences between making and listening to music are not necessarily clear-cut. For example, many people 'sing along' or drum the table whilst listening to music on the radio, or take part in karaoke, without considering themselves to be 'musicians'. Nor is listening to music a purely passive undertaking even when it does not involve such joining in (see, for example, Middleton 1990, pp. 93–8). But it is nonetheless reasonable to draw a distinction between music-making and music-listening, in so far as the former is geared mainly to the production of music, and the latter mainly to its reception.

The relative paucity of music-makers by contrast with the plenitude of music-listeners today is not the result of pure chance. Sound recording and reproduction technology, the expansion of the music industry and mass media into major international concerns, and the Internet have made music ever more accessible, widespread and even unavoidable for the listener. But whilst the music industry and the media have increased music's availability, they have simultaneously dictated norms of performance and composition that result from such high levels of capital investment as to be virtually impossible for amateur musicians to attain. Most people are involved in music as consumers and fans, alienated from the majority of music-making activities, and operating instead as spectators on the sidelines of a game in which, if circumstances were different, many more could play a part. For some, whether or not they consider themselves to be musicians, the idea of being required to make music in front of, or even alongside other people, inspires little other than feelings of dread and embarrassment.

What music do most people listen to? Although the terms 'jazz', 'classical', 'popular' and 'traditional' music are marked by many overlaps and omissions, I will use them to depict the main music categories of the world, being more specific as and when the need arises. Most people agree that the term 'world music' is absurd, but it is nowadays almost unavoidable, and I will use it occasionally in addition to the four terms above, in its generally accepted sense to mean music of virtually any kind *except* Western classical music, Western popular music and jazz (always with exceptions to the general rule). Over 90 per cent of global sales of music recordings consist of popular music, including traditional forms such as folk and blues, with classical music making up only 3 or 4 per cent, and jazz even less; whilst figures for radio listening and concert attendance paint a very similar picture. For example, Table 1 shows percentages of world album sales by musical category for the year 1997. The figures vary from country to country but are nowhere radically dissimilar to the general picture given here. (See IFPI 2000 for further details.)[2]

During the last hundred and fifty years or so, many societies all over the world have developed complex systems of formal music education based on Western models, common to most of which are one or more of the following: educational institutions from primary schools to conservatories, partly involving or entirely dedicated to the teaching and learning of music; instrumental and vocal teaching programmes running either within or alongside these institutions; written curricula, syllabuses or explicit teaching traditions; professional teachers, lecturers or 'master musicians' who in most cases possess some form of relevant qualifications; systematic assessment mechanisms such as grade exams, national school exams or university exams; a variety of qualifications such as diplomas and degrees; music notation, which is sometimes regarded as peripheral, but more usually, central; and, finally, a body of literature, including texts on music, pedadogical texts and teaching materials. Although many musics have developed through formal education systems specific to themselves, as Campbell makes clear 'music education practices in much of the world today are based on Western models' (1991b, p. 205).

Table 1 Percentage global sales of albums, 1997

Pop	34.3	Other	1.4
Rock	25.7	Jazz	1.2
Dance	11.8	Children's	1.1
MOR/Easy listening	8.3	Spoken word	1.0
R&B	7.7	Reggae	0.8
Classical	3.6	Folk	0.7
Country	2.1	Blues	0.3

Source: Dane and Laing 1998, p. 10, based on BPI (1998)

The teaching strategies, curriculum content and values associated with Western-style formal music education derive from the conventions of Western classical music pedagogy. For a large portion of the twentieth century music education was almost exclusively concerned with classical instrumental tuition outside the classroom, and classical music appreciation and singing inside the classroom. At the beginning of the twentieth century and beyond, influential composers and music educators such as Cecil Sharp, Zoltán Kodály and Ruth Seeger worked to include European and North American folk music in the school curriculum. In various guises, most notably settings by classical composers, folk songs have had a place ever since. During the last three or four decades of the twentieth century in many countries, classroom music teachers, lecturers, and instrumental and vocal tutors from the primary school to the university underwent a gradual yet massive swing towards recognizing and incorporating an ever-increasing variety of musics in their work.

Jazz began its entrance into formal music education in the 1960s, first in the USA. By the end of the century it occupied a major position in several countries, especially at higher education levels, was supported by dedicated instrumental grade exams from beginner to advanced standard, and had spawned its own pedagogic texts and research literature.[3] Popular music first gained support from educators during the late 1960s. The subsequent development of new curricula materials and teaching strategies put it firmly in the curriculum of many countries during the 1980s, and soon afterwards it entered further, then higher education.[4] World music has taken up an increasingly central position in Western formal education, supported by publications and conferences under the auspices of the International Society for Music Education amongst other forums, and following influential arguments from scholars such as Christopher Small (1980, 1983, 1987). In England, where the research for this book was carried out, the swing towards musical diversity can be described as little short of overwhelming, and similar changes are taking place at different rates in other countries as far apart as the USA, Canada, Sweden, Japan, Brazil, Scotland, Hong Kong, Australia and Cyprus.[5]

Whilst formal music education has become increasingly available and diverse in content, it has not managed to stem the ebbing tide of involvement in music-making, particularly in the lives of adults after they have left formal education. Indeed, those societies and communities with the most highly developed formal music education systems often appear to contain the least active music-making populations.

Alongside or instead of formal music education there are always, in every society, other ways of passing on and acquiring musical skills and knowledge. These involve what I will refer to as 'informal music learning practices', which share few or none of the defining features of formal music education suggested earlier. Rather, within these traditions, young musicians largely teach themselves or 'pick up' skills and knowledge, usually with the help or encouragement of their family and peers, by watching and imitating musicians around them and by making reference to recordings or performances and other live events involving their chosen music. Amongst the variety of vernacular musics that are passed on in ways such as these, popular music has always formed a major category. Some popular musicians have never been offered any formal music education, but many of those who have been offered it have found it difficult or impossible to relate to the music and the musical practices involved (see, for example, Bennett 1980, Berkaak 1999, Cohen 1991, Finnegan 1989, Horn 1984, Lilliestam 1996 and later in this book). Overall, despite its widespread provision in a large number of countries, and notwithstanding the recent entrance of popular music into the formal arena, music education has had relatively little to do with the development of the majority of those musicians who have produced the vast proportion of the music which the global population listens to, dances to, identifies with and enjoys.

In referring to a distinction between 'formal music education' and 'informal music learning', I do not wish to imply that these are mutually exclusive social practices. They can be conceived rather as extremes existing at the two ends of a single pole. In some countries and some musics, formal and informal music education sit side by side in the nature of an apprenticeship training (see, for example, Berliner 1994, Nketia 1975, Merriam 1964). Many musicians who are mainly brought up in formal settings engage in some informal learning practices, such as teaching themselves to play an occasional popular song by ear and without any guidance. Similarly, many musicians who have learnt largely by informal means have experienced a certain amount of formal music education. Some musicians are 'bi-musical' (McCarthy 1997), having been brought up both formally and informally. Community music programmes such as youth employment training courses and traditions such as brass bands, gospel choirs or samba schools stand somewhere between the two spheres. Nonetheless, there are some significant differences between the formal and the informal approaches to music learning and teaching, the networks they involve and the attitudes and values that tend to accompany them. For a number of people the two rarely, or never, come into contact.

The literature on jazz and jazz education is increasingly concerned with questions about how jazz musicians learn in the informal realm, and to some extent, how this relates to formal education (Beale 2001, Berliner 1994, Monson 1996). Scholars working on world musics in education have likewise paid attention to the formal and informal teaching and learning practices that go along with a variety of world musics, and to their differences from and similarities with Western formal education (Campbell 1991b, Lundquist and Szego 1998).[6] Some music education researchers have also taken a close look at how children acquire musical skills and knowledge in their informal playground cultures (Campbell 1991a, 1998; Harwood 1998a and b; Marsh 1995, 1999; Wemyss 1999; Glover 2000).

By contrast, despite the prominent position of popular music in formal education, and even though most of the literature supporting it shows full *awareness* of the learning practices of popular musicians, detailed investigations by music education researchers into the specific *nature* of popular music learning practices or their relationship to formal music education have been relatively minimal.[7] Likewise, there is a small but well-established body of anthropological, ethnomusicological and sociological literature on popular musicians' social practices, most notably the significant contributions by Bennett (1980) and Cohen (1991).[8] However, although they do pay attention to the musicians' learning practices, and in some cases they consider such practices in relation to formal education, the main concerns of these texts lie elsewhere.

Therefore, although each and every popular musician knows how he or she went about their own learning, there is very little common knowledge or recognition of how popular musicians *in general* learn, or of the attitudes and values they share in relation to music learning. It is one thing to bring popular music into the music classroom, instrumental studio and lecture theatre, but if for want of knowledge and understanding the music is then stripped of the informal learning practices by virtue of which it has always been created and passed on, such an oversight could have the effect of introducing a peculiar 'educational' sub-style, bearing little resemblance to any music that exists in the world outside. As Björnberg stated in the early 1990s:

> The open, informal and collective learning processes at work in the everyday practices of many popular styles differ in several respects from those of institutional education. To what extent and how such 'alternative' learning processes can be used (and to what extent they are even necessary) in teaching popular music within music education institutions remains an urgent question.
>
> (1993, p. 76)

In addition, very little research has looked into popular musicians' perspectives as students within formal music education. Although we can hazard likely guesses, we have as yet only a slight knowledge and understanding of the reasons why so many past popular musicians, despite being highly motivated towards music-making, often turned away from both instrumental tuition and schooling. Similarly, whilst popular music has entered formal education during the last thirty or forty years, little is known about the impact that its presence is having on young, developing popular musicians: whether, for example, it has resulted either in changes to their informal practices or in improvements in their responses to formal education, especially in the school. Finally, a serious examination of popular music learning practices could surely provide formal music educators with some new insights and fresh perspectives, not only for teaching popular music itself, but for teaching music in general. If we continue to largely ignore popular musicians' experiences of both informal and formal music learning, educators could be depriving our students of precisely some of that spark which attracts and holds so many musicians and listeners to popular music every day.

The aims of this book are to examine the nature of popular musicians' informal learning practices, attitudes and values; to consider the extent to which these changed during the last forty years of the twentieth century; to come to an understanding of popular musicians' experiences in formal music education, and whether these too changed over the same time span; and finally, to explore some of the possibilities which informal popular music learning practices might offer to formal music education.

The book does not represent an attempt to 'convert' those people who already think that popular music is worthless, nor is it intended to compare and contrast the value of popular with classical or any other kind of music. Happily, these undertakings seem barely necessary nowadays, and there is anyway a fast-growing literature which, along with ample recordings, would soon put paid to any doubts a reader might have concerning the quality, skill and diversity that characterize popular music as a broadly defined field.[9] It is not questions concerning the value of *music* that I am interested in here, but questions concerning the benefits of different approaches to music *learning*, specifically focusing on popular music. I share the belief of many people that music and involvement in music-making are of unique value to humanity, and I do not intend to argue that point. Having been a music pupil and music student in school and higher education, a piano teacher, school music teacher and music education lecturer and writer within various formal settings all my life, I am also in no doubt that formal music education offers wonderful experiences and opportunities to millions of children and adults worldwide. But this should not prevent music educators from stepping back and re-assessing certain aspects: in this case, not the gifts offered by music education, but some of the possibilities that seem to be missing from it.

I have focused on particular sub-categories of popular music, engaged in by musicians from one country. Many of the findings and discussions are generalizable to a number of other vernacular musics in other times and places. But there are also some significant differences in, for example, instrumental and technological skills, group interaction, values, lifestyles and so on, not only between popular music, jazz and world musics, but between different sub-categories of popular music. Similarly, although the trend towards diversity in music education is widespread, the content of curricula and the nature of education systems are very varied across the world. In short, the issues raised in this study are by no means presented as being of universal applicability, but rather they bear comparison – of both similarities and differences – with other musics, other education systems and other parts of the world.

Research methods

The research begins from interviews, which took place between October 1998 and May 1999, with fourteen popular musicians living in and around London, aged from 50 to 15. In the first place I kept a fairly open mind as to how many musicians to interview, on the grounds that I would continue interviewing until the responses kept on raising the same issues without introducing new ones (or in more technical terms, until the data were repeating themselves). This began to happen relatively quickly, after only five or six interviews, and by the time I had completed fourteen I felt satisfied that the areas relevant to my research questions were sufficiently saturated. In addition, the findings corresponded with knowledge gained from two other areas: my own immersion in networks of practising musicians, music students, educators and musicologists, many of whom are in the popular music field; and existing academic research, particularly ethnographic studies of rock musicians such as those mentioned earlier by

Bennett (1980) and Cohen (1991), music education researchers, and others (see notes 7 and 8).

The reasons for choosing an age span from 50 to 15 were threefold. One was to enable an assessment of whether the musicians' informal learning practices had changed over the forty years or so that they covered. Another was to see how the attitudes and values of older and experienced professional musicians corresponded with those of younger and beginner musicians. The third was to compare the impact of the changes in formal music education that have occurred over the last forty years in England, especially the introduction of popular music, on the musicians' informal learning practices, attitudes and values. The oldest six musicians were aged from 50 to 27, which meant that their school years had spanned 1954 to 1985, that is, before radical changes occurred which challenged the central role of classical music in English music education during the mid-1980s. Two who were in-between the oldest and youngest groups were aged 23 and 21, and were therefore in attendance during one of the most turbulent periods of curriculum change, 1986 to 1990. The youngest six were aged 19 to 15, which meant they had entered secondary school from 1990 onwards, after the development of popular music instrumental grade exams and the official recognition of popular and 'world' music in the school curriculum. My main concentration is on instrumental tuition and school class-teaching, but I also looked into the musicians' experiences of applying to and taking further and higher education popular music courses from the early 1980s to 1999.

Other than the numbers and ages of the musicians, I applied only the following four selection criteria. First, the musicians should not be friends, or personally acquainted with me prior to the interview. Second, they should have attended school in England.[10] Third, those in the older age group should be professional or semi-professional popular musicians, and those in the younger age group should either play in a band (professional or otherwise), or be just about to start one. What exactly is meant by 'professional' in the case of musicians is far from clear. (See Everitt 1997, pp. 39–40, and Finnegan 1989 for good discussions of this issue.) Whereas a more precise notion of the musicians' status will emerge during the course of the book, for now, by 'professional', I mean that they make a living or part of a living from playing and in some cases also composing and/or arranging music. The expression 'semi-professional' refers to a variety of work contexts and can mean that 'sometimes you get paid and sometimes you don't', or that the musicians are paid, but not enough to live on even if they worked every night of the week.

Fourth, I selected musicians who were involved in what can best be described as 'Anglo-American guitar-based pop and rock music'. In many cases this extended outwards. The most experienced musicians in the sample had played anything from blues to charts pop, music for advertising, country, soul, progressive rock, punk, jazz, pantomime music and many other styles and sub-styles. The youngest musician was interested mainly in rap and soul (a slight exception there, which emerged during the interview), although the music he played was also reminiscent of London-based post-punk. The instruments they played formed the standard guitar group line-up of electric guitar, bass guitar and drums. Some of them played all of these, although everyone specialized. In addition, several played keyboards although no one specialized in that area; one was a professional vocalist and the youngest musician played the saxophone. Whereas the sample could reasonably be described as 'rock musicians', I have referred to them throughout by the more general and inclusive term 'popular musicians', except where the context demands more specificity.

I avoided interviewing rap artists, DJs or musicians involved in purely or largely synthesised/sampled fields of production, for reasons of focus as already explained. Musicians in such fields do not go about acquiring their musical skills and knowledge in the same ways as each other, or in the same ways as, say, rock musicians. It is probable that many basic learning practices as well as attitudes and values towards learning are shared across various sub-categories of these musics, with differences occurring mainly between the details and the amount of emphasis placed on different aspects of learning, rather than between altogether different 'kinds' of learning. As just one, very general example: solitary learning is likely to be prominent in connection with purely synthesised dance musics, but this does not mean that group learning practices are totally absent; by contrast, group learning is particularly vital for rapping, but this does not mean that rappers never learn in solitary ways; meanwhile rock learners are likely to employ both a solitary and a group approach in complimentary ways. Further research is needed to look into the precise learning practices of musicians in different areas of popular music. The research in this book is intended to provide simply one study, focusing on guitar-based popular and rock music, which is hopefully of interest in itself, and which can also be used for comparative purposes with other areas of popular music.

In Chapter 2 I will consider some of the characteristics of different categories of popular bands and the musicians who play in them, particularly the categories 'covers', 'function' and 'originals' bands, and 'freelance' and 'session' musicians. Although many players will at some stage in their lives experience more than one of these categories, the differences between them can be very significant in terms of not only the skills and knowledge required but also the self-conceptions and aspirations of the musicians involved. Most importantly, these skills, knowledge and self-conceptions all impinge to some extent upon the learning practices of the musicians. The oldest and most experienced musicians I interviewed had worked as session musicians, stable band members and in some cases, songwriters with a number of stars and famous bands. These include Joan Armatrading, Long John Baldry, Jeff Beck, Eric Burdon of the Animals, Ian Carr, Georgie Fame, David Gilmour of Pink Floyd, Isaac Hayes,

Hawkwind, Van Morrisson, Leo Sayer, the Stylistics, Danny Thompson, Pete Townshend of the Who, and many more. Others of the interviewees were primarily freelance musicians, some were in covers and function bands, one was in a tribute band and others were or had been in their own originals bands. The oldest five were or had been full-time professionals, the next six were semi-professionals, two of the three youngest were in their first rehearsal bands with schoolfriends, and the very youngest was planning to form a band soon.

I did not interview any major pop or rock 'stars'. Although their lives as star musicians may be rather different to the lives of the musicians I interviewed, there are no reasons to suppose that their *learning practices* have ever been significantly different. Furthermore, there is, of course, a category of stars who have risen to fame more by virtue of luck, looks, ambition and manipulation by the music industry than by virtue of any particular commitment to acquiring musicianship; and it is the acquisition of musicianship, rather than fame, that I am interested in. Behind these kinds of stars, there are nearly always session musicians, without whose skills the music would not be possible and very likely not commercially successful either. (Session musicians in popular music are not always themselves popular musicians, of course, as string sections and even entire orchestras of classical musicians often provide ballast on the recording. However, their position is very different from their colleagues in popular music, a topic which is illuminated in an interesting article by Brewer (2000).)

The circumstances and musical involvement from which each musician spoke are highly relevant to an understanding of their perspectives. It matters, for example, whether the speaker is a 51-year old session musician or a 15-year-old school pupil. However, rather than trailing laboriously through a description of each individual before starting my main project, I wish to allow a picture of the musicians to emerge gradually. (A summary profile of basic information about each one is provided in the Appendix, pp. 219–20.) There is no need for readers to memorize individuals' names and backgrounds, as I have tried to provide whatever information is necessary to the discussion as I go along. One aspect of presentation which may be helpful to bear in mind is that where I refer to more than one musician in order to illustrate a variety of similar perspectives, the discussion and the quotes are presented in order of the age of the speakers, starting with the oldest first. Although I am not always interested in comparing experiences across ages directly, this procedure acts as a helpful organizing principle.

The interviewees lived in London, Reading, Surrey and Middlesex. Their parents' occupations ranged from the professions to scrapyard merchants and factory workers. Their own occupations and educational backgrounds also varied widely. For example, one had left school at the earliest opportunity with no qualifications or certificates at all and had spent many years unemployed or in unskilled jobs; others had gone straight into semi-skilled manual work, apprenticeships or low-grade clerical work; and one had become a higher education lecturer in popular music. All but one attended state schools, some of which were selective and some comprehensive, one went to a famous public school and some went to university. They were all white, and comprised twelve males and two females. Clearly my own social class, gender, ethnicity, geographical location and so on affected the sampling. If I were black, or if I had sought musicians through a black music network, there would undoubtedly have been black musicians amongst the sample. If I had sought interviewees through a women's music network, there would obviously have been a lot more females (although the sample corresponds with the relatively low numbers of women and girls in popular music; see, for example, Bayton 1997, Clawson 1999a, Cohen 1991, Gaar 1993, Green 1997, O'Brien 1995, O'Brien 1994). However, given that I applied only general selection criteria as mentioned earlier, I am satisfied that the sample represents a reasonably typical cross-section of English popular musicians involved in Anglo-American guitar-based rock. Furthermore, although issues of class, ethnicity, gender, nationality and other sociological factors are clearly of enormous importance to the ways in which music is learnt, detailed differences connected to such factors lie at the edges of this book's central concerns.

I sought out the musicians by various means. One of these was to tell acquaintances, colleagues and friends that I wished to interview popular musicians. Over the ensuing two or three weeks, I was kindly put in touch with seven musicians from various sources. These included Leo, who was the son of one of my colleagues (not himself a music lecturer), Michael and Richard, who were the teenage children of acquaintances of friends, Andy and Nanette, who were students at universities where I had friends among the staff, Rob, who was a colleague of a colleague in another institution, and Emily, who was a school pupil of an ex-student of mine. I interviewed two musicians whom I knew as students on courses I teach – Bernie and Will (see Note 10). Terry is the father of one of my son's primary school classmates (although I did not know him before the interview), I met Brent completely by chance and I was put in touch with Peter by Will, and with Simon and Steve by Andy. Peter and Will played in the same seven-piece band, and Andy, Simon and Steve played in the same five-piece band. Other than that, the musicians were not personally acquainted with each other.

Lasting from an hour to an hour-and-a-half, each interview was tape-recorded and transcribed. Starting with the present day, then going back to their first experiences of music-making, I asked the musicians detailed questions concerning the nature of their skills and knowledge; how they had gone about acquiring these skills and knowledge; how they had developed as musicians; what attitudes and values they attached to acquiring musicianship; what experiences they had as pupils and students in formal music education; what opinions they held concerning the current position of popular music in education;

and what experiences some of them had as teachers. The interviews were intended to record the first responses, memories and opinions that floated to the top of the musicians' consciousness, and the analysis takes note not only of direct responses to questions, but of asides and unintended and unexpected outcomes and topics. I asked open questions and did not prompt any answers by making suggestions or giving examples of the sorts of replies I expected. When on occasions I 'drew a blank', I repeated the same question, trying to put it in different words. If there was still only a minimal response, I passed on to the next question. Given this lack of any prompting, as well as the diversity of their ages and backgrounds, I have taken it to be of general significance when several of the musicians made similar statements. Where there are differences of opinion, these are included in the analysis, often providing points of discussion.

A diverse and fascinating set of stories, drawn from different perspectives in the lives of professional, semi-professional and beginner popular musicians, was revealed. Some things were said which I have been forced to leave out of my analysis because, although rich in provocation, they were not always relevant to the focus of the research. It is worth giving an example of this to orientate the reader to my approach. Here are two experienced session musicians, Bernie Holland, a guitarist, and Rob Burns, a bass player, although both of them compose, arrange and play other instruments as well:

Bernie   You know, there's one difference I've noticed between English musicians and American musicians. This is a generalization, but you know, there's one thing I've noticed, that English musicians tend to be very eclectic, they tend to do a bit of this, a bit of that, you know, they have a lot of colours on their palette. Well you know, it's so competitive and you really need to be versatile. Whereas American musicians, it's interesting this, they tend to pick one particular style or area, and go for it in a big way, and become really amazing at that, whether it's country guitar, or whatever, and they become absolutely phenomenal at that one thing: but that's all they can do.

Rob   Now obviously you have to have some sort of artistic sense to know that you can overplay or underplay. Fashionably most people would prefer that the bass was underplayed. I remember in the seventies there was a big move towards, well British bass players moving towards being Americanized; and American bass players tended to be much more economical with their notes; and I found I got much more work when I started adopting that kind of approach, basically trying to sound like an American bass player, which included slapping.

Differences and similarities in the skills adopted by or demanded of British and United States musicians, and the relationships of these skills to the particular working conditions within and between these two nations, could form a fascinating area of research, which to my knowledge has received very little attention. However, from the existing published research, much of which was conducted in the USA, there are no grounds for presupposing that the general *learning practices* of the musicians are very different. I will therefore overlook, or only briefly mention, issues which, like this one, are tangential to my central research interests, even though they may at times appear in the text as the necessary context of what was said.

I have presented the quotes so as to make them as accurate a reflection of the musicians' views as possible, without including every 'um', 'er', repeated word or every interjection from myself. However, when 'umming' and 'ahing', pauses or my interjections are necessary to understand the syntax, or add anything to the significance of the speech in terms of the analysis I am conducting, I leave them in. Cuts in the conversation are represented by ellipses. Ellipses within a paragraph indicate the omission of one or two sentences or phrases; ellipses followed by a paragraph break indicate a different part of the interview. Otherwise, punctuation is designed to correspond with syntax or, occasionally, slight pauses in speech. Long pauses are represented by [pause]. Some statements by the musicians are examined more than once, in different contexts and for different reasons, and there is of necessity some overlap in the topics under discussion between sections.

Amongst the fourteen musicians, only Nanette was a singer. When referring to her music-making I will, of course, be specific, but in general I will use the word 'playing' to include singing as well as instrumental playing, and the expression 'instrumental teaching' to include vocal teaching. This is out of no disrespect to singers, least of all Nanette; rather, it avoids the need for cumbersome sentences such as 'all the musicians played or *sang* in …', 'their playing or *singing* was …', 'instrumental *and vocal* teachers do …', and such like.

After and sometimes during each interview, I listened to commercial and home-made recordings of the musicians' music, watched some of them playing live, and kept in touch with them all in various ways during the period of writing. In the course of discussion it occasionally becomes pertinent to make comments about the quality of their music-making, although I only ever found it appropriate to make positive comments. In all cases I have played the relevant music to at least two other people who were musicians, music educators or musicologists, sometimes quite informally at home and sometimes during post-graduate teaching sessions or conference presentations in the UK and overseas. The judgements of these people were either in broad or complete agreement with my own. However, apart from these checks, such comments can only be taken as my opinion.

All the musicians were given the opportunity to read and comment on the penultimate draft of the book, and all gave their approval. Some made editorial adjustments to their quoted speech in order to clarify their meaning. No one made any criticisms of the text and the majority gave explicit positive feedback, some of which was very enthusiastic with statements including 'fascinating and enlightening', 'fantastic', 'impressive and comprehensive'. Although it may be that some of them were too polite to express criticisms, from those who did give feedback the main message seemed to be that not only classically trained musicians and teachers, but popular musicians themselves are able to learn something from the study. Even though many of the musicians were busy freelance professionals, people doing a day job on top of their night work as musicians, impecunious students or school pupils, every one of them responded affirmatively and without hesitation to my initial request for an interview. I contacted fourteen musicians, and fourteen musicians immediately agreed to give up their time, with an enthusiasm and a generosity that was heart-warming. I would like to repeat here my enormous appreciation of their involvement and the encouragement and interest they have shown in this work.

Terminology

A few words of clarification concerning the terms 'learning', 'teaching', 'training' and 'education' are in order before going any further. The concept of learning necessarily implies the occurrence of some cognitive or psycho-motor shift in the learner, whether this shift results from an associated experience of being taught, educated, trained or any other similar experience. Whilst learning may thus stand as a concept independently of these other concepts, the latter – that is, the concepts of teaching, training and education – are not so easy to separate out, either from the concept of learning or from each other. For example, if the activity of teaching a class on a Monday morning results in no one in the class learning anything, then the activity cannot properly be referred to as having been one of teaching after all, but only as having been one of attempting, unsuccessfully, to teach. What if, as a result of the activity, half the class learns something and the other half does not? How can we then describe the activity? What if some or all of the class learn something as a result of the teaching, but not the same thing as the teaching had been designed to teach? Was it still teaching?

The concept of education implies the notion of causing worthwhile, ethical learning to occur. But in practice this result is not always forthcoming, or is only partially forthcoming, which is what makes it reasonable to speak of a 'poor education system', or of a person's having been 'badly educated'. Whilst teaching is often a part of education, it can occur outside of educational contexts, such as when the young burglar is taught to pick locks, depending on whose concept of education as a worthwhile and ethical pursuit is being invoked. By the same token, education can occur without any teaching having been involved, as is implied by Mark Twain's quip, 'I never let my school-work interfere with my education' (Noble 1995, p. 251). Training is distinct from both teaching and education only by matters of degree concerning factors such as the breadth of knowledge covered or the degree of autonomy allowed the learner, and is equally subject to being either entangled with or disentangled from the concept of learning. This book does not engage further in a philosophical discussion of these concepts and issues (for a classic treatment of which see Peters 1978), but I will now give some brief indications of how I use some central terms.

By 'informal music learning' I mean a variety of approaches to acquiring musical skills and knowledge outside formal educational settings, as the latter have already been defined (pp. 3–4). I will in general terms refer to informal music learning as a set of 'practices', rather than 'methods'. This is because, whilst the concept of 'methods' suggests engagement which is conscious, focused and goal-directed, that of 'practices' leaves open the degree of conscious, focused and goal-directed engagement. Informal music learning practices may be both conscious and unconscious. They include encountering unsought learning experiences through enculturation in the musical environment; learning through interaction with others such as peers, family members or other musicians who are not acting as teachers in formal capacities; and developing independent learning methods through self-teaching techniques.

I will use the expression 'formal music education' to refer to instrumental and classroom music teachers' practices of teaching, training and educating; and to pupils' and students' experiences of learning and of being taught, educated or trained in a formal educational setting. The term 'practices' in relation to formal education again denotes a wide range including conscious and unconscious, intended and unintended practices; whilst the term 'methods', as in 'teaching methods', refers to specific, conscious, focused or goal-directed activities designed to induce learning.

Lave and Wenger (1991) provide a fascinating discussion of apprenticeship learning, also known as 'situated learning', offering insights from anthropological investigations of apprenticeships in various contexts, such as becoming a midwife in Yucatán, Mexico and becoming a tailor in West Africa. One of their central concepts is that of 'legitimate peripheral participation' in a community of practice, slowly turning into full participation. The acquisition of musical skills and knowledge in many traditional contexts could form a model for similar studies of apprenticeship learning, although Lave and Wenger do not mention music.[11] However, informal Western popular music learning practices tend to be marked by certain differences from both traditional and apprenticeship music learning contexts, particularly in the following two senses. First, most young popular musicians in the West are not surrounded by an adult community of practising popular musicians, and therefore 'legitimate peripheral participation' of the sort studied by Lave and Wenger is largely unavailable to them. Hence they tend to engage in a significant amount of goal-directed solitary learning. Second, in so far as a community of practice is available to young popular musicians, it tends to be a community of *peers* rather than of 'master-musicians' or adults with greater skills. A comparative study of popular music learning with apprenticeship and traditional music learning in many world music contexts and jazz could form an interesting topic, although I have not attempted it in this book.

Concluding thoughts

At present the measurement of 'success' in a musician so often seems to be virtually synonymous with 'full-time professional'. In the field of popular music the quest to 'get signed' by a (preferably major or well-known independent) record company, combined with the chaos and unreliability of the music industry, so humorously but tellingly described by Negus (1999, pp. 1–14) has led to the disillusionment and exploitation of thousands of aspiring young 'acts'. Surely musical success ought to be measured by factors other than being a professional, let alone fame and commercial gain? Such factors come to life from time to time in movements like the folk revival of the 1960s, the do-it-yourself punk of the 1970s, rap, or many urban dance musics. They involve valuing not fame so much as enjoyment, a sense of community, a sub-cultural, ethnic or gender identity, a lifestyle, expressing sexuality, voicing political or moral views and appreciating a musical tradition. Such factors can be achieved through part-time, sporadic or semi-professional involvement in bars, at local functions and on street-corners, and moreover, through amateur music-making not only in public places but in the home. My own belief is that whilst such musical values, related not only to popular music but to all kinds of music, are shared by huge numbers of people, their realization in practice is not as widespread as it could be, or once was.

In this chapter I have suggested that music educators should examine, on one hand, the informal learning practices, attitudes and values and, on the other hand, the formal educational experiences of popular musicians, in themselves and in relation to the changing position of popular music in education over the last forty years or so. Otherwise, we could be deprived of the means of acquiring the skills and knowledge that are necessary to the production of some of the very music that is purported to be represented in formal music education; we could continue to bypass those children and young people who are nonetheless highly musically motivated and committed in their lives outside the classroom; and we could ignore a potentially worthwhile, accessible and inspiring repertoire of approaches to music learning. Informal, vernacular music learning practices will never be lost so long as human beings continue to be human beings. However, these practices are currently under threat. I believe that popular music will play an important part in the future of vernacular music learning practices, and that its role in this respect should not remain beyond the limits of formal music education.

In the next chapter I discuss some of the conditions necessary for informal music learning of any kind to take place, especially in terms of the musical enculturation of children; then I move on to examine some of the skills and knowledge that are normally required of professional and semi-professional popular musicians. The chapter closes with a consideration of some of the practices, attitudes and values that are characteristic of musicians working in and across different sub-categories of popular music. Chapter 3 considers the nature of the learning practices employed by the musicians in this study over approximately the last forty years of the twentieth century, looking into how they went about acquiring their skills and knowledge from their earliest contact with an instrument to their entrance into professional music. Chapter 4 enquires into the attitudes and values which popular musicians attach to their informal learning, and the nature of the satisfaction they gain from their musical practices. In Chapters 5 and 6 I take a step into formal music education environments, in order to consider the changing nature of instrumental tuition and the school music curriculum in England over the last forty years, from the perspectives of popular musicians who took classical and popular music instrumental lessons and who attended school from the 1960s to the end of the twentieth century. I also present some aspects of their experiences of further and higher education in popular music. The final chapter compares characteristics of informal popular music learning with those of formal music education and considers whether the learning practices, attitudes and values of popular musicians, as articulated throughout the book, may or may not reasonably be adapted and included within formal music education, in a move to help re-invigorate the musical involvement of the populace at large.

Notes

1. Many countries produce statistics on musical participation which can be accessed through libraries, government and privately sponsored research agencies. For a variety of statistics relating to Britain see, for example, Research Surveys of Great Britain Ltd (1991), Everitt (1997) and National Music Council (1996, 1999a and b). Statistics vary depending on how they are collected. For example, one UK survey in 1991 found that 5 per cent of adults played a musical instrument, whilst another in 1993 found that 24 per cent of adults did so (Research Surveys of Great Britain Ltd 1991 and Associated Board of the Royal Schools of Music 2000 respectively). In the latter case it is not clear whether the adults played the instruments regularly, or only when they were children.
2. The largest percentage of classical music sales given by the International Federation of Phonographic Industries (2000) is 11 per cent in Russia. Not all countries are listed by genre, but some other figures for classical music are Australia 5 per cent, Germany 9 per cent, the UK 4 per cent and the USA 4 per cent. Popular music in its narrow definition is considerably less popular than rock, rap/dance/R&B and country in the USA, with 11 per cent sales as against rock's 25 per cent, rap/dance/R&B's 21 per cent and country's 11 per cent.
3. For a helpful overview see Beale (2001, Chapter 2), and with specific reference to the USA, Berliner (1994, pp. 55–7) and Volk (1998, pp. 82, 95–6 and 111).
4. It first appeared in formal education contexts in Sweden (see Tagg 1998) and became accepted in many British schools during the 1970s, following arguments, curriculum materials and teaching strategies put forward by Swanwick (1968), Burnett (1972),

Farmer (1976), Vulliamy (1977a, 1977b) and Vulliamy and Lee (1976, 1982). Also see Green (1988) for a critique. In the USA the central forum, the Music Educators' National Conference, staged a major discussion of popular music and education in 1969 and again in 1991 (see Cutietta 1991; Volk 1998, pp. 82, 95–6, 111; Newsom 1998, Herbert and Campbell 2000). For work mainly in Australia see the special issue, *Research Studies in Music Education* (1999), Dunbar-Hall (1996) and Dunbar-Hall and Wemyss (2000). Popular music has been taken on to varying extents in the formal education systems of different countries, (see, for example, Byrne and Sheridan 2000, Ho 1996, Koizumi 1998, 2002, Maryprasith 1999 and Stålhammar 2000 for information on developments in Scotland, Hong Kong, Japan, Thailand and Sweden respectively); at times causing uproars such as those examined in Shepherd and Vulliamy (1994) and Gammon (1999).

5.   For scholarly treatments of the introduction of world musics and the diversification of curricula in many countries see Campbell (1991b), Lundquist and Szego (1998) and Volk (1998). Also see note 4 above.

6.   Also see Cope (1999), Dunbar-Hall (2000), Elliott (1989, 1990, 1995), Farrell (1990), Floyd (1996), Kwami (1989, 1996), McCarthy (1997, 1999), Nwezi (1999), Oerhle (1991), Small (1980, 1983, 1987), Stock (1991, 1996), Westerlund (1999), Wiggins (1996) and many more in journals such as the *International Journal of Music Education*.

7.   The only English-language book-length consideration of the relations between popular music learning practices and formal music education that I know of is Small (1987) who concentrates on what music educators can glean from the African heritage of communal and improvisatory aspects of African-American popular music. Amongst articles/dissertations on such themes in the English language, Björnberg (1993) and Lilliestam (1996) consider popular music in relation to higher education courses in Denmark and Sweden respectively; Horn (1984) looks at community-based popular music courses in the UK; Newsom (1998) discusses issues facing a rock instrumental programme in a middle school in the USA; Byrne and Sheridan (2000) look at popular music in upper levels of schooling, further and higher education in Scotland; Oliveira (2000) presents an educational project involving the informal music-making of Brazilian children; Wemyss (1999) considers Australian indigenous popular music in connection with children's playground culture and schooling, also see Dunbar-Hall and Wemyss (2000); and Campbell (1995) and Finney (1987) present studies of school-aged rock bands in relation to formal education in the USA and UK respectively. Lilliestam's (1995) book would undoubtedly be beneficial for those who can read in Swedish. Despite such valuable work, and despite the awareness of earlier and contemporary supporters of popular music in education, explicit emphasis on the informal learning practices of popular musicians is not a central part of music education research and literature.

8.   Also see Berkaak (1999) for an illuminating study of a Swedish rock band; Finnegan (1989, Chapter 11) for a comparison of classical music education and popular music learning practices; Negus (1999) for a sociological perspective on the interface between musicians and the music industry; Toynbee (2000) for a theory of creativity and generic change in popular music as 'social authorship'; Kirshner (1998) for a plea to combine ethnographic work on popular musicians with theoretical work on popular music; Gomes (2000) for a consideration of the learning practices of street musicians in Brazil; Bayton (1990, 1993, 1997) and Clawson (1999a and b) for sociological considerations of women's experiences as popular musicians.

9.   Good standard texts include Brackett (1995), Middleton (1990, 2000), Moore (1993), Walser (1993) and journals such as *Popular Music*, *Popular Musicology*, and *Popular Music and Society*.
10. There were two exceptions to the first criterion. One interviewee, Bernie Holland, had been a student of mine several years previously and another, Will Cragg, was a current student. However, I did not know either of them very well because I had been on maternity leave during most of Bernie's course, and Will had only just begun his. Will also presented an exception to the second criterion, for he had lived abroad until he was 9 or 10 years old; however, this did not significantly affect findings.
11. For discussions of music learning as a form of apprenticeship see, for example, Nketia's (1975) classic study in relation to Africa. Merriam (1964, pp. 150–61) provides a scholarly account of work in the area; Campbell (1991b) provides a helpful overview of literature, and she and Volk (1998) also provide more recent discussions of a variety of relevant 'world music' education systems. Berliner (1994) lays bare the emphasis which the jazz community in the USA places on apprenticeships and 'sitting in' with more experienced players. Some areas of popular music are more marked by apprenticeship learning than others. For an example see Stolzoff (2000, p. 153f.) in relation to young boys learning the skills of DJ-ing in late twentieth-century Jamaica.

Chapter 2

Skills, knowledge and self-conceptions of popular musicians: the beginnings and the ends

This chapter will first consider the very beginnings of musical skill and knowledge-development for popular musicians – 'beginnings' in the sense of the experiences and opportunities that tend to be in place at the start of the learning process. Then I will leap to the 'ends' of musical development – 'ends' both in the sense of 'aims' and in terms of the kinds of skills and knowledge that are required of professional popular musicians in order to maintain their careers. Finally, I will consider some of the different self-conceptions and aspirations of the musicians in this study, from beginners to professionals, according to the bands they play in and the type of work they do. This discussion of the beginnings and ends of playing popular music, and of the self-conceptions and aspirations of popular musicians, then provides the context for the next two chapters, which look in more detail at how, having started at these beginnings, the older musicians had arrived at these ends; and at how the younger musicians were going about the process of working towards them.

Although the title of this chapter contains both the word 'skills' and the word 'knowledge', and although throughout the book I refer at times to skills and at other times to knowledge, I do not consider the two concepts to connote completely distinct areas of human activity or consciousness. Skills are often associated with motor control, such as the ability to play fast scales, whereas knowledge is connected with notions of understanding or acquaintance, such as appreciating in what ways psychedelia influenced the history of rock or 'knowing a song'. But the notion of skills also includes the execution of purely mental acts of interpretation, such as recognizing chord progressions by ear or reading notation 'in the head'. Similarly, a covers band musician's knowledge of a song, when put to use in music-making, is the necessary condition for motor activity: without the knowledge, the song could not be played. I do not wish to go into the distinctions between skill and knowledge as a philosophical problem, but rather to acknowledge that it is sometimes more reasonable to refer to one of these than the other, as in the common usage of the two words.

The 'beginnings'

Musical enculturation: playing, composing, listening

The concept of musical enculturation refers to the acquisition of musical skills and knowledge by immersion in the everyday music and musical practices of one's social context.[1] Almost everyone in any social context is musically encultured. It cannot be avoided because we cannot shut our ears, and we therefore come into contact with the music that is around us, not only by choice but by default. It is helpful to conceive of three main ways in which we engage directly with music: *playing* (to include singing), *composing* (to include improvising) and *listening* (to include hearing). Each of these is discussed briefly below in terms of its role in enculturation towards music-making.

Part of musical enculturation involves the early exploration of sound using either the voice, musical instruments or other objects. In many societies, musical enculturation has a particularly explicit and valued role in children's upbringing. Imagine a baby banging a spoon or some other object on a table in the kitchen of an indigenous white London family. Any adults in the vicinity are liable to take the spoon away or by some other means get the baby to stop. By contrast, as John Blacking has made widely known, if a baby repeatedly bangs an object in a home amongst the Venda people of South Africa, surrounding adults and other children are likely to voice warm approval and join in, converting 'the spontaneous rhythm into intentional musical action by adding a second part in polyrhythm' (Blacking 1985, p. 46, cited in Swanwick 1994, p. 24). In each case, the baby is undergoing enculturation in the music-making practices of (or their absence from) the social context into which he or she was born.

Most people have at some stage banged an object repeatedly on a table, experimented with a few notes on an instrument, hummed a made-up melody and such like. For a few children enculturation into playing music may never proceed much beyond that. But when it does proceed further, there comes a point where the path forks. Along one route such enculturation may turn into formal music education, which involves the introduction of new or unfamiliar skills and knowledge of sorts that are not normally assimilated in ordinary daily life. In Western contexts this usually occurs through formal instrumental tuition or other special educational programmes. The other path, by contrast, involves a continued journey along exploratory lines, turning imperceptibly into informal music learning. This is the path taken by many of those who become popular musicians.

Here, for example is Emily Dicks, a 16-year-old lead guitarist who at the time of the interviews was in her first band with schoolfriends:

Emily   When I practise guitar sometimes, it's not actual playing, but I've got an amp with a few knobs on it and I don't know what they do, so I spend time just twiddling them and seeing what sounds good, and seeing what styles you can get out of the amp and that, so that's all like, experimentation.

Or Andy Brooks, lead guitarist in an originals band Deepvoid, talking about how he had progressed in the early stages:

Andy   It's a very basic thing. I mean, you'll play something and you'll just work out what sounds good. You don't even know what scales you're playing. You don't know what progressions work or anything. To some extent I believe it's what you've heard already, and you're just taking it in.

I will use the term 'composition' to encompass a range of musically creative activities, including improvisation. Early experimentation with music-making of necessity involves not only playing as discussed above, but also some level of composition in the form of improvisation. For as soon as the young child's repeated banging of the spoon turns into music-making, it is an elementary improvisation. If the child then proceeds along a pathway towards informal learning, the act of improvisation also becomes a precursor to other kinds of composition. For example, Andy described his development at around the age of 8, with a friend of the same age:

Andy   I was using the simple chords that I'd learnt, and jamming with this other guitarist ... We started playing the guitar at the exact same time ... just learning together, and every now and then we met up for a little jam. That proved quite good.

By the time of the interviews, Andy, along with others of his colleagues in Deepvoid, was making a major contribution to their eclectic and imaginative group compositions. The roles of group improvisation, jamming and composition are of great significance in the development of popular music skills and knowledge, and will be considered again later.

Notice Andy's allusion to listening above – 'it's what you've heard already and you're just taking it in'; and although Emily uses the word 'see' as in 'just twiddling' the knobs and 'seeing what sounds good', she *means* that she is *listening* in order to make choices about which sounds to use. (People speaking or writing English often use the word 'see' when they mean 'hear' or 'listen': it is perhaps one of many symptoms of our alienation from the sonic environment.) In the activities of playing and composing above, musicians are listening to *their own* musical product during the time that they are making the music. As distinct from this, we also of course listen to music made entirely by other people. I wish to distinguish three main types of such listening, specifically related to the learning practices of popular musicians.[2]

First, *purposive listening* has the particular aim, or purpose, of learning something in order to put it to use in some way after the listening experience is over. It is the sort of listening that any musician would employ when, for example, learning to play an exact copy or cover of a song, making a mental or written note of the harmonies, the form or other properties of the song in order to be able to use them in another context, undertaking an analytic exercise and so on. Second, *attentive listening* may involve listening at the same level of detail as in purposive listening, but without any specific aim of learning something in order to be able to play, remember, compare or describe it afterwards. Third, we can distinguish *distracted listening*, when the music is being attended to on and off, without any aim other than enjoyment or entertainment. Within this type it is also feasible to include *hearing*, which occurs when we are aware that there is music playing, but are barely paying any attention to it at all. Different types of listening are not discrete. A listener can easily pass from one to another or even experience all the types suggested here during the course of one piece of music. For example, a listener may be listening purposively when someone walks into the room and starts talking, which results in distracted listening or hearing; a listener may wish to listen purposively to one particular passage and will then listen to the rest of the music in other ways and so on.

Listening of any kind is a crucial activity for all musicians. Purposive listening, in particular, is a part of both informal music learning and formal music education. However, for those who become popular musicians as well as other types of vernacular musicians, all types of listening – including attentive listening, distracted listening and even hearing – also form a central part of the learning process. Moreover, in what follows it will be seen that listening is a fundamental part of the enculturation that is intrinsic to the development of popular musicians, from their earliest attempts at making music right through their professional careers.

The influence of parents

In the example of the two babies mentioned earlier, it is clear that adults and other surrounding people, including siblings and friends, have a profound effect upon the ways in which infants and young children are encultured into music. Research in the psychology of music suggests that parental encouragement of various kinds is one of the most crucial factors in the formation of classical musicians.[3] Findings from the present study suggest that similarly, although larger-scale research would be required to verify it, the likelihood is that parents play a prominent role in the formation of popular musicians. Indeed it may well be that due to the increased emphasis on enculturation in popular music learning practices, it is *more* likely that popular musicians will come from musically interested families. Here I will consider the role of parents, leaving that of same-generation relatives and friends for Chapter 3.

As youngsters, thirteen of the fourteen musicians in the study had parents who gave them verbal encouragement, lifts to and from gigs and rehearsals, financial help in buying instruments and/or direct musical advice. The parents of Bernie, Brent, Andy, Michael and Emily organized lessons for them on their choice of popular music instrument; Nanette said she 'couldn't have done it without my Mum'; Brent's father bought him his first drum kit and his mother took him to lessons and rehearsals; Terry's mother and brother-in-law bought him his first kit; the fathers of Will, Steve and Leo played the guitar, Richard's father played the piano, and all these dads showed their sons chords and other rudiments. Michael's father was an active musician and bandleader in the church and taught him the basics of guitar-playing, showed him chords on the piano and helped in other areas (although Michael was primarily a drummer). At the same time as this parental input, only one of the musicians had a parent who was or had ever been a professional popular musician: Brent, whose mother had been a nightclub singer before he was born.

Only Peter mentioned that he did not come from a musical family, and it is worth noting in the present context that he did not become interested in music or in playing an instrument until after he left his parental home to go to university, aged 18. Rob was the only one who had experienced major confrontations with his parents over his musical career aspirations, although they had encouraged and provided instruments for him in the early stages. The conflict lead to ill health by the time Rob was 17, and continued to be a problem for some years:

Rob   My father never forgot that I didn't become a doctor, not for a long time, until he came to see me playing with Pete Townshend in the stage version of *Tommy* and then he let up a bit and realized I'd actually *done* something.

Terry experienced a certain amount of parental disapproval when, at the age of 17 he gave up his chance of involvement in the family scrapyard business to join the cult psychedelic rock band Hawkwind. A British version of the Grateful Dead, Hawkwind is described by Hardy and Laing (1990, p. 350) thus: 'A free performance outside the Isle of Wight Festival in 1970 confirmed Hawkwind as the mascots of Britain's underground media and burgeoning alternative society'.

Terry   Everyone was really disappointed, 'You're absolutely mad' and you know, I looked awful, taking lots of things and staying up all night and you know, and I suppose I was in a bit of a state and they were appalled really. Because you know that was a good business we had going, and I was sort of turning my back on it for something that might happen or you know, the chances are it probably wouldn't, you know; and living in a squat and all this and that, and up and down the motorways and things … I mean they, you know they didn't force me or anything, force me not to do it but yeah. I mean you know it was my decision and they thought it was the wrong one. Financially it might well have been [laughs] but I had a good time.

But prior to that, he had been encouraged.

First instruments

Although early enculturation experiences through contact with other people are vital, musical progress also relies on the will to play an instrument and the accessibility of an instrument. Whilst parental encouragement was present in the majority of cases, all the interviewees had at the same time been entirely self-motivated in their choice of instrument and in their decision to play. Some started playing after having been inspired by some music and, in particular, the sound of the instrument. Notice that listening is significant in many of these cases, in so far as the young musicians were attracted to a piece of music, to the performance practice of a particular instrumentalist, to the sound qualities of the instrument or a mixture of all these.

Rob (referring to being about 9 years old)

> I can almost remember the day that I became aware of pop music, because I heard 'Love Me Do' by the Beatles on the radio, so it must have been '62 and something clicked; I just thought 'Wow! That's good.' Because up until then, my parents had music, I mean often had music on in the house – but music for me was not a novelty – it wasn't a passion. And as I say this 'switch' went on in my head, it was like a, a bolt of lightning.

Peter   I was completely obsessed with music. I saw a performance by Gil Scott Heron and it was amazing, and the bassist from that group did some remarkable things with the bass line that I'd never heard anyone else do. So the excitement of that particular performance stuck with me. I knew I wanted to play some kind of instrument. Strangely enough I couldn't decide whether I wanted to play flute or bass … I had no idea that the obsession would reach the point where I wouldn't be satisfied doing anything else.

Will (who started on drums but became a guitarist)

> [I chose guitar] possibly because of the music I was listening to at the time … there were some great guitarists around at the time and I think that maybe that's something to do with it.

Michael   … well it was mainly through the other drummer at church because I used to admire him very much. I used to like his drum kit and he sometimes let me play it and that was always good fun. I was quite impressed by him and he actually gave me a few lessons before I got the drum kit. This was on his drum kit and I really enjoyed that.

Richard   Before, I wasn't really into much music, I sort of, I'd hear some Blur stuff on the radio and think 'That's alright', but then I really started getting into that about this time two years ago. And I just listened to it and thought 'I have got to play the guitar' because I just loved hearing them and so, I don't know if my Mum told you but I went and got a paper round so I could buy a guitar and an amplifier and stuff. And just went on from there. And started playing.

As well as the sonic components of the above experiences, motivation was also enhanced by the presence of a real instrument which the embryonic musician was able to hold and touch. As is already apparent, many of the musicians saved up or begged for an instrument of their own. In several cases there was an instrument already in the house – their fathers' electric guitar in three cases – and at least three of the musicians' families owned pianos.

Bernie   Right, well, my first encounter with anybody else playing an instrument was when I was about 6 or 7 years old, and I had a brother about four years senior to me, who had got a ukulele … However, that wasn't enough for me. I wanted a six-string guitar. I wanted a proper six-string guitar. I saw one in a shop in Cheltenham and pestered my mother and father. They got me this six-string guitar, and that was it, I mean I was just, just, you couldn't, I was just you know you couldn't get me off the thing, day and night, I was just playing this thing.

In Terry's case the 'instrument' that was available to him at the start was a large array of scrap.

Terry   My parents owned a scrapyard so I was always banging on something … saucepans and stuff.

Rob   But I didn't give performing music very much thought until I was in the Boy Scouts and our troop leader had left and I used to go visiting him at his Mum's house, and he'd bought an electric bass guitar. And again it was another one, the second 'switch' went down. I held this thing and I just thought, 'Wow' … And then I watched his band rehearse, and that was it. I thought 'This is, this is fantastic, this is wonderful' …

    … I was determined that I ought to have a bass guitar and my parents bought me a guitar, because they took advice that it was best to learn the guitar first, which gave me my first kind of, 'These are the chords'. And then I brought a home-made bass guitar and sort of went on from there. My parents bought me a proper one for Christmas, and there was a progression of instruments until I ended up using Fenders and Gibsons.

For Nanette the instrument was her own voice, which she used so much from the age of 7 or 8 that it 'drove my family nuts'.

Brent   I was, oh, how old was I? Probably I was about 8 or 9 when I got the drum kit. My Mum apparently reckons when I was really little I had one of those little toy kid's drum kits that apparently I trashed but I've got no recollection of that. Basically one Christmas they said 'What do you want for Christmas?' And I said 'Oh, I'd like a drum kit please.' I was fortunate enough to get one.

Will   Drums – I first came across drums when I was young [about 8]. A friend had a drum kit and it was loud which was a pretty good thing. At school there was a drum kit and it was less frightening than other instruments: you didn't have the pitch thing. With piano chords, I didn't know what I was doing; the guitar was just, I just thought it was a horrible instrument, didn't want to know about it and I couldn't see the point of it, I couldn't see how it worked. I couldn't see the fret-board, didn't understand it at all …

    … And then I was just walking along the street one day and I saw a classical guitar in an Oxfam shop and just, for some reason it completely reversed, and I just thought – 'Absolutely wonderful instrument! Well I'd like to have one of those' …

> L: Why did you change your mind, do you think?
> W: Um, I've often thought about that – I don't know. Possibly because of the music I was listening to at the time.

Andy first came into contact with drums through the instrument of a friend when he was 5 years old: 'He had a snare drum – that was all it was', but it was enough to form a small band, and with that, to ignite Andy's determination to become a guitarist.

Michael   [I] must have taken up the drums seven years ago [aged 10]. I'd shown interest in it for a long time. I mean I got a snare drum for Christmas – just the one drum. And I had that for about a year and I saved up and bought the whole drum kit, and then I got another drum kit since then which I saved up for, and it was all sorts of Christmas presents and birthday presents and stuff.

Out of the fourteen musicians, only one mentioned school as having been the trigger for his interest in playing a popular music instrument. This was Simon who, as will be seen later, started secondary school in 1990, at a time when popular music was well and truly a part of the curriculum of many schools, and whose particular school had a notably positive attitude towards it.

Simon   I was at school and there was just a music class basically, and they had a drum kit there and I hadn't started drums yet. I wasn't really that interested and he said 'Play along with the music.' Because my old music teacher was really into [pause], the sort of people, I don't know, if I said 'who were talented' that would sound a bit big-headed; but he said, you know, 'See if you can play the drums without any lessons whatsoever.' And I done it and won the competition in the first year.

Professional musicianship: the 'ends'

I will now make a leap from the musicians' experiences of the beginnings of their informal music learning to the 'ends' or, in other words, the knowledge and skills required of a successful popular musician – successful in the sense of being able to maintain a playing career – in a variety of contexts.

Playing covers

Session, covers band and function band musicians, in particular, have to be aware of the norms and variations of a large number of sub-styles of popular music, and to be able to translate these norms and variations into their playing. Such awareness and ability derive from purposive and attentive listening, but musicians also pick up songs purely by distracted listening and hearing.[4] Apart from a few highly professional function bands and session musicians, popular musicians rarely use music notation, and whether they use it or not, they must always be able to play without it, on the basis of what has been learnt through listening. Amongst the sample of musicians here, only Bernie, Rob and Brent used notation fluently in professional scenarios. Sometimes listening is geared to producing an exact copy; at other times it involves looser imitation or the adaptation of stylistically suitable components from one song or one stylistic context to another.

Covers band and session musicians must be able to play, sometimes at a moment's notice and in any key, a large number of songs drawn from a standard repertoire, or what are known as 'covers'. Covering songs is a skill perhaps most readily acquired in the early learning stages by drummers, for whom a number of songs share common patterns. However, when a drummer intends to produce a detailed, direct copy of a particular recording, this relies on precise memorization of the fills, breaks and so on, as well as the dynamics, touch and feel of the original. Knowledge of covers is also relatively accessible for the bass, chordal and melody instrumentalists in cases where standard chord progressions are in use such as a 12-bar blues or a I VI IV V sequence. But the majority of songs require more specific knowledge of the particular pitch and harmonic structure of the original recording, as well as the timbral, textural and rhythmic qualities. Covers band and session musicians, whether they read or not, often know by heart their own instrumental part and the overall structure of a large number of songs, ranging from fifty or sixty to several hundred.

In some cases musicians are obliged to acquire player-knowledge of covers in a short period of time. An example is provided by the early career of Nanette Welmans, who became a professional singer when she was 17, working with resident bands in local Top Rank and Mecca entertainment centres. 'At the beginning of the week, you'd get a tape of say eight or twelve songs and you had to learn them all off by heart.' These songs were in the charts, therefore a period of familiarity extending much beyond a week was often not possible. Each one had to be sung in such a way as to sound as close to the original as possible, requiring knowledge not just of words, melody, decorations, breathing and so on, but also of vocal timbre, 'feel' and other more nebulous aspects, which will be returned to in due course.

In other cases, musicians are required to play such a large array of songs, often without advance warning, that they would be unable to become familiar with the whole repertoire by any means other than distracted listening or even hearing. For example, Terry, who was the drummer of Hawkwind in the early seventies, found himself playing in a covers band for the first time in his life, several years after having dropped out of Hawkwind and out of music altogether. I asked him how he had felt about it, and whether joining the band after such a long gap had necessitated preparatory listening to a lot of records to refresh his memory.

Terry   No … because it's like, you know, the bass player or someone would say, 'Oh
           it's High Heel Sneakers' and there's loads of songs that are the same as 'High
           Heel Sneakers' for the drums to play; or it's a shuffle, you know, and I'd just
           do it from that.
           L: And you do the fills and stuff from feel?
           T: Just feel, yeah.

The demands of professional musicianship in covers or session work also
encompass the ability to 'busk' to previously unknown songs, sometimes whilst
playing live on stage.

Terry   L: And do you do things like, I mean, have you found yourself in a position on
           stage where somebody says 'Oh we'll play this number', and you've never –
           T: And I don't know it? [Laughing]
           L: And you don't know it?
           T: I have, yeah, I have.
           L: So how do you – you just gauge what's going to happen, do you?
           T: Yes, and generally play a bit quieter! [Laughter]
           L: You get to breaks, you get to middle eights –
           T: Yeah, I mean, you can feel it, more or less, you know what I mean.
           L: Yeah, and when the song's coming to an end, what, you communicate with,
           you've got an MD or somebody.
           T: Eyeball, yeah.

In the case of pitched instruments, Bernie Holland provided an example of a
similar situation. His favourite musician is the North American jazz pianist Mose
Allison, so fortunately Bernie had been immersed in his music for some time
when the following happened:

Bernie   … the phone went, and it was Van Morrison in Bristol, and he said 'Are you
           available?' and I said 'What do you mean am I available?' and he said 'Oh I
           need a guitarist, I've got to do a gig with Mose Allison, blah blah blah.' So I
           said 'Yeah all right.' So I got in the car, drove down the M4 in a blizzard, and
           I got there just in time to get out the car and go on stage. I didn't have time to
           wash or anything. I'd never played with Mose Allison in my life.
           L: So what did you do?
           B: I just got on stage and listened to him. He was playing all these things I'd
           never heard in my life before.
           L: So what did you do?
           B: I just listened once, tried to cop the sequence he was doing, let him play the
           first chorus and get it in my head, yeah, and then I'd improvise over it.
           L: Did you have to do solos?
           B: Yeah, I did a solo. It came out on television, about ten minutes of it is on a
           thing, I've got it up there amongst all those hundreds of videos. So the thing is
           like, there again, because I'm a great fan of his, I'd heard all his albums, even
           though this was a new piece, I knew the sort of thing, I knew roughly what he
           was up to, and what he was interested in. But that for me, was the greatest
           thing ever, to this day, the greatest thing ever was to play with him.

As well as having to produce a drum part in a cover of something that you have never played before, or improvise a guitar part over a previously unknown chord progression, Brent, a freelance drummer, gave an example of having to play along with songs he knew but without anyone having told him what they were going to be:

Brent   Sometimes people just start playing the song; you don't even know what it is when they start so it's – you just have to listen basically and –
L: You mean they do that on stage?
B: Yeah, sometimes.
L: So what happens to you when that occurs?
B: Well, depending on what it is, I mean sometimes people will count you in, so at least if they count you in you've got an idea of tempo. If they've not told you what they're playing at all, which I don't particularly like, then I'll just try and play a pulse really I suppose, and within a bar you'll have a vague idea of what sort of feel you're going for and then gradually embellish that until hopefully it, you know –
L: And would you always know the song or do you sometimes –
B: No, not always, no, sometimes you're just going through stuff and you don't know it.

Below, Brent mentions both what I have referred to as attentive and distracted listening, in terms of the preparation required for playing covers, depending on the situation. I asked him how he went about getting songs inside his head, and also whether he always copied recordings loosely, or whether he sometimes aimed for an exact, detailed copy of the original drum track:

Brent   It depends on the situation. I listen to quite a lot of stuff and have done ever since I was a kid. In fact I probably listen less to current popular stuff than I did, you know, I'm probably much better off knowledge-wise on seventies and eighties stuff. You know, it varies. If it's a tune that I've listened to a lot and I know what the drum part is, maybe not note for note but give or take a note, know what the basic feel is, know where the fills are, know the form, then obviously you're going to play it close to the original. Or where the drum feel is an integral part of it you know, for example, Paul Simon's 'Fifty Ways to Leave your Lover': I mean that's such a *part* of the song that, you know, unless you're doing a completely different arrangement then that, that needs to be played exactly.

Bernie and Brent illustrate below that purposive, attentive and distracted listening are also all a part of the preparation for a session or contract:

Bernie   I got asked to do several concerts with a chap called Leo Sayer [a famous British singer-songwriter in the seventies]. Now this chap dressed up as a clown at the time, and went on stage. It was a pop, a pop performance. So I'd heard him, he'd had some hits and I'd heard him, and I knew what he did and I was familiar with it … So basically, with a situation like that it was easier

because I was already familiar with his music ... Now in the event where
there's somebody that I'm not familiar with their work, they usually send me
a tape with either the rough demos [demonstration tapes] of what they're
doing; or if we're going out to do some gigs and we're going to be performing
stuff that they've already recorded, that I haven't heard, they'll send me a
copy of the tape, or an album.

Brent   If it's a case of you just turning up wherever, it's cold and you've never heard
it before, then sometimes I might take a tape machine along and record things
in order to practise along with it or listen to it later ... If you get a tape ahead
of time, again I might write a chart beforehand and that may be a more detailed
chart, depending again what's on the demo. If they've got an original demo or
something that you think they're actually going to want to go with pretty much,
then I'll write something to that effect.

The importance of 'feel'

Whatever the instrument or situation, and whether the music is a precise copy or
a looser interpretation, internalization and reproduction are not restricted to the
pitches, rhythms and forms of the music. For, equally importantly, they also
encompass exacting attention to ephemeral details, often referred to as 'feel'.
This includes the precise timing of notes on and around the beat, the exact and
often changing sound or timbre of each instrument, the sensitive interrelations
and responses between the instruments and many other subtleties. Every player
has to know exactly how and where to fit into the overall 'groove', that is the
basic rhythmic qualities that characterize the piece. For a musician who plays
covers or works with an endless variety of outfits, this relies on a high level of
versatility and style knowledge. Will Cragg, who was one of the youngest of the
professional musicians I interviewed, played lead guitar in a seven-piece
function band (one which did not use notation) and also in a two-guitar duo:

Will   I used to think each style was a million miles apart – which they are – but just
on one instrument, as I've realized, it's only just tiny little things that are
different. Such as the amount of vibrato you give or the way you bend the
string, or the way you hit a note, sliding, all that sort of thing. This realization
has made getting to grips with new styles a lot easier, because you notice the
little things much quicker and you can sort of, almost like a bluffer's guide to
it, you can approximate what it's trying to do and people will go 'Oh, he's
playing that' ... I think you have to be pretty familiar with the music, with the
general style.

The demands of fine variations between styles are multiplied when a covers
band is switching from one style to another within a live set. The sound of each
instrument needs to be an accurate copy of the original recording, such that, for
example, in a country number a particular timbre and playing technique are
required to make each instrument sound like those played by country musicians;
in a rock'n'roll or heavy metal number different sounds are needed. As well as

the individual sound of each instrument, the overall sound of the band also has to be similar to that on the recording. An audience having a meal or dancing whilst a covers band plays may not consider whether the sound for each song is right; they will notice pretty quickly, however, if it is wrong. What they may not be aware of is the speed and accuracy with which timbral, textural, rhythmic, metric, pitch-inflected and technical decisions have to be made. Finally, where session or freelance work is involved, as indicated by Rob, Brent and Bernie in some of the quotes above, familiarity with a large repertoire of memorized songs, basic song structures and knowledge of the required sound and 'feel' of individual styles is not enough, for musicians may also need to adapt their normal approach according to the idiosyncrasies of whoever is hiring them.

The roles of the instruments and players

Rob Burns explained how the bass relates to the other instruments in the context of different musical styles and historical periods. It is worth quoting him in full to give an example of the kind of awareness with which the more experienced musicians approach their work. I asked him to illustrate the role of the bass guitar by giving two contrasting examples.

Rob The bass guitar function in most situations links the chordal instruments with the rhythmic instruments, so in other words it's the link between say the drums and the rest of the band. And that's the way it should be because you're providing feel, providing groove and so on ...

 ... Let's look at reggae and then look at fusion. Now in reggae the bass is kind of the anchor along with what is called the 'one-drop' on the bass drum. Now reggae kind of loosely falls into two areas – very very loosely – there's the kind of more melodic pop lover's rock, which is Aswad, UB40, that kind of area, and then there's the more politically orientated rockers and steppers, which is much more Black Uhuru, certain aspects of Peter Tosh, Bob Marley and probably where modern kind of dance – I use the term advisedly – meets reggae and has a 'ragga' and 'chat' – which are two forms, new forms of reggae, which are much more London Black music orientated. But in all of those, the bass is so fundamental, it underpins – it might only play two notes, it might just play the root and the fifth – maybe just the root note – and it would just be placed in certain areas of the bar, accenting what the drums are doing. Very, very simple, but if you were to take it out, you wouldn't have the finished product ... If the bass drum is just playing 4s on the floor, 1–2–3–4, the bass is much freer then. If the bass drum is going to happen on beat 3, which it quite often does in 'one drop', the bass might just be playing a simple figure around that, but obviously *with* that beat 3 as well. Very, very simple, but an art form in some senses because you either can do it or you can't – there's no halfway point. There are bass players who specialize in this ...

 ... Now with fusion – by fusion I mean where jazz harmony meets rock and funk rhythms – the bass is much more liberated these days because, I suppose, of the pioneering work of people like Jaco Pastorius and Stanley Clarke – where the bass can become much more melodic, in terms of say using the fretless, you can play melodies and solo – it isn't confined solely to locking in with the rhythm and underpinning root notes and chords, and because of that, has become much more of a, shall we say a front-line instrument. Whereas say in the '60s – I have to say this really – in the late '50s and early '60s – the bass guitar was something for the failed guitarist – it was the instrument that you gave to the guy in the band whose Dad owned the van so you couldn't sack him. And because of people like Jack Bruce, Paul McCartney, John Entwhistle, it's become much more of an instrument to be taken seriously. Well, because of all the development that's gone into the playing styles since it was invented around 1950, we're looking now at what, forty-eight years of an instrument growing and being used in a variety of different ways; so much so that nowadays despite the kind of retro-pop aspects of it, it's become very much a lead instrument in the same way as the guitar and the saxophone and the keyboards; and there are exponents playing the thing nowadays who would have been considered to be almost heretical in the late '60s and early '70s, where you're not supposed to do that on the bass guitar – you just play the root note.

Rob himself was an exponent of the instrument in ways described above, a virtuoso player with a huge repertoire of techniques at his fingertips, and the author of a regular column on advanced bass technique in the player magazine *Guitarist*.

As well as the instruments which Rob refers to above, every other instrument is situated in a similarly subtle role depending on the style, period and performance context of the music. The drums can control the tempo and any tempo inflections, and they provide a dominant contribution to the groove. Whereas they are hardly ever used as lead instruments they paradoxically have a leading role to play. Lead melody instruments, including the voice, may float around the beat, hitting or sliding onto pitches before, after or on it depending on the style of the music. Most popular music is sung, and the lyrics often form an important part of the song, such that not only singers but also other instrumentalists are liable to inflect both pitches and rhythms, and to use timbral variations according to the meanings of the lyrics. Rhythm guitar, keyboards, backing vocalists, horn and string sections in general keep to a more stable groove, but can enhance the general feel when they step out of it for a moment.

Along with considering the roles of the instruments goes another vital aspect: that of contact between the musicians. Inter-player awareness and interaction are brought into play in a variety of ways, depending on the style and period of the music, the performance context, and the prior familiarity and interpersonal relationships among the band. The examples below are all taken from drummers. The drummer can choose to 'go' with any of the instrumentalists, the choice being determined by a variety of factors including friendship and familiarity, as will be discussed in more detail in Chapter 4. 'Going' with others can take the form, on one hand, of following and responding to another instrumentalist or, on the other hand, of introducing an inflection which 'pushes' another instrumentalist into making a response. At best, such interaction involves neither always following nor always pushing, but takes the form of a musical conversation involving both.

Terry, who was playing in a Hendrix tribute band called Little Wing at the time of the interviews, emphasized how much he enjoyed interacting with the lead guitarist. Whilst the band played exact copies of the Hendrix recording for the main part of each song, they usually improvised during the breaks. Terry and the lead guitarist played complex solos which were at times virtually ametric.

Terry   I mean like the three-piece set up I'm in now is particularly good you know, and it's very much like the Hendrix thing you know, like the guitar and the drums go off, Pffff, you know what I mean, and the bass player is sort of the anchorman, you know what I mean; and um, he used to get really worried in case we didn't come back. [Laughing] He used to get really worried – he hates improvising … But he's alright now, he's got used to it.

On a live recording of the band covering 'Purple Haze' there is an example of the interaction between drums and lead, when at the end of the improvised passage both instrumentalists simultaneously articulate a subtle but powerful rallentando, or slowing up of the tempo, coming out of the improvisation and back into the main riff of the song. This pulls the music up for a moment and emphasizes the reprise, adding something to the original recording in which the drummer goes straight through the passage without observing any tempo inflections.

Simon Bourke and Michael Whiteman were, like Terry, drummers: in their case young, very good semi-professional covers/originals band members where the relationships between the musicians were well established. They also talked about interaction within the band, in terms of something they said they found hard to put into words, concerning an immediate understanding and non-verbal communication between the musicians. The relationships in each of their bands were different according to both non-musical factors, including friendships, and musical factors such as the style of the music or the proficiency and experience of different band members. Simon's band Deepvoid, which had given up doing covers to become a fully-fledged originals band a few months before the interviews, had an eclectic approach drawing on a large array of styles. (At the time of the interviews they had two guitarists, who swapped over the roles of lead and rhythm for different songs. One of these was Andy, and another member was bass player Steve, both of whom are also interviewees in this study.) I asked Simon who he primarily communicated with whilst playing:

Simon   Everyone. Apart from – not so much Robbie, the lead singer – everyone else though, always. I'm a lot with Steve the bassist, and Illy [lead/rhythm guitar] as well. And even Andy [also lead/rhythm] because I know Andy. With Andy though we can, we know how each other's going to play, because – I know it's a bit strange, but we can sort of read off each other – without you know just, we'll just *know* sort of thing. But Illy definitely, I read off him, and Steve; but no, not Robbie. I mean he's at the front anyway on stage so I can't see him – see the back of his head but that's it.

L: So how do you do that communication, how does it take place?

S: Don't know really. Look I suppose. Body movement stuff, you know, body language. You just think 'Now is the time', whatever. Let each other know. Definitely.

Michael's band was a heavy metal/progressive rock band called Rising Star, introducing about four original songs for every six covers in their set. On listening to a tape of some of their songs which Michael sent me a few days after the interview, my high expectations were surpassed by the technical proficiency of both himself and the 17-year-old lead guitarist Dave Addis who, as Michael said, 'is incredibly good. Because he's quite into that sort-of, the top-notch guitarists that are around so he's influenced by them quite a lot.'

Michael   The most important thing to me in, well in pop music certainly, is empathy with the rest of the band. And my band I play in we're very empathetic, um whatever that word is. Having played with the guitarist for five years of course it helps that. Occasionally from time to time I'll think, 'Triplet run coming up here', and I'll play a triplet run and the guitarist will also play a triplet run without having communicated beforehand, and that – I think that's absolutely excellent when that happens. And little things like that, just having the bass part following the bass drum, and every so often the drummer will do a double bass drum bounce or something, and the bassist will also do a double thing. I think that, that really makes music for me: just the little attention to detail that will bring the music to life.

Unlike the three drummers above, all of whom played in originals bands, Brent was a freelance drummer who frequently found himself playing with complete strangers. Here, contact between the musicians takes a different form, being approached more clinically, as a necessity rather than an outcome of friendship and familiarity, although that does not prevent it from offering a 'lift' to the musical experience, similar to those described above.

Brent   I mean, if somebody knows that you're coming in to do a gig that you haven't done before, then usually somebody is going to try and cue you; whether it's, you know a bass player who's going to bring the end of his guitar down for stops, or they might say at the beginning, you know, 'There's some stops, watch me'; or they might turn round and sing a phrase to you that's the end phrase just before the end's coming round, or they may be playing – you know, you kind of get to know when you're getting towards the end of a song, so if there's a repetitive phrase or something that's going around sometimes they'll give some indication, whether it's eye contact or whatever, to indicate 'This is the end.'

Dealing with equipment and acoustics

As already mentioned, one task for covers bands is to replicate the sound of the original recording. This involves not only the ways in which instruments are played individually and together, but all the equipment in use, and the acoustics of the room or hall. Whilst recordings are usually multi-tracked and engineered to a high degree, the live covers musician has to reproduce the original sound as closely as possible, using equipment which is not likely to be the same, in an acoustic which is not possessed of the properties of a recording studio and without the benefits of post-hoc sound engineering. On top of that, the electronic relay of sound means that the musicians can only hear themselves through monitor speakers and are unlikely to be hearing the same thing precisely as the audience hears (see Bennett 1983, pp. 140–45 and 160–68 for a helpful discussion of such areas). Problems can arise, such as Brent recalled on an occasion when he was playing live on television. There was very little rehearsal time, and because the monitor speaker was placed in front of him, he could hardly hear the other musicians. The music 'fell completely apart on the run-through, but for whatever reason we did it right when it actually came to it'. In the interim Brent did not consider it wise to 'make waves' by asking for the monitor to be moved.

I asked Nanette to talk about microphone technique, for example, gauging the distance between the mouth and the microphone according to the required volume, tone (such as breathy or focused) and the range (high or low notes).

Nanette   Well for live mike technique, the whole thing about pulling back and everything – that's something that takes a few years to, you know, to get off pat. But once you do, your life is a lot easier [laughs]. Otherwise they [the other musicians] hate you. Absolutely hate you if you're blasting in at the mike and it's all distorting, yeah, it's terrible …
    … So the mike is actually an extension of what's actually happening with you internally, I suppose really …
    … Well, singing live, your mike is – I mean, gosh – it's so important because when your mike sounds great, you feel comfortable and you sing better, and obviously the better the mike you're singing through, you know, the better sound you get, then the better you sound. But there has to be a point where even if it's a terrible sound, you still have to try and create something from it. So your microphone can be your best or worst friend really.

Ideally, she likes to be able to hear the sound less through the monitor speaker than through the auditorium speakers.

Nanette   … because then you can also mix that in, so if you're too loud and the instruments are too soft, then you can actually do your mixing while you're doing it, as it were. But for the studio – thankfully the studio mike that I use has got different settings, so for any BVs [backing vocals] I take this little cap off, making it omni-directional, and for any solo work I just put the cap on, changing it to uni-directional, creating a slightly different sound. So all those little things help.

Popular musicians, like all musicians, also have to judge their output levels according to the requirements of the occasion. Although Michael's main band played progressive rock and heavy metal, he also played hymns every Sunday in his local church.

Michael   Of course the congregation size varies tremendously so at Easter I can afford to actually play quite loud although I, as a drummer I actually play very quiet for a drummer, I'm not a very loud drummer at all. But yes, at Easter I can afford to play loud because there's a whole congregation there, there's the organ and there's all the brass parts and everything's going full pelt because it's a joyous occasion. But then at things like Good Friday which is very close to it, it's much more sombre and sensitive and I've got to show that in the drumming. And I think, I think that's one of my main strengths – my sensitivity towards the style.

Notation

In popular music, notation includes conventional staff notation, guitar tablature, drum notation and chord symbols, all of which are often referred to as 'charts'. Although, as will be seen in the next chapter, notation in one form or another plays a role in learning for many popular musicians in the early stages, it is always heavily mixed in with aural practices, and used as a supplement rather than a major learning resource.[5] After the early stages, published scores are used only by some function bands and session musicians, some of whom may have sight-reading abilities. Unpublished notation is used in a variety of circumstances, such as when a musical director or bandleader may hand out their own pre-written charts, or may 'scribble' something down and pass it to the musician during the session itself. In the latter case, the notation has the status of a mere instruction and is liable to be thrown away as soon as the instruction is internalized by the musician. Notation is also used as a memory-jogger whereby musicians may prepare themselves for a session after having worked with a demo or other recording, or may write down ideas and instructions for themselves during a session. In all these latter cases, notation does not have the function of preserving or passing on the music for, as already seen, these practices occur primarily through aural means which pay attention to musical aspects that are not readily notatable. Partly because of this, published scores, particularly songbooks on sale in music shops, are usually very inaccurate. A circle is created because the musicians who play the songs do not use the scores that are available in shops, so there is no need for the scores to be accurate. This in turn, of course, provides another good reason for avoiding them. At the time of writing, more accurate transcriptions of popular music instrumental parts are becoming increasingly available on the Internet. Although none of the musicians in this study mentioned using them, they may well presage some changes in how popular music is passed down in the future.

Rob Burns had a grounding in staff notation when he was a youngster, through classical trumpet lessons which included learning to read the treble clef. But he was entirely self-taught on the bass, and never connected what he was learning formally on the one instrument with what he was learning informally on the other. Then, during his first professional engagement, the following occurred:

Rob   As far as reading bass goes, it was an ordeal by fire, because I'd just got a gig in this band that backed soul artists, the Stylistics, and it was the first tour I ever did, and they had an MD who took no prisoners, and he just gave us all the charts, counted us in, and – I learnt to read bass clef in an hour!
L: You understood the principle of it before?
R: Oh yes, I knew treble clef pitch, it was only a question of reading everything a third down, but it was nerve-wracking. But I was determined not to fail.
L: Was it a completely notated part, or sort of just partially –
R: The majority of it was completely notated. I was just flying on adrenalin.

Brent, who learnt to read drum notation from his first teacher when he was 11 or 12 years old, used notation in various ways, although like all the others he never relied upon it, but mixed it with internalization and various approaches to listening:

Brent   With the pantomime you're basically reading charts – you may not have to play every note as written – it may not be that heavily written anyway but you're still having to play fairly standard sort of things ...
L: So are you, would you say that you would normally be furiously reading for the first two or three nights at a panto and then you get to know the music, or do you, do you internalize it before the –
B: I probably would be reading it, but you kind of do internalize it to some degree but I learnt to read basically when I started to play and I kind of use music kind of like a safety net. If I've got music I pretty much always stick it up. Er, whether I look at it, you know, or, or probably I'll just kind of glance to see anything like: is this three times round, four times round, or what's the ending? You're just going to glance and confirm.

He also sometimes used notation in his practice routine:

Brent   ... generally if I'm playing along with something it'll either be something I've listened to, or occasionally if I get a new book or something that's got some charts with it, I just might not listen to it and just stick the charts up and just play along and see what happens.

Nanette had maintained a very successful career without ever having been able to read except with difficulty (and as it happened, a few months after our interview, she was diagnosed as having notation dyslexia). As can be seen below, difficulty in reading notation had been stressful, but had not deterred her. Tiring of her early work in covers bands, she had decided to stretch herself after a couple of years:

Nanette   And from that I went on, I ended up doing a lot of BBC Big Band sessions. And that was a different discipline again because you had to, you were just given a score, and I couldn't read, so I'd have to take it away – they were live sessions – I'd have to take it away and literally pick out the notes one by one … When I was 11 I did have a few piano lessons so I did know the difference between C and D. I would take away the vocal part from the BBC library, and actually work out the melodies for myself and then just keep on counting from the intro sections and, as you know, you have hardly any rehearsals or anything so it was pretty nerve-racking.

Although in session work the ability to read notation is an advantage, and sometimes a necessity, it is by no means a sufficient skill for popular musicians to build up their repertoire or to join in previously unheard material. As seen earlier, Rob became a proficient sight-reader, but this did not help him at all to get work during the mid-seventies punk era when such things were less than requisite.

Rob   … going through the punk era, '76 to '77 where I'd got my technique to such a point where I was almost unemployable because of the fact I could, I had long hair and I could sight-read and I could do all these other things which were utterly unrequired.

Some popular musicians, of which Terry is one, consciously avoid notation.

Flexibility and adaptability

Freelance and session musicians must ideally be able to produce songs in any key required by the bandleader, play back melodies, riffs, chord sequences or rhythms immediately by ear and remember them, improvise over familiar and unfamiliar chord progressions, and contribute original ideas to new songs, also in a variety of musical styles, performance or recording contexts, sometimes with very little or no rehearsal. Much of this again requires basic familiarity with style. It also requires high levels of flexibility and adaptability.

Later on in his career, Rob became Head of Bass Guitar at one of the first dedicated popular music institutions in British higher education, the 'Guitar Institute and Bass Tech' in Acton, West London. Here he ensured that versatility was emphasized in the organization of the course. 'It's no good being what I call a "one-trick pony". In other words, "I'm a jazz guitarist" – well fine, wait for the phone to ring, let's see how lucky you are.' Bernie Holland made the same point in describing the dangers of concentrating too single-mindedly on developing flashy technique at the expense of branching out:

Bernie   ... you know, there's so many youngsters who go and see this stuff [for example Joe Satriani, Stanley Jordan] and they think 'That's it, that's what I've got to do!' and in the end they go down a blind alley, because at the end of the day they're not going to be able to – you know, if somebody rings up and says 'Look I've got a job doing a restaurant, I've got a vocalist who sings like Ella Fitzgerald, who does all these Gershwin songs', then, where are you then?

Although flexibility is a must for freelance, session and covers band musicians, it is not absolutely essential for all popular musicians. Originals bands, by definition, concentrate on developing an idiosyncratic musical identity. For example, Bowman (1995) provides a fascinating account of how musicians in the Memphis Stax studios during the 1960s learnt together laboriously by trial and error to produce a highly distinctive sound. Members of originals bands who play together over a lengthy period of time are liable to gain flexibility through sheer experience and the need to develop their style for personal fulfilment, professional development and to maintain their listeners' interest. But it is not essential at the time of their early development.

From copying to composing: a continuum

Playing popular music is inseparable from a variety of activities including memorizing, copying, jamming, embellishing, improvising, arranging and composing. In this section I will examine these concepts as points along a continuum.

Popular music is often described as involving a high level of improvisation, but this word is used loosely to connote a range of different practices.[6] What may be called 'pure' improvisation occurs when players make up music as they go along, without reference to any pre-agreed formal structures, chord progressions, modes or other organizing properties. This is rare, virtually non-existent in popular music, and found mainly in small pockets of post-1950s jazz and avant-garde classical music. Normally referred to as 'free improvisation', it is most readily available to a player who is unaccompanied, such as in the free solo improvisations of Lol Coxhill. When free collective – as distinct from solo – improvisation occurs, it is likely to include a limited set of pre-agreed components, such as making modal, metric, timbral or speed changes at particular, pre-identified moments, using particular notes or rhythms as signs from one musician to the others, observing speed levels, dynamic levels, physical gestures, eye contact or other factors as indicators for musicians to respond to each other, and such like. Even with free improvisation, either unaccompanied or collective, it is necessary to acknowledge that for sounds to be counted as music, they must be recognized as such, and therefore must either bear reference to a style or be contextualized by social conventions such as placing them on a concert platform, in a rehearsal or on a recording sold in a music shop.

In popular music of many kinds, improvisation usually involves the insertion of improvised passages into a pre-designated structure. The improvised passages may take the form of a solo accompanied by other instruments, which continue to play the pre-designated music. Here again, we can distinguish various points along a continuum of types of improvisation. At one extreme there is what might be conceived as an 'original improvisation', in that the music has never been played before. At the opposite extreme is a 'memorized improvisation' in which what may have started off as an original improvisation on the part of a particular player is intentionally or unintentionally memorized and then repeated with more or less exactitude by that same player, at each rendition. In memorized improvisation, what began as fluid and changeable, and may well sound like an improvisation, takes over the character of a composition, in that it has become relatively stable and fixed. In a median position between these two extremes there is a 'changeable improvisation', which is where a player significantly varies the pitches, timbre, feel, shape or other elements of a memorized solo each time it is played. The concept of improvisation can also include that of embellishment, although there is no definite line where embellishment stops and improvisation begins. Embellishment tends to connote a less extended or more local variation on pre-existing fixed musical components, and in many ways overlaps with the concept of 'changeable improvisation'. From the listener's point of view, it is not always easy to distinguish an original, memorized or changeable improvisation one from the other, the safest means being to listen to two or more takes, that is different recordings of the same song.

When songs are being covered, musicians have a variety of options concerning how they approach improvisation. In some cases, especially where the original recording contains a very famous solo, the covers musician may copy it exactly. But this is not the norm. For example, out of forty-five or fifty songs that he played with his function band, guitarist Will Cragg only played two solos in a way that was identical to the originals. This was because he felt the solos were particularly good or particularly well known. More often, whilst the main part of the song is copied as exactly as is possible or desired, covers musicians will intentionally move away from the original recording during the improvised passages and insert their 'own' improvised solo, which may be either an original, a memorized or a changeable one. Players might also make passing reference to well-known improvised solos as part of their own solos.

Improvisation has no clearly defined boundaries marking it off from jamming. The two activities are distinguishable mainly in terms of the degree of freedom accorded players, as against the extent to which they are playing over pre-arranged patterns. Free collective improvisation, as the most extreme or 'pure' type of group improvisation, tends to be based on agreements that are minimal and idiosyncratic to the group. By contrast, jamming tends to occur on the basis of high levels of agreement as to the harmonies, rhythms, structure and other elements of the music, and is based on patterns that are not peculiar to the group or the particular piece in question, but that are on the contrary, well known and frequently employed in the musical tradition from which the musicians are drawing.

In popular music, jamming will normally occur over standard chord patterns, typically 12-bar blues progressions or other very common progressions. Without any verbal discussion whatsoever, any notation or other stimulus, a whole band, including a group of people who might never have played together before, can launch into group music-making on the basis of such progressions. If desired, they can agree substitute chords by merely saying a couple of words before starting; but prior verbal agreement is not necessary for changes to be made to the set patterns, for a player might introduce a variation, such as a substitute chord or a new distinctive riff, during the playing, with the intention that the others will pick it up and respond to it without any discussion; or they may shout out an instruction or suggestion. Improvised solos in jams may also depart from pre-set structures and involve inter-musician communication concerning, for example, when the solo is to end. The issues discussed earlier – particularly feel, groove, timbre, sensitivity to style, the roles of the instruments and players – will all come into play to varying degrees of finesse.

As will be seen again in later parts of the book, jamming is a fundamental activity for popular musicians. It does not take place only at the beginning stages, but throughout a career, usually for fun. In many cases, especially at the early stages, jamming can lead to the formation of a band, but some of the professional players in this study also mentioned jams that took place when there was spare studio time at the end of a recording session or in other similar circumstances. Today it is becoming increasingly common for record companies to issue previously unreleased recordings of sessions, sometimes including jams.

Many covers are presented as conscious interpretations of an original song, perhaps using different instruments or involving a different groove, feel, tempo and other factors. These then move along the continuum towards a place that might be referred to as 'arrangement'. Record companies and some performing outfits make use of arrangers, either appointed as external personnel or drawn from within the band. In the case of groups that are 'created' by the music industry, arrangers will be provided by the record company; in the case of originals bands, one member might take precedence over others in the arrangement of the music. For covers bands, an arranger is required to varying degrees depending on the needs and experiences of the musicians in the band. Will Cragg's seven-piece function band learnt songs by aural methods akin to those described by Bernie, Rob and Brent earlier. But for his duo, Will makes detailed arrangements; a task which is not easy given that it usually involves reducing music originally made by a number of musicians and instruments to a copy by only two (and the duo do not use a pre-recorded backing track or drum machine).

Will   In the function band, we give everyone a copy of the song on tape. Everyone goes away and learns it, apart from the guy I do the duo with – he's the singer in the band as well. He plays acoustic. So I arrange his parts. Because I'm playing electric in it, I've got to cover usually the string section, the brass section and all the guitar parts. I just arrange it myself, but again it's picking out the important bits.

L: Yes, so you do a sort of acoustic trick – a sort of deceptive thing on the audience.

W: Yes. Well, again like with 'Hotel California' there are three guitar parts doing all this twin lead stuff all the way through and you just pick out the famous bits, because I've always found that people don't notice it – it's like, they fill in the bits themselves. It's so famous, but they don't realize it's not twin lead, it's just a lead ...

... Say something like 'Good Vibrations' which has got, I don't know how many tracks on it. For the most important bits, I figure out what the chords are, write down the chords for him, give him the chords ... He'll play the chords, I'll play the bits that people recognize, like the bass line at the beginning and all the sort of widdly bits in between ... We try and arrange it so that we're not playing in the same part of the neck, otherwise it just sounds boring, so he'll play maybe down the neck; I'll put a capo halfway up the neck and – we use different voicings, different harmonies.

A much younger musician too:

Richard   L: OK so could you say, not how did you get the cover onto your recording, but how interested were you in copying not just the chords and the structure of the song but, you know, some of the details and how did you go about learning them?

R: OK, um, if it was say an Oasis song – the lead guitar doesn't play that important part – it's kind of always there, but with some songs there was an important bit that needed that riff. You know, do you know 'Film Star' by Suede? There's this riff at the end and it's kind of important – it needs to be part of the song. It's a bit – everyone recognizes that bit. So we tried to get all those important bits and if they went wrong we just did them anyway.

Finally, the concept of composition itself cannot be distinguished from many of the other activities mentioned above, except in so far as it connotes two further aspects. First, it tends to suggest that the work is the product of an individual rather than a group; second, it implies the creation of a piece of music whose formal properties remain largely fixed. Popular music has many individual songwriters, but nonetheless, their end-products are nearly always the result of a combination of people, and are subject to major improvisatory changes by different musicians. In some cases, the songwriter will produce a demo recording for the musicians, each of whom will then respond to the recording through musical actions that can be placed somewhere along the continuum from changeable improvisation to embellishment. In other cases, the record company might employ an arranger for all or part of a song, so that the final product is again the work of more than one person. Not only that, but the opinions of 'A and R', or 'Artist and Repertoire' personnel, managers and most particularly the role of the producer or sound engineer are vital to the overall mix, allowing the emergence of auteur-producers such as Phil Spector or Brian Eno. In other cases, such as when Nanette works with her partner Russ Courteney, two or more people will collaborate on a composition from the outset. As will be seen in Chapters 3 and 4, a great deal of popular music composition occurs as a group activity in which every member has a major creative role, and is embedded in improvisatory practices leading to finalized products which are essentially memorized improvisations. So popular music composition is undertaken along a continuum from the individual to the group. This can create tensions including dissension over the ownership of the cultural product, leading to heated arguments including the break-up of bands (of which readers will undoubtedly know some famous examples).

Whereas group popular music composition will be discussed more fully in Chapters 3 and 4, here I wish to mention that the practices, attitudes and values involved in individual popular music composition are not necessarily far removed from those associated with composition in the classical field. A comment by Andy suggests that creative processes identified in some of the literature, including concepts such as 'inspiration' and 'spontaneity', and the notion that worthwhile creative ideas only arise when they are not sought, came to him in very comparable ways.[7]

Andy I mean like I've got problems writing nowadays – I mean I've got to look after the band in other ways now, but I have to take time to sit down and write and I can't – I could never do that. It would have to be – I'd be walking along one day and it'd pop into my head, what I'm going to do. And what I try to do is remember this, and when I get some time I will write it down, but it doesn't really work – to sit down and write is, is just, I don't know. It's a frustrating thing because you can't be creative just because you want to be. It just pops into your head, just like that.

Some self-conceptions of popular musicians

Popular music involves different categories of musicians who produce different musical sub-styles and engage in different kinds of employment, and amongst my interview group were representatives of all the main British guitar-based pop and rock categories. I now wish to consider some of their self-conceptions, looking first at the session and freelance musician, then the covers band and function band musician, and finally the originals band musician. Most popular musicians will experience two or more of the activities involved in these musician categories at various points in their lives, but this is by no means necessarily the case and, indeed, as will be seen, some of the categories are actively avoided by some of the musicians. Self-conceptions arise not only from past and current involvement in music, but also, particularly for younger musicians, from aspirations for the future, and as such they can affect music learning practices in various ways which will be discussed during Chapters 3 and 4.

Howard Becker's famous study of 1950s dance band musicians (Becker 1963) revealed tensions between their involvement with two styles of music: jazz, which was perceived as aesthetically and technically demanding music for the connoisseur, and the popular dance music of the day, which was conceived as inferior music for the undiscerning 'square'. Whereas they *wanted* to play jazz, opportunities were few, competition intense, audiences small and remuneration even smaller; therefore they *needed* to play dance music in order to earn a living (also see Berliner 1994 for a more recent perspective on similar issues). In the world of British popular music (and that of many other countries), a similar split between two large-scale musical 'worlds' is discernible and is often commented upon. One is perceived as demanding and serious, typically including progressive rock, the music of 'indie' bands (bands signed to independent record companies rather than 'majors') or music known as 'Brit Pop'. The other is seen as a commercial sell-out aimed at 'duped' young teenagers and children: in other words, charts 'pop', especially that emanating from hit-factories and performed by 'manufactured' groups. It would be reasonable to surmise that this split would confront popular musicians in ways that are similar to the split experienced by Becker's musicians. However, although some of the musicians in the present study felt strong disdain for certain types of work, others were less affected and rather took pleasure and pride in the versatility required of them in working across distinct musical worlds, including both rock and 'pop', more in the manner of a craftsperson than an inspired artist.[8]

The session and freelance musician

The term 'session musician' in the world of popular music is generally hallowed and denotes one who is freelance and highly proficient. A session musician may be found playing any kind of music in virtually any scenario, including recording sessions for the large companies or live gigs, and is hired on the assumption that he or she will need relatively little rehearsal time in order to produce a flawless performance. The meaning of the term 'freelance musician' is in many ways indistinguishable from that of 'session musician' with regard to the *types* of skill, knowledge and versatility required, but the freelance musician generally enjoys less prestige, is contracted to fewer major record company sessions or gigs by famous bands and more demo recordings (demonstration recordings used as advertising for up-and-coming bands or individuals) and local live gigs. As the type of work they do is in general terms similar, I will treat the session and the freelance musician together under the single descriptor 'session musician'.

As mentioned in Chapter 1, in some areas of popular music, especially certain charts music, a huge gap can exist in the technical ability, versatility, musical understanding, improvisational creativity or general musicianship between the performers. There are many examples of hits which are marketed on the basis of the fame – or intended fame – of the singers or band members, but which rely for their sound quality on the input of session musicians, sound engineers and others whose names are not even credited and who, in comparison to the 'stars', would be receiving a comparatively tiny financial reward for their services. I witnessed a particularly extreme example not long ago on the BBC weekly programme *Top of the Pops*. A new (and short-lived) all-girl band was on stage, the 'live' drummer of which could be seen playing only about a quarter of the notes that were audible.

Session musicians tend to have an attitude rather reminiscent of the pre-nineteenth-century position of the musician as a servant. In Bernie Holland's words:

Bernie   I've always tried to be mindful of the fact that if somebody hires me, because that's what we are, as freelance people we are allowing ourselves to be, we hire ourselves out to do a particular job of work … When I get a job from somebody, I want to find out exactly what they want from me; not what I want from them, not what I want, not how can I do my thing in this – I think that's where some musicians can go wrong is, you know, using a situation as a vehicle to do your own thing, when really you are serving, you are a servant of the person you are working for.

He takes this attitude to the point of avoiding, and implicitly putting down showmanship or self-expression, in a manner that suggests taking a certain pride in humility. I had been trying to get him to answer a question on whether he identifies more closely with a particular style of music than with any other. Eventually he said:

Bernie   I was asked by a lady called Joan Armatrading [a famous British singer-songwriter], I got a call from her, she was doing an album. I asked her, I said 'What do you want?' She said 'Oh, I booked you because of *you*. I've got a track which is a kind of a bluesy sort of thing, and there's a guitar solo, and I

want you to do exactly what you want to do in that solo', you know, 'That's
why I booked you.' Well, in that situation, being a blues, once again having
listened to the track, I had to bear in mind you know, I didn't want to do
something that was going to stick out like a sore thumb, so that I might like, I
might think it's clever and everything but, you know it just might stick out like
a sore thumb on the track. So I have to listen to the track and see the general
sort of feel of it, so I'm going to have to, even though she's saying you know,
'Do exactly what you want to do', I'm going to have to adapt myself to
accommodate a situation like that.

Rob also provided an example of how the work of the session musician
requires an amount of self-effacement. This occurred as an aside in a conversation
during which I was trying to establish some basic facts about his career. As quoted
earlier, he was describing the period of mid-seventies punk as a time 'when I'd
got my technique to such a point where I was almost unemployable because of
the fact I could, I had long hair and I could sight-read and I could do all these
other things which were utterly unrequired'. Later he said:

Rob   I was a kind of freelance hired gun, as it were. Quite often in the kind of late
           seventies and early eighties, with the kind of, what was called the New Wave
           – sort of *après* punk – whereas there were a lot of good songwriters around at
           the time, the standard of musicianship was such that there was always a call
           for people like myself, not necessarily to join the band, but to go and do the
           recording and the showcase and all the rest of it, and then the band would go
           out and promote the single …
              … So I ended up between '76 up to very early '79 just doing loads and
           loads of functions and being a kind of freelance, 'do anything you like' type
           bass player, 'just give me the money', sort of thing.

Brent also revealed a similar attitude, in discussing how he approaches a
contract:

Brent   You know, if you'd never heard the stuff before then you're going to try and
           come up with something that is what they want. I mean usually once you've
           had a couple of run-throughs you should know what's going on, but it depends
           on whether you find something that fits what they want … And sometimes
           people don't, they kind of know what they *don't* want but they don't always
           know exactly what they *do* want. And sometimes they're not always that good
           at explaining; you know in their own head they know what they want but they
           can't actually always explain it.
           L: You're speaking a lot of the time of trying to do what other people want. Do
           you feel that that's your role, to translate their ideas into something as close as
           you can get?
           B: I suppose yeah, to some extent. I mean it depends on what kind of gig
           you're doing. But generally I think if I'm going in to play on somebody's
           original material, then I want to basically do what it is they want. They've
           obviously got some idea of what kind of thing they're trying to do, and I see
           that as my function basically. But if I'm doing, say a jazz gig or more of a

blowing gig then obviously there's more room to sort of maybe thrash around a bit more.

None of the above musicians mentioned any tension comparable with Becker's musicians, but expressed instead a certain pleasure in their adaptability to a variety of demands. However as we will see, others did articulate tensions which bear both similarities and differences.

The covers band and function band musician

'Covers bands' primarily 'cover', or copy, well-known recordings or hits in a variety of popular styles. Their gigs take place mainly in pubs and other similar venues. Often, as well as copying previous hits, they produce their own original music and are able to insert some of it into their set at a proportion of approximately 70 per cent covers to 30 per cent originals. Covers bands are therefore often embryonic originals bands. 'Function bands' can be thought of in the same way as covers bands, except that they will be hired for functions such as weddings and dinner-dances. They are likely to be asked to agree a list of songs before the event, and are unlikely to be tolerated if they introduce original material into a set. The distinction between covers and function bands is often blurred, as the same band may well operate in both capacities in order to maximize bookings. I will sometimes use the word 'covers' to refer to them both, in so far they have in common the practice of covering songs, and it is this that I am concerned with rather than details of gigs and venues. The 'tribute band' is a type of covers band, but it covers the music of only one originals band, which may itself be either defunct or still active. Some tribute bands aim for a precise replication of the original act, including not only every note of the music but also the clothes, hair-styles and stage performance of the band they copy; others place their own interpretation on both the music and the act as a whole; and there are of course various gradations between these two approaches. (For an interesting discussion of the tribute band phenomenon and the North of England pub rock scene in general, see Bennett 1997.)

Session musicians will often find themselves contracted to a covers or function band in order to deputize for a missing player, but by 'covers band musician' or 'function band musician' I am mainly referring to those who are established members of a band containing more or less stable personnel. These musicians are looking for bookings for the band as a whole, rather than looking to fit into a variety of different situations as an individual.

Will Cragg is a covers band musician *par excellence*. His musical tastes, like those of the musicians quoted in the sub-section above, were wide, and as distinct from expressing any shame about playing various sub-styles of popular music, he was quite open about his enjoyment of it. As well as seventies and eighties charts music, he had recently been teaching himself AOR, or what is known in Britain as adult oriented rock (and in the USA as album oriented rock).

Will   That sort of style I've taught myself recently, which is very different from your out-and-out seventies rock. Most people hate it, I think it's a wonderful style of playing.

Despite his allegiance to covers, as we have already seen earlier in the chapter, Will does not usually copy solos, but rather regards improvisation as representing an area of freedom which both covers and session musicians carve out for themselves.

Will   Santana's solo is very famous, but I don't like to copy it because half the fun for me is improvising. I mean, it's lovely getting paid, I need to get paid, but the thing that sort of keeps me going, meaning I want to go out and do it every night, is the improvisation, trying new things, it's always different.

His position suggests a love of the distinction afforded between freedom and necessity, regardless of style.

The originals band musician

In contrast to session, covers and function band musicians, there are 'originals band' musicians, who are dedicated to a particular band and the style of music which is deeply felt to be characteristic of that band. The originals band is one which produces its own *oeuvre*. In the case of experienced, particularly professional originals bands, this will mean only releasing a cover on the general understanding that it is an interpretation of the song with the individual style of the band stamped upon it. In the case of young originals bands, as already mentioned, the repertoire may include covers, or alternatively the band may have left covers behind at a relatively early, and in some cases premature, stage.

   Andy Brooks was one of two lead/rhythm guitarists in the band Deepvoid (although the other guitarist left soon after the interviews). In contrast to Bernie, Rob and Brent earlier:

Andy   My idea of session work is when you're told to play, and you play that. You're paid to do it, fair enough, you're probably paid quite a lot of money and it might be a good living but I couldn't do that – I'd have to put my own interpretation in there somewhere or other. No, session work's never appealed to me, and one of the reasons against it was to get somewhere and to, maybe to influence someone, I mean inspire someone.
             ... There's room for interpretation whatever you do, and you're always going to put your own style into whatever it is. So I mean, the main place you get to do that as a guitarist is when you're doing solo work.

He had, however, regularly deputized for a friend in another originals band. Covering in such a situation is more problematic than usual because, unlike previously released songs, he might not know the music, and there would not be time to work up an exact copy.

Andy   If you had to learn everyone else's solo when you're standing in for them, it's a long task – takes too much time. So you just do your own thing. And sometimes I actually think it sounds better, which is always a plus – it helps, you know.

His attitudes are more akin to those of the musicians in Becker's study (also see note 8), in that they suggest a higher value accorded to the individuality of the isolated genius, as against the need to 'play to the gallery' for financial gain: Deepvoid did covers 'purely to earn the money'.

Michael Whiteman, who was in a band that saw itself as both a covers and an originals band, expressed similar attitudes.

Michael   We compose a lot of our own stuff – it depends what we're doing. The gigs at pubs, we play mostly covers to keep the audience interested but when we're playing for clubs and things we try and play a bit more of our own stuff: sort of 60 per cent our own stuff, 40 per cent covers, to keep the interest, but so we can still expose our own material.

Crossing between covers and originals

After the first couple of years of her career, Nanette tired of doing covers, partly as a result of her position in the band:

Nanette   At the beginning of the week, you'd get a tape of say eight or twelve songs and you had to learn them all off by heart, and the bandleader would probably only use about three or four of them so, you know, you felt you were always on somebody else's timetable, you were always doing what someone else wanted, and so on.

Not only that, she felt constrained by having to sing exact copies of the music, as close to the original recording as possible. Her transition into original music was gradual:

Nanette   Well, it took me a while actually to get into original music because one of the dilemmas, I think, if you're copying all the time is at what point do you stop copying and when do you start to own the song for yourself and put it over as *you*, rather than just as a copy of someone else? And I never forget the day that that happened for me – I was, oh, I was going to sing a song called 'Rio de Janeiro Blues' by Randy Crawford and I'd learnt it off pat, how she did it, and I remember just sitting in the back of my Mum's car and she was just driving to some gig or whatever, and I remember just feeling totally free as I worked through the melody, and finding a new way, and I just threw it completely upside down and found my own way of doing it. And from that day I've always found my own way of doing it. So I think it's, it's something you have to develop.

Terry crossed over the two musician categories illustrated earlier in a drastic manner. At 17 when Hawkwind first started, he was completely committed to its particular stance against the music industry and to the band's preference for giving free benefits, protest gigs and performing on festival fringes. But as the success and following of the band grew, disillusionment with and maltreatment by the record industry caused him to leave Hawkwind about two weeks before their hit single 'Silver Machine' reached number ten in the UK charts in 1973. This was followed by a period of several years during which he either did not play at all or engaged in sporadic work with a variety of bands. Later, in his thirties, he joined a covers band:

Terry   I played with a covers band after not playing for ages. In fact the band I got into, someone just rang me up, after not playing for about seven years ... and I'd never played in a covers band in my life. And this band was atrocious, it was the worst band I've ever played in in my life, but it was hilarious – they were doing things like 'Ghost Riders in the Sky' – it was hilarious, I was screaming with laughter, you know what I mean, and it was really novel. They said 'Do you want to come back and do it next week somewhere else?' 'Yeah OK.' Er, I played with them for about two years and they were absolutely appalling, dreadful band. Although I did meet my current bass player in it, he played with them for a while. But yeah, it was a terrible, terrible band but they just had constant work, you know all the time.

He made a comment similar to those of Will and Andy, above, concerning his need to put some self-expression into his playing of covers.

Terry   It's like when you're playing in an R & B band, or even with the Hendrix stuff you know [his tribute band at the time of the interviews], it's only during the solos that you can put your own stamp on it, do you know what I mean; and then, I very much like to do that you know. But you know, during the rest of it I'm just doing the actual number.

However, personal commitment to the band and to the music being covered went a long way towards ameliorating the more negative perceptions of covering:

Terry   Oh, I give it my all. This is why I so love playing the Hendrix thing, because I can do the same with that, you know, it's wonderful stuff and you know, I totally believe in the guy, so I'm able to give it everything, you know, as opposed to playing in a covers band or, although it is covers as such, or an R & B thing, you know, it's not the same commitment.
L: Yep. Because?

> T: I mean you can enjoy it almost as much but it's not, I can't you know, or one doesn't tend to give it – it doesn't allow one to give as much of oneself you know.

Later:

Terry   Well, that's how I play anyway, I'm a really busy drummer, quite a lot and that's what I like doing and that's when I can you know express myself more, as opposed to just sitting back and tapping away. I like to get really physical with it.

In general, the younger the players were, the more value they explicitly placed upon producing original music. Here 'original' means more than simply 'their own compositions', but denotes compositions that are felt to be idiosyncratic to the band. Ask any young popular musician what kind of music their band plays and the answer one is liable to get is 'It's impossible to describe; it's not like any other music', a comment that is inevitably highly exaggerated, given the necessity for all music to conform to conventions enabling it to be recognized as music at all. Negus (1999 p. 4) includes an interesting discussion of young bands coming to face the reality that they must classify themselves in order to get bookings! But the music will undoubtedly *seem* to the young musicians as though it really is not like any other music, and the reasons for this arise precisely from the experimental nature of the musicians' early learning practices, oriented around the unconscious assimilation of musical conventions, or enculturation. The role of covers in popular music learning practices will be discussed in more detail in Chapter 3.

Music for pay, music for fun and musical aspirations

The demands of the work, combined with a competitive selection process whereby some young musicians become professionals and others do not, suggest that those who do are relatively highly motivated. Apart from Peter, who had not started an instrument until he was about 18, the oldest eleven musicians in this study had become fully professional between the ages of 17 and 22, and semi-professional from 13 and over. They all displayed exceptionally high levels of motivation dating back to childhood or at the latest early teens. For example:

Bernie   I'd always wanted to be a musician. One of the teachers in our school, when I used to bring the guitar in, you know, I think it was one of the science masters, who said 'Holland, if you think you're ever going to make a living twanging that thing, think again' and I said 'Yeah, alright, thanks' you know. So, you know, I'd always wanted, I was, I just loved it you know.

Some of the younger musicians had ambitions of becoming session musicians – Simon Bourke and Michael Whiteman, both drummers, in particular. But as we have already seen, such a role was not attractive to everyone. Even though Andy had wanted to become a fully professional musician since he had first picked up a guitar at the age of 6, he was not prepared to go against his beliefs and musical values so far as to aim for a career as a session musician. The highest aspiration of musicians in this study was to become a 'star', but even stardom has never been regarded by all young popular musicians as a desirable end-point and can, on the contrary, be consciously avoided. Terry provided a strong example of this. He had initially felt committed to Hawkwind partly because the band took a stance against the industry and the commercial construction of stardom, and had left it aged 19 or 20, when he thought it was beginning to move in the opposite direction.

Terry   … when we were in Hawkwind, we used to, you know, put down pop stars as such, you know, 'Look at me' and, you know what I mean. So I was never sort of pushy of myself.

Dreams of stardom were, for obvious reasons, more common to the younger musicians, the main part of whose lives still lay ahead of them. At 21, Deepvoid bass player Steve Popplewell was unconcerned and measured about it:

Steve   If you get famous, you get famous. But I mean it's not the end of the world for me, which is why I've made sure I got my [motor mechanic] qualifications, so I've always got something to fall back on … If you're just going out there just to be famous and it doesn't happen, you got nothing, you just, you got nothing at all.

Some younger hopes were expressed more forcefully, but were nevertheless tinged with realism.

Michael   I'd really quite like to be a very famous musician; my ideal thing would be to practice the instruments I'm not so good at, like the guitar, and also learn the bass guitar, which I can sort of play a bit, but only through my knowledge of the guitar, and become one of the people who record all the parts individually in the studio, multi-layering … that would be something I'd quite like to do. More realistically though I'd like to be a session drummer.

Emily   Obviously we have the dream that I think most, or everyone like, who plays in a rock band can identify with: you know playing, big concert and having everyone marching around to your music and that. You know, the fame, the glamour, that kind of thing. But I think, I know that's not really likely to happen in the near future. I think we're going to maybe support in Camden and see where it takes us. But we do hope to gradually put out singles and albums and that.

Richard   I would like to go on stage one day and you know, when you go to a concert so you have the effect of hearing their music and thinking 'Wow! Imagine for them to have all these thousands of people just screaming "Yeah we love you".' You know, I want to do that on stage sometime.

Youthful aspirations of creativity and fame amongst the younger musicians can be understood in terms of post-eighteenth-century notions of genius – notions that continue to be common-sense assumptions today – as involving the inspired, intuitive outpourings of the isolated individual, autonomous from the social and artistic contexts in which he (not normally she) finds himself, yet able to sum up in his work a universal expression of the human condition, recognized and hailed by one and all. By contrast, most of the more experienced players had either dropped or had never espoused such ambitions and saw themselves more as craftspeople. But for all the musicians, enjoying and believing in what they were doing earned more acclaim than making money, and despite the dreaming, none of the youngest musicians I spoke to ever intended to give up making music, stardom or no stardom, as exemplified below.

Steve   L: Can you see yourself when you're 30 or so – do you think you'll still be playing?
S: I'll still be playing, but I don't know if I'll be in a band. I'll be like my Dad – teaching my son. [Laughs]

Emily   L: Would you ever consider playing in a different band – I mean, if your present band fell through, what would you do?
E: I really hope that doesn't happen, but I mean if this band fell through I'd always be looking to play in another band because I, I don't think I'll give up the guitar. I mean I might not play it, practise it all the time but I wouldn't, I'd never forget how to play and I think I'd obviously be looking to play with somebody else, just in a group.

Leo   L: And what do you hope to do with your music now?
Leo: Um, I'm not quite sure because now I'm leaving school and I have to think about what I'm doing in the future, and I would like to have something to do with music; but then again, maybe there's another profession that I would like to do and I'm not quite sure at the moment; and, but I would like to definitely, I would enjoy to keep it up, to keep on doing music, in whatever way, playing the saxophone, composing or whatever … just doing it for fun, yeah.

One of the motivations behind this book was to contribute to calls for increased amateur participation in music-making, not only by children and school-aged young people, but carrying over into adult life. In order to establish any correlation between informal music learning practices and long-term practical musical involvement, large-scale research conducted over a long period of time would be required. Such research could also consider whether, for example, the session musician attitudes such as those discussed earlier contribute to the likelihood of musicians becoming successful professionals; whether the younger ones who were more romantic in outlook are likely to be prevented by their attitudes from becoming professionals; or whether if they do become professionals it will necessitate a change in their attitudes. In this book, I am not able to address such issues longitudinally, but my aim is to consider how popular music skills and knowledge are acquired. However, I do wish to suggest a hypothesis for future investigation beyond the scope of the present book: that young musicians who acquire their skills and knowledge more through informal learning practices than through formal education may be more likely to continue playing music, alone or with others, for enjoyment in later life. Whatever the solution to the hypothesis, it cannot deny the experiences of the young musicians, during the time that they are involved in music-making.

Notes

1. For a scholarly review of early ethnomusicological work relating to this concept see Merriam (1964, pp. 145–50). According to him the term derives from Herskovit (1948) and is used synonymously with other terms, 'culturation', 'culturalization' or just 'socialization' (pp. 145–6). The word 'acculturation' is also sometimes used, although this normally implies musical hybridization (see Manuel 1988 for a good discussion). For discussions of the concept in relation to formal music education see, for example, Nettl (1983, pp. 323–5) , Kwami (1989), Campbell (1998), McCarthy (1997), Nwezi (1999).
2. For a full musicological discussion of different types of listening, mainly in terms of musical reception rather than playing and composing, see Middleton 1990, pp. 57–60 and passim.
3. See for example, Davidson et al. (1996), whose study of 257 children suggested that those who were the most 'successful' at instrumental lessons had parents who were 'the most highy involved in lessons and practice in the earliest stages of learning'. The parents were also often involved with music themselves, mostly through listening rather than performing. The most musically able children had the highest levels of parental support. For further discussion and debate in this area see, for example, Sloboda and Howe (1991, 1999), Sloboda and Davidson (1996) and Gagné (1999). Within popular music studies parental encouragement is mentioned by several authors for example, Bennett (1980, p. 20), and in music education studies see, for example, Campbell (1998, p. 162f.).
4. See Lilliestam (1996, pp. 201ff.) for a helpful discussion of how musicians aurally memorize material.
5. For helpful discussions of the use of notation in rock music see, for example, Bennett (1980, 1983) and Lilliestam (1996).
6. For discussions of musical improvisation across genres and styles see Nettl and Russell (1998), Small (1987, pp. 281–309) and Bailey (1992). With specific reference to free improvisation in jazz, see Jost (1994); for jazz in more general terms see Berliner (1994), Monson (1996); for a phenomenology, Sudnow (1993); and for a sociological perspective, Martin (1996). Within music education studies and the psychology of music, the journal *Psychology of Music*, vol. 27, no. 2 (1999) contains an interesting article by Sawyer with separate replies by John Baily, Hargreaves and Welch; and for discussions of free improvisation in formal educational contexts, see, at higher education level, Ford (1995), Davidson and Smith (1997); and in schooling, Derek Bailey (1992), pages 118–23 of which are also available as Bailey (1996).

7. For a discussion of creativity in relation to composers in the Western classical tradition see Sloboda (1985, pp. 115ff.), and for further examples of musicians talking about this subject in ways similar to Andy, see many of the popular music ethnographies already mentioned such as Bennett (1980), Cohen (1991) and Berkaak (1999).
8. See Berkaak (1999, pp. 31–2, 41) for an interesting discussion of differences in the originals musician and the session musician attitudes amongst members of the Swedish rock band The Sunwheels (and subsequent bands that were formed out of it). The ethnographic literature on rock is rich in examples of such tensions. See, for example, Bennett (1980), Cohen (1991); and see Negus (1999) for a discussion of how corporate commercial concerns impact on these tendencies.

Chapter 3

Learning to play popular music: acquiring skills and knowledge

The discussion in the preceding chapter, concerning the 'beginnings' and 'ends' of acquiring popular music skills and knowledge, sets the context for examining what went in-between. How do the musicians get from those beginnings to those ends? This chapter will consider the main learning practices through which the professional musicians in the study had arrived at, and the younger musicians were going about working towards, their ends. In interviewing the older musicians concerning this aspect of their experiences, I was relying to a large extent upon their long-term memories. The younger ones, by contrast, were often talking to me about what they had done that day or the week before. All the accounts were nonetheless largely commensurate with each other, age and experience featuring as interesting parts of the musicians' perspectives whilst introducing no glaring contradictions. The accounts also tied in with existing research into popular musicians' practices.[1]

As observed in Chapter 1, informal music learning practices and formal music education are not mutually exclusive, but learners often draw upon or encounter aspects of both. Whilst Terry had received no specialist instrumental tuition in either classical or popular music, the other thirteen musicians had each experienced varying amounts, four in classical music, four in popular music, and five in both classical and popular music. In many cases the experiences involved only elementary tuition, the number of lessons amounting to not much more than a handful or less than two years' worth, and were not felt by the learners to have been particularly beneficial. The main exceptions to this were, regarding classical tuition, bassist Rob who had regular trumpet lessons for two or three years as a teenager, drummer Michael who had piano lessons for three or four years when he was about 8 to 12 years old, and guitarist Emily who had taken cello lessons for about five years from the age of 11 or 12, and was still taking them at the time of the interviews. Regarding popular music tuition, those who had received a continuous course of lessons during their teenage years were Will, who had electric guitar lessons for five years, and Simon and Michael, both of whom had drum lessons for three or four years. Brent took lessons sporadically from the age of about 10 to 13, when he started to do paid gigs. He then dropped lessons until he was 18 when he took them up for a year, then dropped them again until he was 23, a year after having become fully professional. Nanette had taken singing lessons only after she had become professional. A summary of tuition taken by all the musicians is provided in Table 2 of the Appendix (p. 220).

Whilst recognizing that both classical and popular instrumental lessons provided a vital input for some of the players, in this and the next chapter I will focus on the informal practices that made up the bulk of the interviewees' popular music learning experiences, leaving consideration of their instrumental lessons and their classroom music education for Chapters 5 and 6. Therefore, although readers will undoubtedly observe both similarities and differences between informal and formal practices, discussion of these will wait until later in the book.

Learners are aware to differing degrees of the nature and even the mere fact of their learning practices. At one extreme, 'unconscious' learning practices occur without any particular awareness that learning is occurring; they lack goal-directed design, are unfocused and may not be considered, named or otherwise conceptually isolated by the learner. At the opposite extreme, 'conscious' learning practices occur when learners are aware that they are learning, or attempting to learn, have explicit sets of goals combined with procedures for reaching them, such as a structured practice routine, and are able to consider, name or otherwise conceptualize and isolate their learning practices. Musical enculturation is likely to involve relatively unconscious learning practices of the former type. Formal music education places emphasis on relatively conscious learning practices of the latter type. As will be seen in the course of the book, informal popular music learning stretches between the two, varying in the degree of awareness on the part of the learner from virtually unconscious learning by enculturation to highly conscious autodidacticism. In addition, both musical enculturation and informal music learning can of course take place within and as a result of formal music education.

The overriding learning practice: listening and copying

Children not only *copy the behaviour* of adults and other children, but they also *make copies of objects* which they find in the environment. Here, the object in question is music, and its main form of existence for most people most of the time is in recordings and broadcasts in the home, school, college, at work, at social gatherings and in other public places such as shops. Live music is encountered much less. By far the overriding learning practice for the beginner popular musician, as is already well known, is to copy recordings by ear. Bennett (1980) pays considerable attention to the primacy of this practice in the development of rock musicians, and there are also discussions of it in much of the literature mentioned in note 1. It seems an extraordinary fact that many thousands of young musicians across the world have adopted this approach to learning over a relatively short space of time – covering a maximum of eighty years since sound recording and reproduction technology began to be widespread – outside of any formal networks, usually at early stages of learning, in isolation from each other, without adult guidance and with very little explicit recognition of the ubiquity of the practice across the world. All this, despite the fact that it is a historically unique way of learning music, unknown to humankind prior to the invention and spread of sound recording and reproduction technology. At the same time, I would wish to add, it also has aspects in common with traditional formal and informal music teaching and learning methods, as will be discussed in the final chapter.

Many of the musicians in this study were initially somewhat lost for words when I attempted to draw from them a description of how they went about learning to play their instrument. My impression was that although they all did it by copying recordings, many of them had not considered this practice to be a part of *learning*, viewing it rather as something private, unfocused or unworthy of discussion. Indeed, it is unusual for someone to want to talk about it, and Bennett found his interviewees were similarly bemused by his questions on the subject (1980, p. 132). For these reasons, I was to some extent required to pretend that I did not know anything at all about it, and to elaborate on what I meant by the question rather more than I wished to or needed to concerning other aspects of the interview. Once conversation began to flow, most of the interviewees were able to enter quite confidently into detail, but for some, copying recordings appeared to be so much a part of their enculturation that it had always been virtually unconscious. Many indicated a mixture of more or less conscious and unconscious approaches to it.

Copying recordings involves all three types of listening distinguished in the previous chapter – purposive, attentive and distracted – in so far as it is undertaken with varying degrees of self-conscious systematization.

Copying recordings – purposive listening

The most systematic, conscious and goal-directed approaches to learning through listening and copying involve something akin to what I have described as 'purposive listening'.

Rob   L: So between sort of 13 and 17, apart from devising your own technique as best you could, how else did you teach yourself?
R: By listening to other people and copying them. [Pause]
L: On record?
R: On record, yeah. [Pause]
L: And did you do it by, you put the record on, you would try playing along; or you'd listen to the record first and then play afterwards and put it back on, or a mixture or -
R: I'd listen to the line over and over again till I could sing it, the bass line. And then I'd work it out from singing it.

L: I see. And then would you ever put the record back on and play along with it once you'd got the whole thing?

R: Oh yes.

L: So it's a constant process of listening, internalizing, practising, listening, playing along and so on?

R: Precisely, yeah, yeah.

Nanette L: You know when you started singing the jazz stuff – in what kind of ways did that stretch you?

N: Well, in every way because I'd pick stuff that I liked, that I knew I couldn't sing and then it would be a challenge for me to master it. There were no scores – I mean arrangements were done and everything, but I couldn't read and so I'd learn everything just by the tape, literally going over and over and over it to myself. And then no matter what, when it came to doing it live, no matter what the band were actually playing, even if they'd come in with some embellishments – still great, but unrecognizable for me – I knew it so well that it always sort of panned out.

Brent L: Did you teach yourself covers, I mean did you listen to things and then copy what was on the recording?

B: Yeah, I would try and play along with stuff, since I was a kid. Probably at that age I was not listening absolutely intently and trying to get every note to the nth degree. More just kind of going for the feel and form. But yeah, I did quite a lot of playing along to records.

Below, Will talks about how he went about learning the drums, which later came to be his second instrument, and then how he approached his main instrument, the guitar.

Will At that age [*c.* 10 to 12] I was really, really into the Beatles, and a lot of Ringo's stuff is very easy to follow and I was just learning about where you put the bass drum, where you put the snare, where you put the hi-hat, and just, and I was just trying to coordinate the three – to be able to do that.

L: And how did you go about doing that?

W: Putting on different songs – like, one I remember was 'In my life' – and just making an effort to just follow the bass drum and always just – whatever.

Later:

Will I sold that guitar – hang on, yep, I sold that guitar. I bought a slightly better one with the money and that's when I really got into listening to music and went out and found certain, just a few bands I really liked, and made an effort to learn all their songs …

L: So, when you say 'learn all their songs', you did that by learning off the record, in the same way as you had when you learnt drums?

W: Yep. [Pause]

L: You played along, copied, you listened back – and then what happened?

W: Learnt some basic shapes just from hearing what they were doing.

Andy Without even knowing at the time, I'd get a phrase, just one single phrase and I'd copy that, get it perfect and move on to the next bit; and then once I'd got it all, I'd play along with it and I'd keep on playing along with it.

Simon and Michael are both primarily drummers but were talking here about playing the guitar and the piano respectively:

Simon   L: Did you ever do it by listening to records, by copying?
           S: Oh yeah, yeah, copying out, yeah. Definitely. Playing some songs. Sit down and – [pause]
           L: So you would, for example, you'd listen to a record maybe a couple of times would you, and then you'd start trying to play along with it?
           S: Yeah, if I liked the record, yeah, I'd probably know it, know how it goes and like play it and just stop, yeah, play it and then, yeah; so if I wanted to work it out, hear one chord, stop the tape, work the chord out, next one, next one, until I got the song right.

Michael I'd sit in my room determined to do it myself. I'd listen to a tape, stop it and try lots of different chords until I found one that fitted. But now it's more – I haven't got perfect pitch, it takes me a little while to work out what key it's in, but I recognize chord sequences, so I know most chord sequences are based round I IV V in the pop music of nowadays and I can hear patterns and recognize them and know that that's going A, D G and put those in there and play them ...
           ... It would sometimes drift and I'd – by the time I actually got to what I thought was the right chord, I'd start the tape again and realize my recollection had changed it. I usually got there in the end.
           L: And did you test what you'd done by playing along with the record?
           M: Always yes. I usually wrote it down [as chord symbols] as I was going through it and then I'd go back and play through and check it was alright.

Simon had a relatively consistent course of lessons on his main instrument, the drums. I asked him whether, during the time he was having lessons, he would approach the drums in the same way as he approached the guitar, described above.

Simon   S: Yeah, yeah I did, yeah.
           L: You did that by yourself, or with your teacher?
           S: By myself. But I mean my teacher would play something and I'd go after him but then I'd go home, you know, put on a nice, one of my favourite CDs or whatever, and then try and do that ...Work it out, yeah, which is nice. The tricky ones are nice to do.

Further examples, now from the youngest musicians, are:

Richard I had my guitar with me and I usually knew the song quite well ... Um, turn it on and usually leave all the effects off the guitar – just have the basic guitar – then first of all just find what key it's in to start with and work out – I used to work out the bass note of the chord first. Now I can usually do the chord all at once and – yeah I just add on till it sounded right. Sometimes I'd do it by luck or I'd pause it for a minute and play the bit and see if that sounded right. And then put it back on again, start again.

Leo   L: And, do you attempt to play along with the record, or do you listen to the record and then try to play what you heard on the record, or both?

> Leo: Both because I, first I'll listen to the record, and then I might try it the
> second time or the third time playing along with it and learning from that.

Copying recordings – 'just listening'

Other, less conscious and systematic approaches to listening and copying are
akin to what I have referred to as attentive and distracted listening, and even
hearing. I will examine these together here, under the umbrella concept of 'just
listening', which were words that many of the interviewees used to describe
their practices.

In Chapter 2 I mentioned that drummer Terry Ollis had not found it necessary
to undertake conscious preparatory listening to refresh his memory when he was
invited to play in a covers band, despite the fact that he had never played in one
before, or that he had a seven-year gap in playing the drums at the time. All in
all, he indicated far less conscious or systematic concentration in copying
recordings than any of the other musicians, not only in the later stages but during
the early learning process also. I pressed him to say more about his approach to
copying:

Terry   L: Yeah, how did you – between the ages of 10 and 15 when you had your first
            kit, how did you learn how to play it?
            T: I used to play along to records: the Kinks; Dave, Dee, Dozy, Beakie, Mick
            and Titch; and things like that.
            L: Right, so to begin with, did you, you were trying to copy exactly what was
            on the record?
            T: Yeah, I suppose I was yeah, doing the albums and things like that, yeah.
            This is at about 13 I suppose. [Pause]
            L: So you would put the record on, presumably you'd listen carefully and then
            you'd play along, sometimes you'd listen to the record without playing along,
            sometimes you'd play along with it?
            T: Well, I mean I'd be listening to the record anyway so it would probably be
            on the radio or I'd be playing it. It was obviously one that I liked, and so I'd
            know it.

Later we were talking about his first band, which he joined at about age 15.
They did not play covers, but mainly jammed:

Terry   Er, well, it's all what you hear. I mean I was listening to, you know, I mean
            Cream were around then and you know, Hendrix of course.

A question I asked all the interviewees and which will be examined in Chapter 4
was 'Would you describe the process of learning how to play your instrument as
having been a process of disciplined or systematic study?' Despite its
predictability, it is worth citing Terry's response in the present context:

Terry   No.

L: No.

T: Well, um [pause] well I mean only through listening you know. I always listen to the drums and I always have done.

L: Yeah.

T: And I suppose just by taking it in and keeping it there for use, you know, to plunder if I wanted to.

L: Does that require very intense concentration?

T: I suppose only if it's for difficult things. [Laughs] Well, only when you're playing it really.

At another point in the interview, he referred to his Hendrix tribute band, Little Wing. This was the only band he was playing in at the time of the interviews, as by then he had a steady job as a school caretaker.

Terry   It's a bit like the Hendrix stuff, I was saying, because I'd know the stuff so well I could remember how it goes, do you know what I mean?

L: Right. Well that's slightly different though isn't it, if you're doing it by memory without ever having sat down and played along, or listened over and over to the recording, you're not attempting to get exactly what Mitch Mitchell [Hendrix's drummer] did or whoever it happened to be are you?

T: Well I was, well I am you know, we try to play it almost exactly how it's played.

L: Yeah right.

T: As opposed to a band playing Hendrix stuff in *their* style, we play it in Hendrix's style, you know.

L: And you don't have to go back and check your memory very often then now?

T: Well, yeah, I mean you listen to the tape and think 'Shit I'm not doing that!', things like that, you know what I mean.

During a discussion of how he had acquired technique, to be considered later, Terry volunteered that it was just …

Terry   … whatever came naturally really.

L: Yeah, right.

T: So the playing really is almost, I don't know, I suppose it must have been a fair bit of conscious – it was almost all fairly natural really …

L: Yeah.

T: [Pause] It's like, I don't count also, which amazes some people.

L: You don't count.

T: I never count you know.

L: Right.

T: [Pause] Which some people find quite strange.

L: [Pause] So, obviously you never count 1, 2, 3, 4 through a bar, but do you count like larger segments, like you know that there are eight –

T: No, nothing at all no. [Laughs]

L: No.

T: I just feel when the right time is, yeah.

As previously mentioned, his improvisations with the lead guitarist were often virtually ametric, which makes his lack of counting both more understandable on one hand, and all the more extraordinary on the other hand, given the tightness of the band. Such relatively free improvisatory practices were also a mark of his first band Hawkwind. But when it came to covering existing music, his apparently unconscious or unsystematic approach to getting the music off the recording did not detract from Terry's accuracy. I made a comparison between a selection of covers by his tribute band and the original recordings, checking my listening with that of several musicians and music educators privately as well as informally in seminars and conference presentations. The consensus was that, not only was Terry precise in almost all minutiae, but his drumming was musically committed and sensitive to a degree frequently over and above that of the original. (See Chapter 2, p. 35 for an example of how.) He was particularly fêted at a reunion of Hawkwind involving most of the band's past and present membership at London's Brixton Academy in October 2000. Terry, who had never had an instrumental lesson in his life, was hardly able to refer to having ever employed a conscious or systematic approach to listening and copying, does not even count and has had a sporadic playing career, provides the best example of how listening as a part of enculturation can turn slowly and imperceptibly into an ability both to reproduce accurate covers and to improvise with feel and technical proficiency.

Unfortunately, I can imagine many readers suspecting that he was party to an ideological syndrome, supposedly common amongst rock musicians in particular, which involves assuming 'authenticity' by *pretending* that 'it all comes naturally', and attempting to appear 'cool' by disguising the hard grind that goes into the acquisition of knowledge and skills. This syndrome will be mentioned again in Chapter 4, and is also well treated in the literature (see especially Berkaak 1999 and Lilliestam 1996). But for now, all I wish to say is that there are just as many grounds for supposing that the adoption of such an ideology is a habit of rock fans and journalists as there are for linking it with rock musicians; none of the fourteen randomly selected musicians I interviewed displayed such a tendency when asked about their learning practices; nor is it is very likely that Terry who, it will be remembered, avoided and even shunned 'stardom', would bother to put on such airs, especially by the time he was 46. Furthermore, Terry's family became friends of my own family, during which time he has persistently come across as one of the most humble and self-effacing musicians I have had the pleasure to meet.

Notice Terry's expressions above: 'I'd be listening to the record anyway'; 'it was obviously one that I liked, and so I'd know it'; 'it's all what you hear'; 'just by taking it in and keeping it there for use, you know, to plunder if I wanted to'; 'only through listening'; and 'just by taking it in'. As mentioned earlier, the sub-title of this section, 'Just listening' derives from the number of times not only he, but many others amongst the musicians used the words 'just' or 'only' in conjunction with the words 'listening' or 'hearing'. This includes several who, although they had consciously employed listening and copying techniques, as indicated in the previous section, often also emphasized a less conscious approach, an approach which has more to do with enculturation into and enjoyment of music than with any disciplined or systematic learning practice.

For example, earlier I cited Nanette describing how she had learnt the more demanding jazz repertoire by copying recordings. But she also said:

Nanette   I spent all my time just listening really, listening to loads of different types of music and whenever there's a challenge, try to meet it, really. That was the main thing.

I asked Brent how he had developed during the five years he had spent without a teacher between the ages of about 13 and 18, after having lost his first teacher through moving towns:

Brent   I just, you know, I'd always liked music and listened to music so I just carried on listening to music which I'd sort of practise a bit, although possibly not always with any great focus.

In describing his copying practices, cited in the previous section:

Brent   Normally for me if I'm doing it, it's just playing along. Normally I will have listened to the stuff before to have an idea of what should be going on.

Will had five years of uninterrupted guitar lessons whilst a teenager. But this did not mean that he abstained from copying recordings – far from it, as is evident from the quote in the previous section. Here it is worth recalling the closing phrase of that quote: 'I learnt some basic shapes just from hearing what they [the musicians on the recording] were doing.' As a covers musician, he had to know a lot of songs involving different performance techniques, and I asked him whether he'd been 'shown how to do them by teachers or by teaching yourself, or a mixture of the two, or some other method?'

Will   Um, first of all, I would say listening, because I was really listening to rock music; and then I learnt how to play jazz through what I was taught, because I wasn't listening to it really, apart from when I was playing it; and then I was shown how to play country music, the licks, where it was coming from. I was shown how to play singer-songwriter type of thing, but I think I've picked them up from listening, because I listen to a lot more country, jazz and singer-songwriters than I used to. So I think I've picked them up myself and I've taught myself different styles since then, like, I don't know what style you'd call it, um, AOR [adult oriented rock or in the USA, album oriented rock]. That sort of style I've taught myself recently, which is very different from your out-and-out seventies rock.

Two of the youngest players, Richard and Leo, also spoke about an unconscious, 'just listening' approach to copying:

Richard With some songs you think 'Right, I'm going to sit down and learn how to play this bit because I want to do a cover of it', so I did that; and with others, some of them it would just be luck: I was just, 'Hang on, I recognize that', when you're playing around on the guitar ...
          ... You just listen to it and – at that time I just kind of played the, moved the chords around 'til it sounded right ...
          L: So did you, you would put a record on, you'd listen to it a few times?
          R: We [his band] usually did songs that we knew pretty well so that I knew when the chorus was and it would be a lot easier that way.
          L: And then what – you would try to play along with the record, or you would turn it off, try to play something, see if it sounded right, put it back on again – how, you know, can you explain in detail?
          R: Yeah. Um usually, when I'm at home on my own I play along to it just like that and if there's nothing on I'll just think, 'I feel like playing that song' so I just play a bit of it ...
          ... I had my guitar with me and I usually knew the song quite well...

Leo   ... it's what I pick up from what I hear. Then it's just really what I, I don't know how to explain it, it's sort of, I just pick it up from the music, and then change it the way I want it to sound.

The importance of liking, enjoying or identifying with the music being learnt will form a topic of discussion in Chapter 4, but here it is worth noting that ten of the fourteen musicians made unsolicited references to 'already knowing' or 'liking' the records being covered. This relates closely to the importance of enculturation in learning to play popular music, for clearly, when unconscious listening and copying are taking place, the music involved is already known to a large extent, and one reason why it is already known is because it is frequently listened to, the reason for which is that it is liked. Five examples refer specifically to distracted listening or 'just listening' practices. (The other examples are presented in a slightly different context in Chapter 4, [pp. 106–7].)

Terry   Well, I mean, I'd be listening to the record anyway so it would probably be on the radio or I'd be playing it; it was obviously one that I liked, and so I'd know it.
Nanette I'd pick stuff that I liked.
Brent   I'd always liked music and listened to music so I just carried on listening to music.
Simon   ... if I liked the record, yeah, I'd probably know it, know how it goes.
Richard We usually did songs that we knew pretty well so that I knew when the chorus was and it would be a lot easier that way.
Leo   I sort of like writing the compositions, and so I listen to, that's the kind of music I listen to, hip-hop and soul, and that kind of thing.

Listening, copying and the use of notation

For six of the players, copying by ear was mixed in to varying degrees with using notation, but notation was very much secondary to learning by listening. Bernie had one year of guitar lessons when he was 11 to 12 years old, from a local dance musician in his father's factory band who taught him, amongst other things, how to read notation. I asked him how he had helped himself to improve once the lessons had stopped.

Bernie   Listening to records … I'd buy the LP and it would run at thirty-three revs per minute. I had a record player luckily that had a sixteen-and-a-half rpm speed, and what I'd do is, I'd get their guitar solos, and I'd play them at sixteen-and-a-half revs, write them down, because at that speed I could write it down onto paper, and then I'd learn them … I played them at the proper speed. And then, I started to do this with other things as well. I got jazz, American jazz musicians, records of them as well, and I'd write, you know, write their stuff. I've got a book, I mean I've still got them upstairs, all the transcriptions.

Brent also started transcribing when he was in his early teens which, as he said, 'requires concentrated listening'.

Like Bernie, Rob was introduced to notation by a teacher. Note here that he moves very quickly from describing his early use of popular music song-sheets to a later use of notation in order to read and transcribe classical music.

Rob   I would buy lots of song-sheets, because at the time you could still get those old-fashioned, traditional ones. For three shillings you got the Beatles version of whatever. I'd get those. I'd also go and buy, I remember buying [J. S. Bach's] Brandenburg 3 [concerto] because I loved the bass line. This is how I got into prog rock because I used to listen to the Nice which became ELP and when I heard them doing the 'Karelia Suite' by Sibelius I went and bought the score for that, just to see how it worked – or 'Blue Rondo à la Turk' which was, you know, the Mozart rondo – and I became very adept at taking the bass lines out of those pieces of music and adapting them for bass guitar.

Partial notation reading, or the use of chord symbols as distinct from conventional notation, is common, in ways illustrated by Will below.

Will   L: So you got this guitar for Christmas aged about 12 and –
          W: I got a book of, like, I think Pop and Rock – Russ Shipton Book One or something.
          L: Right, was it what, chord symbols?
          W: It showed you basic chords in the open position so you could play – you'd have the lyrics with the chords written out showing you positions – stuff like 'Leaving on a Jet Plane'.
          L: Yes, with the words. No conventional notation.
          W: Mmm.
          L: You were expected to know the tunes already?

W: Yes.
L: And, as you said earlier, your Dad played a few chords and he helped you.
W: Yes.
L: And how did you go from there to -
W: I bought more and more books – bought *The Best of the Beatles* – it helped that I knew all the tunes; I was able to follow them in that I knew how they were meant to sound.

Despite the fact that Steve was one of the five musicians who had received hardly any instrumental tuition (a handful of trumpet lessons, which he did not like at all), self-taught notation reading had been a means to help him in what he saw – unusually – as the failures of his listening technique. He had perhaps been more reliant on notation, although in the early stages only, than any of the others.

Steve   … then I got the amp and just got a few music books and I learnt songs I liked
               – like Nirvana and stuff like that. So I just went to like music shops, saw books
               that I liked and most of them were in tablature and got the chords written
               down so it's easy to read, and that's how I just first started …
                   … Well I thought I knew – when I first started playing along with the tape,
               you think you know what it is, then you get the book and it's totally different.
               So then you learn the proper way. Then you play it over and over again because
               you find it a lot harder than you thought it was. Because what you found was
               totally wrong. You were doing the easy option because it sounded alright, but
               when you got the book, there's so many different notes that you miss out and
               you've got to try to put them in and then – you used to be able to play it quite
               well, but then you can't play it. Then, because you're putting the proper bits
               in, that should be in there. But it's just, keep practising and then eventually it
               comes, doesn't it? …
               L: And did you find as time went by, that you relied less on the book, that your
               ear improved, or –
               S: It did improve, but it's so much easier to read the book than it is to work it
               out by ear. So you just read the book if you need the song. I mean if you need
               one song then you do it by ear, but if you need say five songs on an album –
               just go out and buy the book.

Later he made two other separate comments:

Steve   But nowadays, because I'm playing bass nowadays, you can't buy sort of bass,
               just bass books really, not for a band, not for bands …
                   … I mean I listen to music when I'm learning it to try and, try and learn it
               so you listen out for the bass line only.

Emily and Richard also used notation, mixed in with listening and copying, from early stages.

Emily   … and with 'There She Goes' by the La's, I had a songbook with the chords
               but no lead bits or anything, so I got a copy of the tape so I listened to the riff
               on that and worked it out onto my guitar and put it in the right key and that.

Richard   L: So tell me how you went about learning covers?
            R: It depended. I was having a few guitar lessons at that time, so we did some
            of those songs because that was like all I could play at the time. We got quite
            a few music books, we got them out of, and the other ones that we didn't
            know, we just listened to it and wrote them out, how to play them.

It is significant that amongst the younger musicians Simon, Michael, Emily
and Leo had all learnt to read and play from notation, to varying degrees, partly
through instrumental teachers and partly through taking the music option at age
14 (the GCSE) at school. This will be discussed in relation to the musicians'
changing experiences of formal music education in Chapter 6. For now, I wish
to observe that, despite their education, notation reading nonetheless remained
secondary to copying by listening.

Five of the musicians had progressed to professional status, or were
progressing through earlier stages of learning, with minimal notation reading
skills, or in Richard's case, virtually none and in Terry's case, literally none.

Nanette   Yeah. Interesting. Because I've developed my ear with copying. I struggled at
            first – because I got involved with studio work and most of my work over the
            last three years has been studio sessions and that took probably, I mean that
            took about six years to actually get to a point where I could be the only non
            sight-reading singer employed, but somehow I got by, just by winging it – do
            you know what I mean?
Leo   L: What about notation? Do you use notation at all?
            Leo: Well, not really because as I said it's just on a sequencer, so, notation, I
            don't use it. I'm not actually very good at reading music.
            L: Right.
            Leo: I can read it but it takes me a little bit of time to sort of – [pause]
            L: Yeah, sure.
            Leo: Because I have to sort of, this note, that note.
            L: Do you think you might ever have a use for musical notation?
            Leo: Yeah, it's very useful, it's definitely very useful for when I'm playing in
            the jazz band; it's very useful for that. If I, I wish I could read better, but I
            can't, so; but that's something I'm practising at the moment. But it's very
            useful for jazz music.

All of those who did not read felt this as a lack in some way. Will and Nanette
felt they had to catch up later, and Terry felt he could not be a teacher because of
it. However, they all valued the ear-training which their lack of reading ability
had forced upon them.

Learning with books

There are a large number of technical magazines for popular musicians, many of
which are graded from beginner to professional standard. They carry articles on
technique, critiques of players, discussions of makes of instruments and other

technology, as well as a significant amount of advertising. Although their sales are wide, amongst my sample of musicians no one mentioned them as a learning resource. It was common amongst the younger players, or in the early stages of learning for the older players, to use or to have used books, but to drop them quite quickly after a certain stage was reached.

Some mentioned the use of books as a supplement to aural methods.

Rob   I'd get whatever books were available for bass playing – there weren't that many then – Carol Kaye was very, very good. She was an American session bass player who played with just about everybody – the Beach Boys, Quincy Jones – and she published four books and I worked my way through them; and my friend Laurence [Canty] – who is now an established bass educator and has published several books – he suggested reading up about the Bach cello suites so I had a crack at that; so it was like becoming sort of a voracious reader – anything I could get my hands on that might increase the power of my playing, I did.

Nanette This one book I bought was – Ah! incredible! – by Graham Hewitt, called just something like 'Learn How to Sing' – it's just amazing. I mean anybody who reads that book can't fail to get something out of it.

After losing his first teacher, Brent turned, amongst other things, to 'some books and listening to music'. I asked Peter how he progressed in the early stages after having acquired what he described as 'a few basic techniques'.

Peter   I then went to books. I had one lesson where the teacher recommended that I got particular books, so it was one of the progressive [inaudible] books. It was probably the main one that they do, for beginners to virtuosos. That just got my fingers working. And I mainly learnt from books instead ... That is until more recently when I began to be more serious about developing my ear.

Andy also used books in the early stages:

Andy   L: So after your five classical lessons, how did you then go about learning to play?
           A: Books. Books and self determination. Sit there, seven nights a week indoors just reading through the books and playing this and playing that ...
           ... And then all the other scales came in time and there was a book I bought by, the author was Cliff Douse – and this is like a bible – I don't really use it any more, but at the time I did; it's got about a hundred and eight different scales...

However, he used the book to help him learn to play scales (popular and jazz musicians are familiar with a range of scales and modes), and only as a spur to then developing licks and lines that were always most heavily influenced by listening.

Terry had been given a book on the drums when he was a young teenager, but:

Terry   I never got to reading it, Buddy Rich thing … I couldn't really understand the book at all.
L: You couldn't understand it.
T: It could have been in Chinese. [Pause]
L: So you never tried again with books or anything like that.
T: No, no, I mean I never bought that; I think someone bought it for me.

Apart from Terry, Leo, the youngest, and Bernie, the oldest, were the only other ones who did not mention the use of books at all. For many of the players, books were introduced by teachers, which will be discussed later. For all of them, printed materials were used as learning resources in the early stages only and in all cases any form of written resource appeared to have been dropped during the first months or first couple of years of learning.

The centrality of listening and copying in popular music learning practices

There are a number of indications in popular musicians' approaches to learning that support the generally held supposition that vernacular musicians in general, who have acquired their practical skills primarily through aural learning practices, have very 'good ears'. Some of the musicians I interviewed thought that their creativity and their technical understanding had also been improved through listening-and-copying practices. Bernie had just been describing how he had learnt from slowed-down records, cited earlier:

Bernie   And there were several benefits to that. One, great ear training, great training in listening; two, some of these things were really quite technically advanced, these people were world class players, so it improved my technique no end; and thirdly, it gave me an understanding, you know, it gave me an insight into the way other musicians were thinking, the way they were conceiving, the way they'd approach a problem.

Andy and Richard mentioned similar benefits, with the added element that they were themselves surprised about their own aural capacities:

Andy   And through [listening and copying] you don't just pick up what they're doing, you pick up techniques, pick up common sorts of progressions and so forth. And nowadays I can hear a record and I just know what's coming next – I know exactly what the notes are as well. This is a recent thing. I can listen and I can pick out the pitch – I know that's a C major or whatever. And I never thought I'd be able to do that, the way I've learnt music, you know, it's really strange.

Richard   You just listen to it and – at that time I just kind of played the, moved the chords around 'til it sounded right, but now I can usually tell, like if it's in A it's going to be that chord next because it's got, you know what I mean? It's – I can't explain it.

Michael surprised his schoolteacher:

Michael   I think my ears – it's alright I can, I can often pick out chord sequences just
             from, if I know a song I can play it ...
                 ... I do remember once a teacher playing us two pieces of music and asking
             us what the connection was between these two. And she was quite surprised
             when I said they were both in the same key. She didn't think anyone was going
             to spot that.

Nanette also valued those aspects of musicianship that arose from her aural
learning practices. To extend a quotation from earlier in the chapter:

Nanette   ... I mean that took about six years to actually get to a point where, um I could
             be the only non sight-reading singer employed, but somehow I got by, just by
             winging it – do you know what I mean? You can do that just by training your
             ear to actually pick up what they're doing and just very, very quickly copy.

I mentioned in Chapter 2 (p. 53) that younger players tend to place greater
value on producing original music than on copying recordings, a topic which
will be discussed in relation to concepts of authenticity in Chapter 4. For now, it
is worth noting that at the time of the interviews both Emily Dicks' and Richard
Dowdall's first bands of 15 and 16-year-olds had just given up doing covers,
and at 15 Leo Hardt had already given it up even before forming his first band.
Emily was talking about the need for originality felt by her band:

Emily   People will say to you 'Oh that sounds like der-de-der-de-der' and you feel
             like they like it because it's that other person's song. It's just, if it sounds too
             familiar. It's not like an issue for us yet because we're not getting deals yet,
             but eventually it would be a copyright problem I suppose.

Her band gained two new members about a year after the interview. She sent me
a delightful, enthusiastic email about it, stating that her only worry was that the
new band were doing too many covers.

However, all the professional musicians in this study had a good grounding
in copying recordings or playing covers, and it is not unreasonable to suggest
that this is the prime method of learning, without *some* experience of which,
original music is unlikely to be successful, in as much as style-knowledge,
versatility and adaptability will be relatively limited. Berkaak (1999) provides
an interesting discussion of an extreme case in point. It draws on the experiences
of two band members who were committed to playing originals but had 'great
difficulties in converting their unfulfilled rock'n'roll dreams into adult life
ambitions' and never managed to establish a band that satisfied them after their
first, acclaimed one broke up (p. 31); and another musician from the same band
who had relinquished originality and adopted 'an ideology of professionalism'

(p. 32), going on to become a successful session musician. In my reply to Emily's email I pointed out that originality is born of imitation, and suggested that covers are essential for future development, to which she expressed relief. As a result of the injection of new personnel and the return to covers, I currently expect her band to have a more fulfilling and creative future, whereas if it had retained its earlier approaches I would have expected it to have folded before long.

It is worth citing Nanette on this subject. Her experiences had taken her exclusively to covers at the beginning of her career, and to original music somewhat later. Although she now regarded this with a tinge of regret and ambivalence, she nonetheless recognized the developmental value of covers:

Nanette   I mean in hindsight, if I could have started again, I would have got involved with original music right in my teens – that's what I would have done. It's strange, but you do, you've got to go through all the process that I went through to get a craft together, to be able to get paid, but at the same time you lose something with that. You don't develop that individuality, that something that, you know, that is unique to you.

But she *did* develop that individuality. To repeat a lengthy quote from Chapter 2:

Nanette   … one of the dilemmas I think if you're copying all the time is at what point do you stop copying and when do you start to own the song for yourself and put it over as *you*, rather than just as a copy of someone else. And I never forget the day that that happened for me – I was, oh I was going to sing a song called 'Rio de Janeiro Blues' by Randy Crawford and I'd learnt it off pat, how she did it, and I remember just sitting in the back of my Mum's car and she was just driving to some gig or whatever, and I remember just feeling totally free as I worked through the melody, finding a new way, and I just threw it completely upside down and found my own way of doing it. And from that day I've always found my own way of doing it. So I think it's, it's something you have to develop.

Copying recordings and playing covers are not only related to the development of performance skills but also form fundamental building-blocks in compositional skills. Without the experience gained from copying and covering, original work is unlikely to be convincingly situated within a style recognized as music: music is not a natural phenomenon but has to conform to historically constructed norms, both concerning its intra-musical processes, forms and sound qualities, and its modes of production, distribution and reception. Otherwise, it is unlikely to be recognized as music at all (which I argue more fully in Green 1988). What is learnt from playing covers can be adapted to fit new musical contexts, and thus provides a precursor to original invention. This point is illustrated by Rob's career (also see Lilliestam 1996, pp. 203–4 and 211–13 for a helpful discussion). Rob had focused on 'just doing pop covers' between the ages of 13 and 16, then began to join originals bands which had a main song-writer.

Rob   ... what I would do was apply the kind of lines that I'd borrowed from other people and kind of mould them to fit to new chord structures, or whatever ...

Years later, as a teacher and lecturer, he explains:

> One of the most common questions I'm asked when I'm teaching, say, in a one-to-one lesson is 'How do I invent bass lines?' because most people start, as I did, listening to somebody else and they learnt that person's lines and learnt someone else's lines, and eventually they become an amalgam of certain people. But then, ultimately, somebody's going to say to them, 'Well here's my song, what are you going to play?' And you can either listen to that song thirty times and put the bass line together note by note, which is how people normally end up doing it, or you can say, 'Well what's the drummer doing?' 'He's playing this rhythm.' 'And what's your chord?' 'It's a D minor seven.' So, if the drummer is playing a funky rhythm and there's a D minor seven chord, now anybody who knows anything could then say 'Well, D dorian – sounds funky, fits a D minor seven chord – I'll then listen to what the bass drum, snare drum and hi-hat are doing.' Looking at that as a rhythmic picture, I then just pin my notes onto that drum rhythm. So in its simplest form, the line invents itself.

Nanette's self-composed, performed and recorded songs are wonderful examples of the strengths gained from her early emphasis on listening and exact copying, and have been admired by many musicians, musicologists and teachers (especially singing teachers) to whom I have played snippets. The music is redolent with a strength that can only arise because of having had a grounding in what she refers to above as a 'craft'.

Peer-directed learning and group learning

Learning by copying recordings, reading and writing notation and consulting books in ways such as those described above is almost always essentially a solitary activity. But solitude is by no means a distinguishing mark of the popular music learner. On the contrary, with some notable exceptions, solitary learning practices are accompanied by other equally significant practices which take place through interaction with friends, siblings and other peers. These practices include *peer-directed learning* and *group learning*. Peer-directed learning involves the explicit teaching of one or more persons by a peer; group learning occurs as a result of peer interaction but in the absence of any teaching. Either type of learning may take place between only two people or in groups of more than two; it can arise in casual encounters or organized sessions; it can occur separately from music-making activities or during rehearsals and jam sessions. The different settings in which such learning takes place are liable to flow into each other. For example, a member of one band can show a new lick or chord to a member or several members of another band; a player may learn something by watching or listening to another player, who remains unaware of the fact that any learning is taking place; members of a band are likely to have casual learning encounters outside their rehearsals, the results of which are then consciously or unconsciously brought back into the rehearsals; and so on.

Compared to the styles that were most significant for the musicians in this study, some post–1970s popular music involving the purely or mainly electronic production of sound (sampling, synthesizing) tends to be developed by a solitary musician, in various locations from the teenager's bedroom to the professional studio, and involves fewer or no peer-directed or group-learning activities in bands. However, peer-directed learning and group learning are nonetheless likely to be of significance. No musician or other creative artist can ever be totally isolated from what Becker terms an 'art world' (1963; also see Finnegan 1989), involving not only other musicians but listeners; all composers are deeply encultured in the styles in which their own music is situated and particularly those who are at the forefront of rapidly changing sub-styles are likely to be regularly exchanging opinions with peers. Not only the artistic, creative side, but the sheer knowledge of how to use equipment and where to get hold of it is bound to be acquired partly or largely through peers. Therefore peer-directed and group learning are still likely to be prominent in these styles, but mainly in the form of encounters away from music-making rather than in organized rehearsals or collective music-making activities. Further research comparing peer-directed and group learning across different popular music sub-styles might be illuminating.

Another qualification of the current discussion is that the early formation of bands is certainly more common amongst boys than girls. With reference to a sample of rock musicians taking part in the USA 'Boston Rumble' festival in 1979, Clawson (1999a) shows how very much later in their lives, and less commonly, the girls had formed bands than the boys (the average age for boys was 15; girls waited until they were 21). She suggests that the band acts as a forum which both invites and produces masculinity, enabling boys and men to develop their gender identities and their rock musicianship in tandem with each other, whilst simultaneously constraining girls and women from doing so. Bayton (1997, pp. 81f.) gives a full account and analysis of a parallel situation in the UK. As she makes clear, the much smaller number of girls who take up popular music instruments in itself mitigates against their forming bands as readily as boys, and also has several knock-on effects concerning the make-up and management of the bands. Gender differences in this area are clearly of enormous importance to music learning, but I will not focus upon them here, as they have more to do with the social organization of musical involvement, learning and education than with learning practices in themselves.[2]

Casual encounters

Four of the musicians in this study mentioned peers (usually friends and siblings) who had shown them chords, scales or techniques in the early stages of learning.

Bernie Right, well, my first encounter with anybody else playing an instrument was when I was about 6 or 7 years old, and I had a brother about four years senior to me, who had got a ukulele … and he taught me, he taught me these chords, you see. I mean he only knew about five chords, so once he'd taught me the five chords, that was it so far as he was concerned, he'd taught me. However, that wasn't enough for me.

Rob … I did it all by ear until at the age of, I'd just turned 19, it must have been around March or April when a guitar playing friend of mine said 'Your hand technique's dreadful', and I said 'Well I'm fast, I can do this, that and the other', and he said 'No, no, no, it's dreadful.' And he showed me correct classical guitar technique.

Peter Well, when I first had a bass I didn't know what to do with it at all, and friends showed me one or two things. Most of them weren't bass players themselves. L: Yes. What were they – guitarists? P: Guitarists, drummers. They, strangely enough they knew a bit about what I've now come to regard as great technique. L: How do you think they knew that? P: By having played with musicians who knew.

Emily My cousin, he's a bass player but he also plays guitar. Last summer he wrote down all the different, can't remember what it's called, bit like all the major scales like mixolydian and dorian and stuff … He wrote all those down for me, and the pentatonic scales as well, one of which I knew already, in charts.

As already mentioned, such encounters also take place between band members during and outside rehearsals.

First bands

In most guitar-based popular and rock genres, bands are formed at stages so early that the players often have little or no control over their instruments and virtually no knowledge of any chord progressions, licks or songs. It is by no means unheard of, indeed, for bands to be formed before any of the members even possess an instrument.[3] All but two of the musicians in this study started up a band or a series of bands with peers within a few months or at most a couple of years of beginning to play their instrument. One of the exceptions was Nanette, whose first band was a professional one when she was 17. The other was Leo, who was only 15 at the time of the interview. However, he did express an intention to join a band at the time, and set up an ad hoc one in order to record one of his songs a year or so after the interview.

Apart from this slight exception, early band formation was the norm, and early motivation to join a band was high amongst all the interviewees.

Will	I remember when I was about 13 ... we were trying to get bands together, and that was just the best feeling in the world, even if it sounded awful, it was just the best feeling in the world.
	L: To be in a band?
	W: Yes. To be playing a three-chord song – like 'Wild Thing' – in a band, just three of us, four of us.
Emily	I formed a band with Alex the rhythm guitarist [a female schoolfriend], because we were just both starting ... I mean every guitarist who plays rock music has aspirations of being in a band. Maybe that's not true but that's what I reckon. Because I certainly had dreams from, like, the beginning, of being in a band, because it's no fun, it's no fun to play covers of things on your own after a point, you want to be doing your own stuff, especially if it's rock music because you're going to be influenced by other bands who write their own stuff anyway; and so to some extent it was, well, we formed a band pretty quickly after the first summer. We were about 14 I think ...
	... sometimes the band rehearsals are like the best thing in my week – I just really look forward to them so much.

The youngest age at which band formation occurred was 6 (this involved Andy and Simon together), but the ages between 12 and 15 were the norm for everyone else except Peter, who was a late-starter on his instrument. Although early bands are nearly always formed with peers, age is less important than ability: the band members are normally all at a similar standard. Terry was 15 when he started sitting in with his first band, whose personnel were about ten years older than him, and the same age gap persisted with the founding of Hawkwind two years later. Apart from this, the age range of first bands was nearly always within two or at most, three years of all the players.

As Bennett emphasizes (1980, pp. 24–5), the school plays an important role in the formation of bands, not only through its provision of personnel in the form of other young people with shared musical interests and aspirations, but also through resources such as rehearsal spaces and equipment, and opportunities to perform such as school concerts. Ten of the musicians had formed their first bands partly through the provision of such things by their school (or in Peter's case, through a further education course), the exceptions being Terry, Nanette, Brent and Leo. In all ten cases from the oldest to the youngest, band formation and rehearsal took place during unsupervised activities outside the curriculum.

Group creativity in rehearsal

In band rehearsals, skills and knowledge are acquired, developed and exchanged via peer direction and group learning from very early stages, not only through playing, talking, watching and listening, but also through working creatively together.[4] Not only might members of embryonic bands have little instrumental skill or knowledge of scales, chords, rhythm patterns or other basic musical building-blocks, but at the start they may also be unacquainted with any covers, or acquainted only with different covers to each other, so that jamming is the only activity available to the group. Jamming is then normally combined with other activities, such as experimenting with playing covers based on collective memory of songs that are known and liked.

Richard   When we were rehearsing it I don't think we actually rehearsed it properly because we weren't too serious then, so we just thought, 'Hmm what do the drums sound like?' And we recorded the basic drum beat then went home, and it was songs we knew pretty well – I really like Blur, 'Song 2' that sort of thing – so we knew how it went and just recorded it over the top.

There are also more organized approaches to group rehearsals of covers, such as when everyone agrees to copy their part off a particular recording in preparation for the next rehearsal.

Amongst my sample, group composition occurred, usually by having one or two main songwriters who would come to the rehearsal with ideas which were then embellished to varying degrees by the other band members, such that everyone to some extent, provides an original contribution to the finished product. In Hawkwind, the main songwriter was Dave Brock:

Terry   He'd come along, he'd be busking it – he'd sort of rehearse it with himself while he was busking you know – he'd come along and like do these numbers on acoustic guitar and we'd sort of turn it into electric stuff you know. He'd say 'Listen to this, what can we do with this', you know and off [we'd go] – we played along with it and that was it really.

Deepvoid had a similar approach. They were a very eclectic band, which was characteristic of certain areas of British rock at the end of the 1990s.

Andy   The main writer is the singer – he does come up with all the lyrics – and more often than not he comes up with the basic tune. But as soon as we get into rehearsal it's no longer what he came up with. We pull it apart, we reform it, we re-structure it, add the harmonies, the bass line, the beat, the rhythm, everything to it. And it comes out as a different product. You can still hear the same basic thing, but it's more refined, it's more definite in structure …
             … I'm speaking from my own and the other guitarist and the bassist's points of view – we're likely to add complexity to the rhythm, put in different chord changes or change like a major to its relative minor and so forth.
             … I mean, one person will walk into the room with their own song and by the time we come out, it'll be a different product. So essentially, it is usually the singer, but we all contribute to it.

Where there is no main songwriter, or where another member of the band comes up with an idea, rather than a more complete blueprint for a song, group negotiation is further accentuated. This would also occur in Deepvoid.

Steve   I've only written about two songs. Normally they're just like a riff, and then the rest of the band, we all mix it together. That's what normally happens, someone gets the main riff and then we all put our bits in and it rolls into one ... Everyone likes a different sort of music so it's good. It's good because it all mixes up so you've got a bit of rock, jazz, blues, funk in there so it's all kind of – bit of grunge in there – so it's all, it's a complete mix of the whole lot.

Composition in Michael's band is

Michael   ... very much a group effort, and what most commonly happens is our guitarist comes along with a riff or a pattern of some sort and the lead singer will start writing words to it and they'll, come up with sort of the basic bits of the song and then the structure is more down to me, and I say things like 'Let's have a triplet run here, bit of syncopation', all the things that make it tight, make it – have to practice it a lot to perfect it – and then Dan puts in his bass parts and follows me a lot. We like having the bass part following my right foot on the kick drum – I like that effect.

Emily's band had produced three originals at the time of the interviews, all by the same methods as those for the song described below:

Emily   Well, the first song [on the tape she gave me], the 'Axe Murderer' song is basically, Anna our drummer wrote the lyrics; then we were just messing about and I came up with the bass line while I was playing guitar, I just came up with that; and then we came up with some chords and then someone did the chorus, Ruth, the singer came up with the chorus I think. Then we decided on the form, like there should be a guitar solo here, so I went away and made that up; and then this is, we call it the weird bit, it's basically there's just the guitar playing the bass line and the singer, just before the end.

Likewise in Richards' band, the singer usually writes lyrics only, then:

Richard   Yeah, it's all of us – well the three guitarists compose, the drummer doesn't ...
    ... I always say to myself we've got to get this sorted out, because we write the music and the lyrics separately so we never usually get a really good vocal line. Because I can, I don't know, I really like it when you've got a nice vocal line and a chord change, but you need to fit them both together properly because the three of us – the guitarists that is – we write the music not the lyrics; we kind of leave that to him [the singer] and we shouldn't be doing that. There's nothing wrong with that I know but I just feel we should go together more and get it worked out ...
    ... What we usually do is someone says they've got a new song which it's like in this key, these are the notes, and we all just start playing it and you know, you can tell when it's a good song so – usually I've got like three different bits that need to go together so we start playing that and sometimes you just look at each other and think, 'No, it's not going to work' and we just scrap it, but other times we sort of – some of them we know are good tunes straight away, and then just sort of in the middle like we've got a good chorus

but we need a verse to go with this, and we just can't think of anything right
then or the current verse is rubbish or something ...

... We – none of us have really been taught music properly so we just make
up the songs by like playing around with them and see what we come up with
and if that sounds nice.

Performance, composition and improvisational abilities are thus acquired not
only as individuals but, crucially, as members of a group, usually from very
early stages. Group creativity is by no means restricted to originals bands, for as
we saw in Chapter 2 popular musicians have to be able to improvise, embellish
or provide their own part in a great variety of group contexts including session
work. Thus group creativity continues into many areas of the professional realm.

Watching

Musicians learn not only from listening to each other, but also from watching
each other. Student observation of the teacher is customary in many traditional
classical instrumental lessons, and watching and imitating the actions of more
experienced players are prime activities in the enculturation and apprenticeship
practices of many traditional musics and jazz.[5] However, there is no teacher in
the informal practices of popular musicians, and as mentioned in Chapter 1 it is
also unlikely that most young popular musicians are surrounded by a community
of practising, experienced adult players. Therefore a great deal is learnt from
watching professionals or more experienced players from a distance, and perhaps
more so from watching peers in close collaboration.

Bernie (thinking back to when he was about 15 to 17)

What I would do, there was a club in Cheltenham, where all the touring
musicians would come from America and from London, they'd all come down
to this club and perform, and of course I'd always be watching the guitarists.

Rob   ... I'd become obsessed with technique, and I used to watch every bass player
that I regarded as being an icon at the time ...

Steve   ... I mean I've always been in a band with a bass player in it so I've always
sort of seen how they play it and whatever.

Simon   ... we had a sort of rehearsal room there that we built ourselves ... so I could
look at the guitar, and just through watching people when I'm playing – you
know there's looking at each other – so I just picked up from there how the
chords go.

Finney (1987) pays particular attention to the ways in which members of a young
rock band watched each other in rehearsal.

Talking

Another significant aspect of peer-directed learning and group learning, which occurs both in the form of casual encounters and during group interaction in band rehearsals, is unlikely to be recognized as a learning activity at all. This aspect involves talk – endless talk about scales and harmony, techniques, rhythms, metres, styles, approaches to performance, music history, instruments and equipment. Talk goes on between peers in and across bands, and with others including older established musicians. Below, Bernie had just been explaining how he used to watch live guitarists when he was a teenager, as quoted above:

Bernie   … and of course some very fine guitarists would come down, you know, and I used to get chatting, you know I wasn't afraid to go and you know pick their brains, I mean, and most of them were really, you know, really nice.

Discussion not only of recordings by established bands, but of the band's own music, will begin on the way to the rehearsal, continue whilst the equipment is being packed up, and carry on afterwards.

Will   I don't think it's necessarily snobbish to enjoy people's company who are as passionate about something as you are, and to know that much about it. I mean, say someone like Peter knows a lot about what he enjoys; it's, I think it's funk, jazz, free jazz type, '70s funkadelic type stuff, and he knows a lot about it – Bootsy Collins, etc. I don't know a lot about it, but he does. I mean I've got a lot of respect for him for that. Because he's taken time to find out about it and it means a lot to him. In the same way I can waffle for hours about James Taylor or Joni Mitchell or something; it can bore him senseless, he can do exactly the same thing back to me, and I think that's great.

The centrality of peer-directed learning and group learning in popular music

As with listening and copying, peer-directed learning and group learning form central components of popular music informal learning practices. They involve the early formation of bands, the exchange of elementary musical building-blocks such as chords and scales, the creation and refinement of compositional and improvisatory ideas through group negotiation, observation of other musicians playing during performances and rehearsals, the giving and receiving of advice on technique and information about theory, and talking about music in general. These activities may or may not be consciously geared to learning from or developing alongside other musicians; but inevitably information and ideas of a formative nature are both consciously and unconsciously exchanged between peers in the course of interactions occurring on school sites and in domestic and leisure settings away from and during music-making activities. Furthermore, as will be seen in the next chapter, friendship and the sharing of musical tastes are highly significant to young popular musicians and affect their learning practices in many ways additional to those that have been under consideration here.

Acquiring technique

Instrumental technique is a nebulous concept, difficult to define, but referring in general terms to players' aurally monitored physical control over the interface between their body and their instrument. In common usage, the term 'technique' carries the implicit assumption that technique is of a conscious, conventional nature, involving ways of playing that have been developed over many years – hundreds of years in the case of many instruments – and that are to a greater or lesser extent agreed upon by expert players as being efficacious in executing specifiable aims. In formal music education considerable emphasis is placed on the development of technique, most usually through the regular practice of exercises such as scales, and also through the adaptation of pieces of music into exercises by various means. However, at the same time as being conscious and conventional, in a sense technique is employed in all playing – even the baby banging the spoon is holding the object in some way or other and as such has or is developing a 'holding technique'. Technique therefore occurs along a continuum from what could be described as primary technique, which is relatively unconscious and devoid of conventional influences, to a more fully conscious, conventional technique.

The concept of technique as a conscious, conventional aspect of controlling the instrument or as an aide to development came late to most of the musicians in this study, and was in many cases incorporated into their playing either immediately before or some time after their having become professional. For example:

Rob   L: How did you go about learning your technique?
R: I didn't. I did it all by ear until at the age of, I'd just turned 19, it must have been around March or April when a guitar playing friend of mine said 'Your hand technique's dreadful,' and I said 'Well I'm fast, I can do this, that and the other', and he said 'No, no, no, it's dreadful.' And he showed me correct classical guitar technique.
L: Right. And you were 19?
R: I was 19. And I turned professional in the September … By this time I'd become obsessed with technique and I used to watch every bass player that I regarded as being an icon at the time, and I noticed that the majority of them did use the technique that my friend had shown me …
L: So you managed to actually turn professional with a very bad technique, basically?
R: No, it was quite good by the time I turned pro. I had from March 'til September to really get my stuff together.
L: So you pulled it together in six months.
R: Most things with me, when I like them, are obsessions and so, you know, it would have been something I would have been doing *every* night …
L: So, you basically had to change from one sort of technique that you'd developed by yourself, without even considering the notion of technique, presumably –

R: Exactly.

L: To something that is a thought-out technique shared by other people. Did you find it very difficult?

R: Well, I used to play with my fingers on the right hand for picking and I think I just used one, in fact, and this guitar player friend of mine who was very much a kind of young Steve Howe, so he wanted to be in Yes, showed me how to use correct picking – alternate picking strokes. So, by the time he showed me that and the correct fingering, it was really a question of adapting everything I knew, all my personal licks and lines, all the lines I had in my band, to this new technique. So it wasn't just a question of sitting playing ... I hadn't even thought about the concept of scales and arpeggios, which I'd done on the trumpet – I never thought about adapting that for the bass – it was just a question of adapting my current repertoire. And that I found pretty easy because it was, you know ... to put it in a nutshell, [laughing] I could go faster.

He came to practise scales and arpeggios on the bass at a much later stage, some years after having turned professional, and by the time of the interviews had long been recognized as a virtuoso on the instrument.

Nanette, Brent and Andy shared similar experiences. Like Rob, Nanette was a professional before she became conscious of technique and, again like Rob, both she and Brent were shown conventional aspects of technique by another person (in their cases a formal teacher) at a relatively late stage.

Nanette   Well I learnt the hard way, because when I was employed in the covers band I was actually the second singer, so I was being given the kind of songs that I would not naturally pick at all. They were all much higher than I actually wanted to sing, in a range that was very sort of girlie and quite twee. And I'd find I was struggling an awful lot with my voice, so I had to go to a local trainer.

Brent   I'd never really thought too much about how I was doing things 'til I went to Bob [Bob Armstrong, his teacher in 1986 when Brent was 22]. You know it was like, you would hopefully arrive at being able to do something just by keeping trying to do it but without actually analysing it too much ...

... I see technique really as just a means to an end. I mean you just need enough technique to be able to do what you're required to do.

Andy had five classical guitar lessons when he was about 12, but found 'the progression was so slow', and gave them up. Like the others above, to begin with he was unconscious of any concept of technique and later taught himself a variety of conventional techniques.

Andy   L: So what about, for example, hand technique?

A: There's a major difference as well. When you're playing classical it's a rotation of the fingers, whereas with the pick I mean, when I started playing electric guitar it was with my thumb – I had a thumb the size of a golf ball, the first year, so I started using a pick after that. I never could understand how you could get such a fast technique out of it but it's not to do with the fingers necessarily. If you want a fast pick technique it comes from the wrist. It's the motion of the wrist and a solid grip on the pick. I mean it is true to say that the technique in playing guitar is more to do with the right hand than it is the left, even though the left may appear to be going faster.

Notice that in the citations above, Rob, Nanette and Andy all associate technique with classical music.

The musician who revealed the largest gap between having a fine technique, on one hand, and having any explicit recognition of technique, on the other hand, was Terry, who had never made any conscious attempt to develop technique, and had never had a lesson or used a book or magazine in his life.

Terry   L: So, how did you go about developing your technique?
T: I suppose just playing really, just practising.
L: Did you ever have anybody to help you, like a friend or a teacher? [Shakes his head] Nothing. So you did it by listening.
T: Yeah.
L: Do you, have you, did you give thought to like: how do you hold the sticks?
T: Well, I mean most of the – I had a drum book, but I never got to reading it, Buddy Rich thing … And they all tell you to hold it like a jazz thing, you know, but I found it difficult. I never did, I chose the 'match grip' [grasping the sticks in the same way in each hand] you know, because when I was with Hawkwind I had to use that to get the volume, because there was no miking up the drums then so I had to really thrash hard to be heard, you know …
L: So you had to adapt your own technique according to your needs anyway and so you had to sort of find a way to hold the sticks that was comfortable and that worked?
T: Just whatever came naturally really.
L: Yeah, right.
T: So the playing really is almost, I don't know, I suppose it must have been a fair bit of conscious – it was almost, all fairly natural really.

By the time of the interviews he was using the 'match grip' most of the time, occasionally switching to the traditional or jazz grip, which he picked up by experimenting with what was most effective and by watching other drummers.

Practice

How much?

I asked the musicians how much practice they put into their instrument, both in the early stages and later on in their careers. This varied tremendously from those who practised for five or six hours a day to Terry, who had hardly ever practised at all. Many of them had gone through some periods of intensive practice, interspersed with other periods completely unmarked by practice. All of them approached practice entirely according to their mood, other commitments in life or motivation by external factors such as joining a new band or composing a new song. Practice was something they did so long as they enjoyed it – if they were not enjoying it, they did not do it. For Nanette, singing at home 'was my life really'. For Brent, playing the drums …

Brent   … was always a fun thing to some extent. It was never like I felt that I had to do this or I had to do that, it was just, 'This is something I enjoy, I'll do it 'til it's no longer fun and then I'll go and do something else.'

The following all indicated they had engaged in regular 'practice', driven in some cases by burning motivation or even obsession.

Bernie   … [my parents] got me this six-string guitar, and that was it, I mean I was just, just, you couldn't, I was just you know, you couldn't get me off the thing, day and night, I was just playing this thing.
Rob   R: Most things with me when I like them are obsessions and so, you know, it would have been something I would have been doing every night.
             L: For like, how long?
             R: Oh, I can't, if I wasn't going out with my girlfriend, I would just sit and play. I'd do anything to make sure everything was completely and utterly right, obsessively. Time didn't really come into it – it wasn't a question of , 'I will practise for four hours'. It [the bass] would be in my hands. Even while I was talking to people I would sit and play.

He started practising scales and arpeggios only after having 'discovered fusion', when he was in his mid-twenties.

Rob   I discovered Stanley Clarke and Jaco Pastorius and again that was another sort of blinding flash – '*that's* what else you can do with the bass'.
             L: So you heard them and you thought you'd practise, what, did you practise all the scales and arpeggios?
             R: Unwittingly, yes. I didn't know, I was doing it again by ear and by sound … by that time I could read well on the bass and I was getting a lot of sessions. I realized that a lot of the shapes people use to write things were standard structures. It was like a, like a kind of voyage of discovery.

Some were more self-conscious in their approach to practice. Peter would often put in 'a solid five hours' of scales, and for others:

Brent   There've been times when I've been practising and struggling with something, then you know, the longer you play you reach a point where you realize that the only way you're going to achieve what you want to achieve is by just putting the time in and practising.
Andy   … self determination. Sit there, seven nights a week indoors just reading through the books and playing this and playing that.
Steve   But it's just, keep practising and then eventually it comes, doesn't it?

Simon   I'd say five hours a night, I was doing, or at one stage when I put in the most:
            come home from school straight into the shed [self-styled studio], sort of thing.
            Five hours without a doubt.
Michael   Practice. Lots and lots of practice.

At the same time as this level of commitment, as mentioned earlier, players
also indicated a sporadic approach to practice, dependent on a variety of other
factors. One of these, for older players, was the demands of professional life; for
younger players, there were noise problems or the pressures of school work.

Brent   It really goes in fits and starts depending on any number of things from how
            busy I am, how much teaching I'm doing. I have days when I might start at
            10.00 in the morning and maybe I'll break just to make a few phone calls or
            have lunch but go through till 5.00 in the afternoon. That is probably less
            frequent now than it once was. Also, a lot depends on what else I'm doing. I
            was doing something recently with a guitarist and I had specific stuff to
            practise and it had to be, if not completed certainly improved upon by a certain
            time, so in those instances I might try and just do half an hour or an hour in the
            morning before I have to go off and do something else. Just grab whatever
            time you can. So it really kind of varies.

Will put in about three to four hours a day from the age of 16 to 18, including one
summer when he was doing about six hours a day. But by the time of the
interview, 'I might pick up the guitar maybe once a day for a couple of minutes,
but, nothing like.' However, he was doing intense and demanding two-hour gigs
with his function band or his duo six nights of the week, so practising and playing,
as is typically the case with such musicians, really become one and the same.

Michael   L: How much practice do you do a day on average do you think?
            M: Well, more recently I've been practising the keyboard a lot more than the
            drums because I can't have them both in my room at the same time. There's
            not enough room, and it takes quite a long time to set the drum kit up. And the
            keyboard's set up so I've been playing that but um, I don't know – in terms of
            actual sitting down and thinking 'Right I'm just going to practise this until I
            can play it', I don't actually do that very much. I just tend to play and then
            keep coming back to this idea every half hour or so; and also it's not good to
            play the drums for two hours non-stop because the neighbours wouldn't
            appreciate it I don't think. So I try and play the drums for maybe, in half hour
            chunks maybe twice a day, but I haven't been doing that very much recently.
            But at the keyboard, that's obviously: I can play with my headphones much
            more quietly and I've been playing that a lot. Generally I walk into my room
            and I play the keyboards for maybe ten minutes then go and do whatever I was
            going to do and then come into my room again later and play again for ten
            minutes, so it's quite disjointed. But I do – if there's one little thing I want to
            practise I think it's quite a good way to do it because if I was just stood there
            for two hours trying to play one little thing then I'd get pretty bored I think.
Emily   I don't practise guitar as much as I used to, but like when I do pick it up I'll
            play for about an hour. There will be some weeks when I'll go without

touching it; and then sometimes I'll play it like every day. It really depends on what I'm feeling like. If we've got a new song then I'm more likely to go home and play that through a couple of times and work on it; and if we haven't got anything then we try to write something else; because it's always about expanding our limited repertoire.

Richard   L: Have you got any idea how much practice you do now, say since you've had your guitar, you know?
R: ... Every day just, I don't do much else. I used to play on the computer a lot but I don't do that any more. I just play on the guitar or the drums or –
L: So how many hours is that?
R: Several hours every day – say, I don't, it depends what's going on ... Sometimes I just play till teatime. But usually I stop and do my homework and go out with my friends and stuff.

Terry, Steve and Leo took a different attitude, engaging in less practice than the other players in general. When I asked him how he had developed technique, Terry had said 'I suppose just playing really, just practising.' But there are also signs that he had hardly ever practised, in the sense of consciously sitting down to improve his playing, at all. Regarding the early stages, when he was 15 he moved to a new house:

Terry   ... and I remember one summer's day having the window open and there were some people sitting out the back you know, and I was *slamming* away, and I had the sounds up and I thought they were digging it you know, I was really giving it some; and the next day the police came round [laughing] with a thing to stop me playing.
L: They stopped you playing altogether.
T: Yeah, that was a bit of a – done me in a bit you know.
L: That was a bit – they could have come and spoken to you.
T: Yes, that would have been preferable.
L: So then you couldn't practise after that.
T: Mmm.
L: You had to go round to these other people's houses.
T: Um, I suppose I just stopped playing. In fact I put them up in the loft. I done the loft up on this house, but it wasn't any quieter.

In response to another question on how much practice he had done, both at the beginning, and now:

Terry   Er, not very much, not very much at all. You know I, I um [pause] I don't remember practising at all really, with that band. I mean I've only practised when I was in the early days with Hawkwind really, and prior to sort of joining [my first] band.
L: So you, practise by yourself, you mean. So you did most of your, sort of practising when you were actually rehearsing.
T: Yeah. And I still do [laughs]. I find it really boring ... Well, it's good to practise, because it is so physical, and you know after not playing for two weeks, I feel noticeably rusty. So any time longer than that, it's you know, it's quite a good thing really.

L: Right, you've got to do a bit. If you're out for a month and you go back into a band, you've got to do a bit of practice before you go to a rehearsal?
T: Well I never do. But I should. Well I should practise all the time. I'd be really shit hot if I had done.

Later:

Terry   I'm sure if I had've practised, or if I played, just continually played, you know I mean – when I was playing, Oh, you know we just did like, a few months ago, ten gigs on the trot, and by the end of that we were really hot, you know what I mean, we were really good. So if I'd have continued playing throughout my career as such, I'd be really good now, you know.

He did, however, put in about half an hour's practice a day for one or two weeks before the reunion of the original Hawkwind for a major London gig in 2000.
    Steve's practice was also relatively minimal, and Andy's had been variable.

Steve   S: I should do, but I don't. One, I don't get the time. I get in from work covered in grease. I get in, have a shower and by the time I've done that I've recovered. I do occasionally, but I normally leave all my stuff at the practice room, and my amp's really heavy so by the time I've carried that backwards and forwards [pause]
L: So most of your practice is done when you're actually rehearsing.
S: Yeah. I wouldn't say I sit down and practise. If I've got a gig coming up I'll sit down, like I've got a gig on Thursday, I'll go over the songs just to make sure it's clear in my mind ...
L: Yeah. How much time were you putting into it do you think – I know that now you, you know you've got a full-time job and it's very difficult, but when you were say putting the most time into music how much would you be doing a day?
S: Hour, hour and a half? Well maybe not even every day. Just pick it up, have a little strum and then put it down again and then go out, come back again, and in the evening I'd have a tune, but I wouldn't say I properly sat down.
Andy   I mean, to say that I've been practising every day since I was 12 would be a lie. I mean adolescence kicks in and you go drinking, you experiment with other substances and so forth and I mean there was a certain lack in there ... I was practising once a week maybe and that was with the band, not in my own time.

Regardless of how much practice was undertaken, it was entirely self-motivated in all fourteen cases. Only Leo referred to a significant other as a spur to practice:

Leo   ... my Mum and Dad, they get a bit annoyed with me because I don't practise enough.

However, this comment referred only to his saxophone playing, which was mainly associated with taking formal instrumental lessons. When it came to creative popular music-making on his keyboard and computer, his story was the same as that of all the others.

What sort of practice?

The prominent part played by enculturation in so many of the musicians' learning practices marks not only how much time they spent practising, but also the kinds of activities that their practice involved. I asked Andy how he had progressed from teaching himself chords to playing lead lines:

Andy It is a very basic thing. I mean, you'll play something and you'll just work out what sounds good. You don't even know what scales you're playing. You don't know what progressions work or anything. To some extent I believe it's what you've heard already, and you're just taking it in …
 … not actually focusing on repeating things.

A number of the musicians preferred playing songs, or what might be described as 'real music', rather than systematically focusing on scales or other technical exercises. Nanette stressed the importance of developing both vocal agility and projection, but:

Nanette Well, basically I grabbed any tapes I could for exercises, but to be honest I haven't done a lot of um – I don't follow regimes of exercises. Because I think it's better to spend time actually rehearsing what you're going to sing, rather than spending time stuck doing some unrelated activity, so I spent all my time just listening really, listening to loads of different types of music and whenever there's a challenge, try to meet it, really.

Brent Well the guy who'd originally taught me … didn't emphasize technique too much, certainly for me, although I suspect that might have been to do with the age I was at and he probably thought that if he had me there doing repetitive single stroke rolls or whatever it would bore me. Basically I'd always liked music and listened to music so I just carried on listening to music which I'd sort of practise a bit although possibly not with any great focus. However, practice became more focused with age.

Emily L: Do you ever sit down and practise scales or practise some particular aspect of technique or anything like that?
 E: I feel that I should do … I mean very occasionally I practise those [scales which her cousin had shown her] and try and learn them off by heart, but usually I just go through stuff we've already done, and developing things like chord sequences, because they're the hardest things to come up with originally.

Richard L: Do you play scales at all on the guitar?
 R: Yeah. My guitar teacher – I was only having lessons for about two terms or something. He taught me three scales [i.e. scale-patterns] – the major, the minor and the pentatonic. And I just, sometimes I just sit down and practise them, but that's usually because I haven't done it for a long time, I think 'Hang on I can't do this properly.' I do practise them, it's just, sometimes it gets a bit boring practising scales.

As has already been seen in the previous section, both Terry and Andy preferred to practise with their band rather than on their own. For such players as well as others such as Will mentioned earlier, the concept of 'practice' as an activity in its own right, or as something separate from 'playing', never really presented itself. Indeed, extending a quote from earlier, Andy felt that his best time had been when he was practising least.

Andy   I mean, to say that I've been practising every day since I was 12 would be a lie. I mean adolescence kicks in and you go drinking, you experiment with other substances and so forth and I mean there was a certain lack in there; but that was possibly our best era because we were going out and we were playing gigs everywhere. I was practising once a week maybe and that was with the band, not in my own time.

On the other hand there were those whose approach to practice included a higher degree of conscious and systematic technical exercises. We have already seen how this occurred for Bernie and Rob. Peter was the most unusual in this respect, and was also unusual in having begun to learn his instrument when he was more mature than all the others, which might be a reason for his greater self-consciousness in attempting to improve:

Peter   I find that I spend some time organizing the practice routine, and sticking to it for a while and then thinking, 'I quite fancy another practice routine.' So it changes, the emphasis changes, depending on what I'm particularly concerned with improving that particular month ... In the early years of playing I found the process of practising, particular scales say, to be a really quite meditative, trance-inducing process. And I actually found myself thinking more clearly and more calmly after a good five-hour session of solid practice ... Whether it did me as much good musically as it did in terms of ordered sense of being I don't know. It certainly did my technique some good.

He also set himself conscious goals:

Very often I set myself too wide a target to be able to accomplish enough of what I set out to do to make me feel positive about my playing. In fact very often I feel that when I've been working on too much for too long, I find that I've been focusing on all the negative aspects of my playing for several hours a day for several days and then I think I'm a worse player than I actually am. All I've got in my mind is all those things I'm trying to do rather than what I do already ... It's a matter of appraising one's playing and then having the discipline to set a modest enough goal so that I can accomplish it and therefore feel good about myself and then be a better player.

At the same time as describing a less systematic approach, as above, Andy and Richard also indicated that they had practised scales in the earlier stages. By the time he was 16, Andy could play the major, minor and pentatonic scale-patterns and their modal permutations on the guitar at a rate of about 240 notes per minute. At 15, Richard usually started arpeggios

Richard   ... on G because that's right down the bottom, then I can go all the way up to the top quite easily and I do the inversions, and I just go up and down a few times.

Whilst some musicians hardly ever practised, it is not the case that everybody in the same band has to take the same approach. For example, the bass player in Terry's band had a completely opposite attitude and according to Terry was 'very studious about it all you know, he practises and reads it all up and stuff, yeah, note for note'.

Acquiring knowledge of technicalities

By 'technicalities', as distinct from 'technique', I mean not the psycho-motor skills involved in playing, but the more cerebral knowledge and understanding of what might be referred to as music 'theory'. This includes not *how to play* musical elements such as scales, modes, chords, keys, pitches, metres or rhythms, but *how to understand* their make-up and the relationship between them with reference to musical style, genre, history and other factors pertinent to a wider sphere than one particular feature or piece of music. (See Lilliestam 1996 for a good discussion of popular musicians' understanding of such factors.) Amongst the musicians in this study, knowledge of theory was partly acquired through teachers, as is apparent in some of the quotes above. But even when the players did acquire knowledge through teachers, and especially when it was acquired in relation to classical music, they did not necessarily apply the knowledge to their popular music practices, instead carrying on by feel, ear and trial and error.

An exception to this was Will, who, as already mentioned, was the only one who had continuous popular music instrumental tuition between the ages of 15 and 19.

Will   ... if you're going to get anything out of playing an instrument you have to put the time in and treat it quite seriously, which is where the theory side comes in.

However:

Will   ... I find music theory very exciting – it's a lot of fun.

More often they had what can be described as 'tacit knowledge' (Polanyi 1967, cited in Swanwick 1988, pp. 131–2) of technicalities, in so far as they were able to use musical elements in stylistically appropriate ways, but without being able to apply names to them, or to discuss them in any but vague or metaphorical terms. For example, Rob had learnt to read music and come to grips with some rudiments of theory through his trumpet teacher whilst at school. But it was not for another ten years or more that he related this to his bass playing:

Rob   I think my theoretical knowledge really blossomed in the early '80s when I was playing with Ian Carr ... I'd done it all on the trumpet. I don't know why the two never tied up. I think it was partly to do with the fact that with the trumpet, I could read well, I could play it, but I could never improvise on it. Whereas with the bass guitar, because I hadn't done a standard, structured way of learning, it was much freer.

Further examples are:

Nanette   L: How did you go about finding out about presumably harmony, modes, things like that. Do you sort of 'know what you're doing' when you're writing [i.e. composing], or do you do it all by ear?
           N: No, I basically don't know what I'm doing when I'm composing ... I mean there's lots of different ways of doing it. Probably the most successful for me is to write lyrics first. If someone plays chords, it's actually telling me some lyrics anyway. It's actually giving something off anyway ... So yeah, that process, even though someone can be playing chords I don't think you have to know what the chords are to be able to create.
Will   I mean when I first started playing jazz I didn't know what modes were but it was more about the feel of it.
Steve   L: So how did you acquire your understanding of harmony?
           S: Um. Trial and error. [Laughs] What sounds right. Just get the bass note, the first note that they're playing, then work a scale round that. I mean, I didn't really know many scales when I was doing the guitar, there was only a few scales I know, so normally it was improvisation, then find the one I like and then keep doing that one that I like. So it's sometimes better that way, because if you follow a scale sometimes it starts sounding the same. So if you do your own thing and then one note might be out, so you change that to something else, not in the scale but it sounds right. Just makes the song sound a bit more original rather than follow a scale all the time.

Steve was not familiar with the term 'modes', although he was using them all the time, and the process he describes above was one of working out modes.

Steve   No because I've never done, haven't done anything at music college or anything like that ...
               ... I know what the notes are, I know all the notes of the guitar. So when they play a song, or I'll write a song, or they write a song, you pick out the chords then – [pause]
           L: And how do you go about picking out the chords?

S: Because I know what the chords they're playing are, because I used to play guitar for them.

L: Because of the names or because you see the hand?

S: Both. Well if someone says to me 'What's that note there?', I can tell them. But from there I have to know each chord for each bit of the song, which you'd have to know anyway. So you get that chord pattern. And then from there you just pick out notes in between that you use.

Steve's bass lines are indeed both sensitive to the harmonies and imaginative in a way that enhances the overall effect of the band.

Andy said that when he began playing the guitar, he did not know anything about scales and other technicalities. I asked him how he had gone about acquiring his knowledge and understanding of them.

Andy   After I got the rhythm book, I got a lead book, because I decided I could do something about it; and it had different scales in it, pretty simple ones – major, minor and the main influential one, the pentatonic. And I learnt that. It's like a jigsaw puzzle the way it fits onto the fret-board – you've got five different hand-changes where you can put the scale. And then the way it works is, if you're playing the modes of that scale – but of course I didn't know this at the time, I just looked at the charts and they all linked together – you keep going 'til you come up to the next octave. So I learnt that and I realized, when I was listening back to my records again, that the pentatonic is the most common scale they use in rock and blues playing, so I've really stuck to that a lot.

Notice that although he relied on a book for the theoretical knowledge, he was checking what he learnt all the time by listening. He also acquired knowledge by ...

Andy   ... interfacing with the other guitarist Illy. Because he was taking lessons at the time. I'm still not completely clued up on it but I've got a fair idea.

And on modes:

Andy   There's some we like to use, like the phrygian mode, I like to use that. It's got a very dark feel to it. I tend to find rather than going by precise notation – because most of the time you're playing over a very simple chord progression when you're doing lead – the way I find modes work is, they're either dark or they're bright. The mixolydian is a very bright scale – it's very colourful. I tend to do it that way.

I asked Simon, Brent and Michael whether, as drummers, they felt they needed or wished to know something about what the pitched instruments are doing. They all did. In Simon's case it was 'Just to understand each other and how it all works together.' Brent took some traditional rudimentary theory lessons and exams to help himself. Michael was playing keyboard with other bands to get his hand in, as well as writing and recording his own songs by overdubbing all the parts. As he quite frequently referred to technical terms concerning harmony in the interview, I asked him how he had acquired the necessary knowledge. He had taken piano lessons between the ages of 8 and 12:

Michael   Well, I remembered. It took me quite a long time to remember everything that I'd learnt from the piano lessons but it did come back after trying for a little while …

        … What I do mostly is, I'm just playing chords while the song's going, but then I might have a keyboard solo, by which time I'll make up a melody on top of the chord sequence and yes, that is using things I learnt in my piano lessons, although I didn't ever learn all that much improvisation. It's just really just something I've taught myself recently – most of it is just pentatonic scales, I think – I can go fairly fast doing that up and down in the, the easy keys, that's what I tend to do.

As mentioned earlier, his father had shown him some added-note chords, and by the time of the interviews he was able to aurally recognize simple chord sequences of primary triads by ear.

Michael   L: And what about tetrachords or chords with added notes – can you get anywhere with those?

        M: Occasionally. I can recognize the sevenths and the suspended fourths and seconds which are quite commonly used, but when you get into sixths – I can sometimes recognize a sixth but anything much more clever than that I, I can't really. I still have to get my Dad to help me on those.

Richard talked about keys, so I asked him how he had gone about finding out what key a song is in:

Richard   It just sounded right and it's – I don't know you could, you could play that note all the way through the song and it, it wouldn't sound very good but it would sound right. And then, the notes that they'd be singing or she was singing – that would be the melody in that key.

Summary

I have suggested that young popular musicians largely teach themselves to play music into which they are encultured and with which they identify, through processes of skill and knowledge acquisition that are both conscious and unconscious. One central early learning practice is solitary and involves purposive and attentive listening linked to the close copying of recordings, as well as more distracted listening leading to loose imitation and improvisatory adaptation. Some of the musicians consult books and use conventional notation, tablature or chord symbols, but the written is always secondary to the aural.

Another central practice involves learning from each other in pairs and groups, through casual encounters and organized sessions, both aside from and during music-making. Musicians watch and imitate each other as well as more experienced players, they talk about music and they form bands at very early stages. Through such interaction they copy and exchange ideas, knowledge and techniques, learn to play together, including making covers, improvisations and compositions of original music. All their listening and copying activities feed into both their individual and their group music-making.

The musicians are not particularly conscious of conventional technical approaches to playing their instruments until the later stages of learning if at all. They have a sporadic approach to practice, so dedicated practice regimes during some periods can revert to lack of routine or of any practice at all in other periods. Amounts of practice and the nature of practice tasks also vary considerably from individual to individual. Knowledge of music theory tends to be acquired haphazardly according to whatever music is enjoyed and played. I have suggested that just because the musicians are not necessarily able to talk about or name musical procedures and elements in the early stages, it does not follow that they should conceive of themselves as 'not knowing' about them. Rather, they have 'tacit' knowledge of them.

Indications are that informal popular music learning practices develop, as is to be expected, according to age and maturity; but there is as yet no evidence to suggest that the passing of historical time, and the social, educational and musical changes that have come in its wake, have been accompanied by any major differences in the learning practices of guitar-based popular and rock musicians in England across the last forty years of the twentieth century.

Notes

1. See e.g. Bayton (1997), Bennett (1980), Berkaak (1999), Björnberg (1993), Campbell (1995), Clawson (1999a), Cohen (1991), Finnegan (1989), Finney (1987), Horn (1984), Kirshner (1998), Lilliestam (1996) and Negus (1999).
2. For sociological discussions of women's experiences as popular musicians see Bayton (1990, 1993, 1997), Clawson (1999a and b); for histories of well-known women popular musicians see Gaar (1993), O'Brien (1995), O'Brien (1994). For an examination of the social construction of gendered musical meanings and practices, and their reproduction through education, see Green (1997). For girls' and boys' different attitudes towards and choices of instruments in schools see Bruce and Kemp (1993), Delzell (1994) and O'Neill (1997b).
3. Berkaak (1999, pp. 27–8), Bennett (1980, p. 4 and passim), Clawson (1999a, p. 110), Finney (1987, p. 32) and Horn (1984, p. 116) all quote musicians making this point; also see Cohen (1991) and Finnegan (1989). See the discussion on p. 77 above for the provisos that more synthetic forms of music do not involve band formation and that girls do not tend to start up bands as early as boys.

4. See especially Cohen (1991, pp. 28, 135ff.), Bennett (1980, pp. 59ff. and 145ff.) and Finney (1987) for detailed observations and discussions of group creativity in rehearsals. Lilliestam (1996, pp. 204ff., 209ff.) contains many interesting discussions and quotations from famous popular musicians concerning group creativity.

5. For a literature review and research findings on classical piano teachers' approaches to demonstration see Lennon (1996, esp. pp. 158–65). For information on learning by watching other musicians in a variety of traditional and art non-Western musics see especially Merriam (1964, pp. 145–63), which is a scholarly account of the literature up to that date, Campbell (1991b, pp. 186–206) for a more recent overview, Berliner (1994) in relation to jazz, and see Chapter 1 note 11.

Chapter 4

Attitudes and values in learning to play popular music

In the previous chapter I concentrated on learning practices concerned with the acquisition of executive and technical musical skills and knowledge. In the present chapter I will look at some of the attitudes and values that go along with those learning practices. Experientially, of course, such practices, attitudes and values come across as more or less inseparable. But in analysing our experiences, it is helpful to separate them out. For example, a learning practice might involve listening to a recording and attempting to copy it; an attitude towards this practice might involve commitment or carelessness; whereas the values placed upon the practice might involve a belief that it is a significant or an insignificant part of life. I will also include discussion of emotional responses to music-making, particularly enjoyment, in relation to attitudes and values in this chapter.

Discipline and osmosis

> we teach classical music because it requires disciplined study. Expertise in pop, on the other hand, can be acquired by osmosis.
>
> (Roger Scruton, 1996)

This opposition between 'disciplined study' related to classical music, and 'osmosis' related to popular music, suggests a broader split between 'culture' and 'nature'. For the implication is that disciplined study is the necessary, un-bypassable route to the acquisition of culture, of which classical music is a part; whilst osmosis occurs without any conscious application and so represents the workings of nature, to which popular music is relegated. Whereas culture is implicitly linked with what is worthwhile and ethical, nature is associated with inevitability and therefore amorality. But looked at in another way, nature can be understood as beautiful, authentic, timeless, and, indeed, the rock ideology of 'authenticity' draws on just such an understanding. Viewed in these terms, Scruton's juxtaposition of classical music as culture and popular music as nature contains an implicit, and unintended, positive evaluation of the popular. Music itself is natural to humanity: no society, tribe or any other social organization has ever been discovered that did not make music. The fact that many people to whom music education has been unavailable, only partially relevant or even antipathetic, have nonetheless learnt to perform and compose to widespread public acclaim is surely cause for celebration.

I have no argument with Scruton's assertion that classical music requires disciplined study, and to some extent I can agree with his depiction of popular music as being acquired by a process of osmosis: the learning practices of the musicians are indeed more natural than many of those associated with formal education, more akin to the ways in which very young children pick up language, and draw more heavily on enculturation experiences. (Berliner 1994, p. 22 also uses the word 'osmosis' to describe the early learning of jazz musicians.) But I cannot accept Scruton's crude opposition of 'discipline' and 'osmosis', nor the notion that skills and knowledge which are acquired largely by 'osmosis' are for that reason, unworthy of inclusion in or recognition by the processes of formal education. Provoked, on the one hand, by this dismissive attitude towards the learning that goes into the acquisition and development of popular music skills and knowledge and, on the other hand, by the ideology that rock musicians are more 'authentic' when they play without conscious design, I asked all the interviewees the direct question 'Would you describe learning how to play your instrument as having been a process of disciplined or systematic study?'

Terry's response has been quoted in Chapter 3 (pp. 64–5) and was a predictable 'no'. Some of the others associated the word 'discipline' with work and something unpleasant. Because their musical involvement was shot through with enjoyment, they therefore could not tally the two.

Steve   No.
             L: How would you describe it?
             S: Just pleasure.
             L: Just pleasure.
             S: Yeah. Just playing when I felt like playing. I suppose it's a bit systematic when you just want to learn a song and you want to learn it so bad so you can play it … But I wouldn't say I sat down properly and studied it. Just pleasure completely – nothing else.

For many of the others, the learning process was indeed considered to have been disciplined, or in some cases they preferred 'systematic', but again, they were careful to distinguish the notion of discipline from any association with unpleasantness.

Rob   It wasn't disciplined that I had to force myself, you see. Because I was so completely wrapped up in it, it didn't feel like work, it was just – 'Oh, I'd better make sure I can do all this' …
             L: … Then how about, not 'disciplined' but 'systematic'?
             R: Systematic would be a better word, yes.
Nanette   Yeah, definitely. Definitely. It hasn't been the kind of study that music students go through, but it's um, it is definitely disciplined, because if you stand up in front of people and mess up, the opinion that they have of you is then set, you

know, you don't get another chance to impress really. So it's by trial and error and you're learning as you're going; and it certainly sorts you out, you can't make mistakes, you know. So in some ways that's quite good. You've got to do the homework and you've got to be disciplined about learning stuff and committing all of it to memory, because that's a really important part of it as well. When I started off, learning eight to twelve songs a week, you know just getting over that hurdle of actually physically disciplining myself to learn all that stuff and memorize it, words as well as melodies, I mean it was fantastic schooling.

Brent   Yeah, I suppose so, I mean not always totally disciplined but it's always been something that I've wanted to do and if there've been times when I've been practising and struggling with something then you know, the longer you play you reach a point where you realize that the only way you're going to achieve what you want to achieve is by just putting the time in and practising, so yeah. It sounds a bit of a grand terminology, but I suppose that is what it involves, although mostly it's something I enjoy doing.

Peter   L: Would you describe your process of learning the instrument and the musical knowledge that goes with it as a process of disciplined or systematic study?
P: Yeah.
L: Can you elaborate on that at all?
P: Um. Sometimes I have to force myself to start. Once I've started I don't have to force myself to stop. Yeah, and I think it's more than disciplined study
...
          ... but I'm still having trouble disciplining it properly ... It's a matter of appraising one's playing and then having the discipline to set a modest enough goal so that I can accomplish it and therefore feel good about myself and then be a better player.

Michael   [Pause] What do you mean? Um, I think so yes, because I set myself aims. I want to be able to play this thing that I've heard or this thing that my drum teacher has shown me or this piece of music and I work towards that and when I've achieved that I go on to look towards the next thing I want to be able to play, and getting more and more difficult as they go through – is that what you mean?
L: Yeah.
M: Yes, in that case, yes.

In response to the same question, both Will and Simon distinguished between having 'fun' with their second instrument and being 'disciplined' with their first instrument:

Will   Drums, no; guitar definitely.
L: What's the difference?
W: The drums has always been fun, it just feels great.

But with reference to the guitar:

Will   ... if you're going to get anything out of playing an instrument you have to put the time in and treat it quite seriously, which is where the theory side comes in.

Simon   Disciplined study I would have thought. Well, on the drums it is. Definitely,
            you do have to have self-discipline big time. But the guitar as you know was
            for myself, it wasn't really for anyone else, I just was interested in it … But
            yeah, discipline, definitely on the drum side, definitely, without a doubt. You
            have to make time for yourself – you need to do it.

In Rob's memory, although his approach became disciplined after a time, it
was not to start with.

Rob   Not initially. As I said, when I first started doing it, it was to improve my
            social stature … I think it only really dawned on me that I'd have to be very
            good at it when I saw what the competition was like professionally, and then it
            stopped being something that was just a bit of a local bass hero in Hemel
            Hempstead into 'You're going to really have to pull your socks up'; and so in
            other words I would say from about 1973 I really started to work.

Similar experiences of clouds apparently parting over time were also described
by two of the younger musicians, Andy and Emily, who answered with a 'yes'
and a 'no', appearing to be at a watermark between the two positions:

Andy   No, not at all. Not at all. The way I look back at it nowadays, it does seem that
            everything's just fallen into place, like certain bits have come from here and
            there; but when I look at it, it isn't in a linear sort of way that it all came
            together …
                … Well, no, it wasn't an intentional, it wasn't an intentional, systematic
            process [pause], but I mean, it would appear to have been. I mean the way I
            was going, I wasn't saying 'I'll do this, I'll do that, I'll do this and that.' It just
            all came together.
Emily   Well I think it's a mixture really … We've recently got more strict about
            rehearsals and this year we've had them weekly, once a week, and I suppose
            you could say that's quite disciplined because like, everyone has to turn up,
            everyone has to be there and I really look forward to that, which is, like, quite
            good…
            L: … And in what ways has it not been disciplined then?
            E: Well, I think quite a lot of it is experimentation actually, because like I was
            saying earlier, you know, with the band I just play what sounds good … And I
            think, really like, because I don't learn [that is, take lessons], that's one of the
            ways it's like, undisciplined because it's, I don't know, it really has to come
            from *me*, because if I didn't enjoy the guitar I wouldn't be playing it.

The very youngest musicians did not see their practices as disciplined or
systematic at all:

Richard   [Laughs] It's just – you picked it up as you went along and you missed bits out
            and then you go back and fill them in later. I probably would've done it
            differently if I'd known what I was doing at the time and – too late now. It's
            not the best way of learning things really … it was just a mish-mash. Yeah.

Leo   Er, it hasn't really been disciplined I don't think, because my Mum and Dad they get a bit annoyed with me because I don't practice enough. But I don't know really; it hasn't been disciplined but I've learnt stuff; but it just hasn't been very disciplined.

Overall, the musicians shunned the notion of discipline in so far as it was associated with something unpleasant, but recognized it in so far as it related to the systematic ways in which they approached learning. The level of systematization seems to have become increasingly apparent to the musicians as time went by. It is plausible to hypothesize that informal popular music learning begins as a jumble of relatively unconscious processes. In some cases, such as Terry's and Steve's, the skills and knowledge involved gradually become so familiar that the learners cannot effectively conceptualize or analyse what they do. In other cases – including the majority of the musicians in the present study – as time goes by and learning progresses, different aspects begin to fall into distinct places, elements become distinguished one from the other and greater levels of conscious systematization develop.

It is not only anti-rock critics such as Roger Scruton who assume that rock musicians acquire their skills and knowledge entirely through 'osmotic' or natural processes requiring no conscious application. For as mentioned before, rock musicians themselves, their fans and the journalists who write about them often operate within an 'ideology of authenticity', which includes the romantic assumption that their music is a natural outpouring of the soul involving no commercial interest, no artifice, no imitation of anyone else's music and no work on the part of the musician.[1] Here again we touch upon an area that is marked by radical differences depending on the style of the music, the ethnicity and nationality of the musicians and other factors. My comments in this context are specifically concerned with rock ideology. None of the musicians in my sample expressed this ideology strongly, so to illustrate it I will quote a musician from Berkaak's research:

> I mean that the music I make is the music I make! It goes all the way back to when I learned to play the guitar. My friends who play the guitar sit at home for hours every day practising and copying solos note by note from other guitarists. They draw their inspiration from all other people. But I have been completely in my own bag all the time. I have only played things that come from here (points to his chest).
>
> (Berkaak 1999, p. 37)

The ideology of rock authenticity arises in part precisely from the fact that the musicians have acquired their skills largely outside of formal education, which lends the appearance of not having ever consciously or purposefully 'learnt' them at all. For example, quite a few of the musicians in this study stated that they 'had not *learnt*' something, meaning they had not *been taught* it. Below are snippets from previous quotations, with italics to highlight the points relevant to this discussion.

Rob	L: How did you go about learning your technique?
	R: *I didn't, I did it all by ear* ...
Steve	No [I don't know what modes are], because *I've never done, haven't done anything at music college* or anything like that.
Emily	... that's all like, experimentation. And I think, I think really like, because *I don't learn* [that is, take lessons], that's one of the ways it's like, undisciplined because it's, I don't know, it really has to come from *me*.
Richard	I can't remember [distinguish between] everything that I've *taught myself* and something that I've learnt ...
	... We – none of us have really *been taught* music properly so we *just make up* the songs by like playing around with them and see what we come up with and if that sounds nice.

The lack of recognition that music learning can occur without music teaching looks in two directions. On one hand, it feeds into the ideology of authenticity, for it involves a concealment of the social, conventional nature of all musical practices and all music. On the other hand, it suggests that musicians themselves unconsciously overlook and downgrade their own learning practices, in line with Scruton's denigration at the beginning of this chapter. The musicians in this study thus often presented themselves as and considered themselves to be or to have been 'ignorant'. I will suggest in Chapter 7 that such an attitude risks riding roughshod over a potential goldmine of approaches to music teaching and learning in general.

Enjoyment

Whereas the concept of 'discipline' is associated with something unpleasant, enjoyment was, as has already been made apparent, a major aspect of all the musicians' learning practices, so much so that it is impossible to do full justice to its centrality and all-pervasiveness in a dedicated section without repeating a good deal of data considered elsewhere. For that reason, I have restricted myself to picking out just one or two comments from each musician, most of which are also cited for other reasons either earlier or later in the book, giving an indication of the enthusiasm and enjoyment they describe. Some of the comments refer explicitly to having fun or enjoyment, others indicate enthusiasm in different ways by, for example, talking about how they '*loved* doing' something or '*would love* to do' something.

Bernie	I've always tried to be mindful that, first of all, I always think it's very lucky to be working as a musician, to be doing something you enjoy doing, when a

lot of people in this world have to do jobs that they don't like doing, so I'm always grateful for that.

Terry ... it's like the early days of Hawkwind and the Pink Fairies, everyone was doing it, you know, just jamming you know, and it's great, I love it ...

... I mean I always remember if I had died at that point, at any time when I was playing, I couldn't have died doing anything better, you know I'd have been completely fulfilled, if you like, doing my utmost for something I believed in you know, it was great.

Rob I can still walk into certain music shops and it's still like being 15 – it's like 'Oh, wow! Want one of those, want one of those too' ...

... And all of it is just fretless up at the – what I would call the dusty end of the bass guitar – very, very high melodic stuff with complete rich kind of piano chords underneath. That was great fun because it was a challenge and it took me out of having to play lots of beat notes which is the accepted kind of role.

Nanette I would love to be able to create an Aretha Franklin type sound, you know those kind of areas ...

... I would really love to be able to master a classical aria, say Puccini or Mozart ...

Brent It's always been something that I've wanted to do ...

... it was always a fun thing to some extent. It was never like I felt that I had to do this or I had to do that, it was just, 'This is something I enjoy, I'll do it until it's no longer fun and then I'll go and do something else.'

Peter I was completely obsessed with music. And I saw a performance by Gil Scott Heron and it was amazing, and the bassist from that group did some remarkable things with the bass line that I'd never heard anyone else do. So the excitement of that particular performance stuck with me.

Will The drums has always been fun, it just feels great.

Steve I enjoyed listening to the guitar and if I could mimic the guitar and it sounded good, then it made me feel good. It sounded good, and it was just enjoyable ...

... I do it for fun, I mean I'm not like, waiting for the money after a gig or anything like that.

Andy There's like, there's a level you get to 'Wild Thing' – you can play the three chords to 'Wild Thing' and you think 'Yeah, that's great.'

Simon L: What are your aims for your future as a musician?

S: Oh I don't know. I want to play in a band you know. Earn money through it would be nice, definitely. Enjoy myself ... I wouldn't be there now if I wasn't enjoying it.

Michael ...occasionally as with my band it just sort of happens, because we feel that there needs to be a triplet run or a bit of syncopation there and we all do it together and I, I love it when that happens – that's really great.

... I used to like his [drummer at church's] drum kit and he sometimes let me play it and that was always good fun.

Emily If I didn't enjoy the guitar I wouldn't be playing it; because my parents don't force me to play it; I mean they don't care, because I saved, after the first guitar, I saved up for the electric guitar, I saved up for the amps, so there's no actual pressure on me.

Richard I do practice them, it's just sometimes it gets a bit boring practising scales and I wasn't learning the guitar to learn music in, I was learning it for fun, not to you know become great at it. I wanted to get better but I wasn't I mean – just for fun ...

> ... like, when we're all there in a group, like I said some songs just – it's boring, it's not happening. But then other times we just, if we're all in the right mood and we're all sort of psyched up and we just play and it's really fun, just playing and that, and that – then you don't care if anyone thinks you're rubbish. It's just – that's important, that. When you're enjoying it as well then that's the best bit.

Leo   I would like to definitely, I would enjoy to keep it up, to keep on doing music, in whatever way, playing the saxophone, composing or whatever ... just doing it for fun, yeah.

As is evident in Chapter 3, playing together in a band can also be associated with a great deal of enjoyment.

Emily   ... sometimes the band rehearsals are like the best thing in my week – I just really look forward to them so much ...

Will suffered abuse from his contemporaries at boarding school as a result of his interests in music: they would hang his guitar out of the dormitory window and splatter paint on his posters of Elvis. But he paid little attention to this because, as cited in Chapter 3

Will   ... we were trying to get bands together and that was just the best feeling in the world, even if it sounded awful, it was just the best feeling in the world.
            L: To be in a band?
            W: Yes. To be playing a three chord song, like 'Wild Thing', in a band, just three of us, four of us.

Fun rubs off: even music theory was perceived in terms far removed from drudgery. Rob and Brent described studying for and taking theory grade exams as 'Great fun. That's where I learnt my initial arranging skills' (Rob); 'it was kind of good fun' (Brent); and Will found 'music theory very exciting – it's a lot of fun'.

Not only enjoyment of the activity of music-making alone and in a band, or of learning about theory, but enjoyment of and identity with the music being played are vital. The centrality of enculturation in informal learning goes hand-in-hand with the fact that the music covered is selected from the styles, or the music created is *in* the styles which the musicians like and identify with. We saw in Chapter 2 that all the interviewees had started off by playing instruments they liked, often because they had heard them being played in ways they found inspiring, or had heard them playing music that they found inspiring. In Chapter 3 (p. 68–9) I noted that ten of the musicians referred to playing music that they liked. The point there was to illustrate the importance of enculturation in listening and copying practices which draw not only on purposive and attentive listening geared to close copying but also on distracted listening (or 'just listening'). Here is a different selection of quotes, now presented in the context of simply illustrating the central role in the musicians' attitudes towards learning of *valuing* the music played.

Nanette	Well, … I'd pick stuff that I liked, that I knew I couldn't sing and then it would be a challenge for me to master it.
Will	I bought a slightly better [guitar] with the money and that's when I really got into listening to music and went out and found certain – just a few bands I really liked, and made an effort to learn all their songs.
Steve	You can pick a song you like … then when you've got a guitar in front of you, you've got your teenage idols there and you can copy them and do it how they do it, and it just makes you feel good, doesn't it?
Simon	You know, as long as I enjoy it, I don't want to be stuck in, you know in a rut, you know just – I don't want to be playing music that I don't enjoy playing. I don't think that's worth it. I wouldn't be there now if I wasn't enjoying it.
Michael	[My Dad] said 'Well put in this, this F in the C chord here and then make it go down to the E' and I thought 'Ooh, that sounds nice.' I started doing it all the time after that.
Richard	… you enjoy playing something more if you like it, I've found.

As a corollary of making music for enjoyment and making music that they liked, the musicians were quite explicit in avoiding activities or music which they did not like. As Brent, Emily and Richard had said, quoted above:

Brent	It was always a fun thing to some extent; it was never like I felt that I had to do this or I had to do that; it was just, 'This is something I enjoy, I'll do it 'til it's no longer fun and then I'll go and do something else.'
Emily	If I didn't enjoy the guitar I wouldn't be playing it; because my parents don't force me to play it …
Richard	You enjoy playing something more if you like it, I've found.

Valuing musicianship

I asked every interviewee the question 'What aspects of musicianship do you value most highly in another musician?' Their answers fell into two broad categories, both of which were expressed by the same person in several cases.

Valuing 'feel'

One of the categories, which was explicit in the responses of twelve of the musicians, came as no surprise to me, and is likely to be shared by musicians of all kinds all over the world. This involved valuing the ability to play with 'feel', 'sensitivity', 'spirit' and other comparable attributes which the musicians found it difficult to put into words, and valuing such qualities over and above technical ability. For example:

Bernie   [Long pause] My answer to you: if you'd have asked me this question twenty
            years ago, I would have said, 'Great technical ability, great confidence,
            supreme confidence, great technical ability', you know, 'Very powerful'. Now
            you're asking me the question now, I would say [pause] – humanity. I would
            say the fact is, if they are a musician, it's given that they can play. We're taking
            that for granted, that they can play their instrument; they know their music,
            they know what the chord sequences are, they know the key signatures,
            basically they know their nuts and bolts and they can run scales, you know,
            they know all that. I would say I'd look for a depth, a depth of character, and
            also, somebody who cares about what they do, not because it's going to make
            them famous or a lot of money, but they care about what they're doing, and
            that what they're actually doing at that time, matters to them enough for them
            to forget other things for that moment.

At the same time, Bernie decried flash technical playing which he felt was
devoid of the qualities above.

Bernie   ... to give you an example of a chap who's done this, there's two chaps who've
            done it, one is Joe Satriani, who's got this sort of technique where he taps on
            the neck of the guitar and he plays these very, very fast things – but that's all
            he can do! That's all he can do! Now the thing is, I went and saw, not him, but
            I saw somebody like him, I went to a whole night of them at Ronnie Scott's, it
            was Stanley Jordan, and for the first half an hour my tongue was hanging out,
            my jaw dropped, but after that I thought 'Well was that it, well come on what
            else?' And it was rather like a circus act. And I thought 'Well hang on a
            minute.'

Later:

Bernie   ... you've got this chord sequence and you've got these bars and you've got to
            make sense of it, and be musical as well. It's not enough to be clever and
            technical. You've got to be musical, you've got to sing, you've got to be
            lyrical, you've got to make your instrument sing.

He described a vehement argument he had had with another musician who
said that singers, including Ella Fitzgerald, were not 'musicians':

Bernie   I would gladly give up all my abilities on all the instruments I play, to have
            that skill, to be able to sing in such a way that you just go straight, direct, into
            someone's heart; just nothing in the way, no obstacles, straight to the heart,
            you know. I'd give everything up to be able to do that, because the human
            voice is the greatest instrument ... When I hear someone who's a really, really
            great singer, I mean you know someone like Stevie Wonder, you know, I think
            'Wow that's just absolutely marvellous.' Another person whose singing I
            loved, always loved was Joni Mitchell. These people, they are what I call
            'bulls-eye people', they're straight there and 'Bulls-eye!', without even trying,
            they hit the centre, all the time.

Rob expressed similar sentiments, and a similar journey to Bernie:

Rob   I've always been a Zappa fan and learning 'Peaches en Regalia' by ear from the original Max Bennett bass line ... just made me realize there was a lot more to music than playing minor pentatonic scales very fast ...

        ... [When I was younger] I had this belief that anything that was demanding, tough to play, took some practising – that was how I'd define the quality of the music. What changed my view was when I first heard Fairport Convention's 'Liege and Leaf' which I didn't like at first. When I later started to have an appreciation of British folk, I thought, if this was sung by what I regarded mistakenly as being rustics – wrong [laughter] – if this was sung by people who had no musical or formal – say formal musical education – even that's a contentious area ... – um, how come they could sing this stuff without anybody saying, 'Ah, but that's a crotchet and that's a minim and this is a C and this is a D.' They didn't know anything about that, they sang something that was passionate to them. And I kind of tied that up with the fact that I used to like guitar players who played loads and loads of notes – John McLaughlin, Alan Holdsworth – that sort of thing; then I heard B. B. King and I thought, 'Hang on, if he can make something shoot up my spine by playing two notes, how is it that I just listen to those guys and think, "Wow, there's loads of notes for you?"'; and it started to change. I think it also ran kind of in a contrary motion: as my own technique became more and more advanced, for want of a better word, I realized how meaningless that actually was, because – fine, I could do all these wonderful things, but 90 per cent of the time when people ask me to play something I'm playing something ridiculously simple, and just making it feel good. And so I started to think, 'Well, all the music that I really rate now doesn't have that kind of thing', you know it's nice to have the technique, but you don't have to use it all the time, let's put it like that.
L: Mmm. So what has it got, instead of technique: can you find words, or a word for that?
R: Passion I think, I've got to be moved by music.

Many others from the oldest to the youngest also espoused the value of 'feel'.

Terry   I think with all music, it's the feel that makes the music, you know you could be technically brilliant and as boring as anything. I think it's what people put into it really.

Nanette   I value that individuality, that something which is unique to you ... [When she is teaching, she emphasizes] the whole thing about personality and how the students would interpret a song; put away how someone else is doing it, get them to write out the lyrics and sort of, just underline the words that really mean something to *them* and get them to speak it, you know, so it's like developing the meaning of the song.

Brent   Spirit, I would say. Spirit or feel or whatever, however you want to describe it, the way in which they play, the way they attack things for want of a better word. You know, you can get people who don't have much technique but really have a great feel about what they do, and you can get people who've got phenomenal technique who are just totally soulless. So you know when it comes down to it I think it's feel or spirit.

Peter   I was about to say 'spontaneity' but it's a particular kind of spontaneity, so it's not standard but it's the ability to directly apply what they're thinking to their instrument in a way that I don't think comes from just practice. It's a naturalness. Yes. I was talking with a saxophonist who is frequently asked to be involved in one project or another, and she hardly ever practises because she doesn't have enough time to – she's a single mother – and she was being very negative about her standard of technique on the instrument and I was pointing out to her that she's another of those people that – they don't want her for her good technique, because her technique clearly isn't good; they just want her to play because what she does try to play she gets right – simple ideas drop out of the end of her saxophone without any effort seemingly.

Andy   Feeling. The way they can convey themselves – what they truly mean through the music. If it comes across then I think it's brilliant. There's so much commercial corporate stuff out there which I wouldn't give a second thought to; but I mean even then, with that sort of stuff there's a commercial aspect to it if the players are feeling ... More than technique, I mean along emotional lines.

Simon   You have to feel the music definitely, that's a big one – I think you should know how that sort of, that piece would go. You know, I mean you can, you can read music fine, I mean but you have to, you need to have the feeling of the music so that you can play it well.

Emily   I mean all the sort of flashy people like the glam rockers and stuff, they're quite technically good but you know, it doesn't have to be all about how good you are, it's about, like, I don't know, it's not one of the main things.

Leo   I'm not quite sure. I think, more what they're playing, especially if it's improvisation, then the melody, or *how* they're playing it, how they've interpreted it, is more important than their actual quality of playing.
             L: Right, so, what do you mean by 'how they interpret it'?
             Leo: Well, whether they play it, say, just if they put their own life into it like, I mean like, interpret it their own way so, play it differently, but not totally differently so it's not off the original part, but it's kind of, the way they've actually played it and the way it's meant to be correspond, but they've added something extra.

Of the three youngest musicians, Emily, in a different part of the conversation to that cited above, and Richard put their answers more in terms of creativity than feel:

Emily   ... if their songs, sorry about the pun, if they strike a chord with me ... I think creativity is really important, obviously.

Richard   Being inventive ... I know most things have already been done by now but like – Oasis, it's kind of more scales on top of chords and stuff, but Radiohead with 'OK Computer' – at least that was partly new, it was something a bit different, and there was probably stuff like it out there but it was just – I really liked that because it was completely different to anything I'd heard. It's inventive. And like 'Paranoid Android'– it's, well there probably are scales in it but I can't recognize the kind of scales. They play what sounds right and I like that. And Blur's guitarist – it's a kind of mixture of scales, chords and jumping about the guitar all over the place. And I like that because it's, well it's inventive, it's more interesting than just chords.

Although 'feel' was high on the agenda, we have already seen that the musicians also valued technical ability and strove to achieve it. For example, at the same time as valuing 'individuality' above, Nanette also values:

Nanette   Skill. I really respect people who can play an instrument, I really do, whether it's voice or whether it's brass or rhythm section, I really respect skill, you know, because I know what time has been sacrificed in having to develop it.

There is a complex relationship between feel and technique. No musician can play with feel unless they have at least enough technique to *put* feel into the actual sounds they are making. But whereas feel relies on an amount of technique at least sufficient to what is required for the physical execution of the music, technique can be superlative and yet totally devoid of feel. Overall, technique is respected but placed second to feel. In the statements below this tension is apparent.

Will   I would say technique, when you start to play with them, how they respond, how they follow you, their sense of timing, um, in a way, their musical knowledge of what they enjoy.

Emily also expressed both sides, by adding to her statement above that 'being good' is 'not one of the main things':

Emily   I mean obviously you have to be good to some extent, I do value that, you know; it's quite frustrating when people don't get things which seem quite obvious to you but, because I'm not really that good I can't really stand there and judge them, their technique.

Bernie and Rob, in the quotes above, had described themselves as having been rather dazzled by technical prowess when they were young. The three youngest musicians in this study did not appear to share those sentiments, but the fourth youngest, Michael, did to some extent. I would not be surprised if Michael were to become a professional musician. In the absence of a very large sample and the passing of several years it is not possible to do more than speculate on this subject, but it is worth considering that the high value which Bernie and Rob had placed upon technique in their youth was a necessary stage in the development of their own technical skills to a standard sufficient for them to follow successful careers as professional musicians.[2] At the same time, one suspects they are being hard on themselves with hindsight.

Valuing each other

I mentioned above that the musicians' responses to the question 'What aspects of musicianship do you value most highly in another musician?' fell into two categories. One of these – the ability to play with feel, as just discussed – was no surprise to me. But I did not anticipate the other. This was expressed in different ways by eleven of the musicians, the exceptions being Terry, Nanette and Leo. It involved placing value, not upon what I would normally consider to be an aspect of musicianship as such, but rather upon personal qualities perceived in other musicians.

Steve   Attitude – like a nice person. That's it.

Many of the responses involved allusions to empathy of various kinds, as a crucial component of relationships within a band.

Bernie   The depth comes, when I'm with somebody, working with them, you know, after a reasonable amount of time, I can, I can feel where that person is. And there's some people that I've worked with, I've thought 'Well, I'm glad I'm never going to work with them again'; and there's other people I've worked with I've thought 'What a great honour.'

Rob   L: How would you describe those aspects of musicianship that you value most of all in another musician?
             R: Broadmindness ... I also think that from my touring experience, I suppose it's a very utopian attitude, but people that can sit in a tour bus or on an aeroplane week after week and not drive everybody else insane or make you have murderous thoughts. I have been on the road with people like that, but a lot of my friends who I've toured with, I'm happy to say I'd tour with again given half a chance, because we had a great sense of sort of a bond. Otherwise you end up killing each other.

Of course, relationships in bands are by no means always smooth, especially in the professional world, where incentives such as being able to play with the 'best' musicians or to gain money or fame may outweigh the importance placed on good working relationships. Many bands which have achieved fame, wealth or both are known for extremely bad relationships within themselves. But in the absence of either the reality or the dream of such 'big' success, there is little incentive to stay in a band which is suffering incurably unpleasant relationships. When musicians in a band let others down, or when arguments take place, such problems are either overcome or tolerated, otherwise the band will sooner or later cease to exist. (See especially Bennett 1980, pp. 26–45, Cohen 1991 and Berkaak 1999 on friendship relations in bands.)

For the older players when they were young, or for the younger musicians in the study, good relationships were important, not only for intrinsic reasons but because the ability to get along together is essential to the very survival of the band. Band members must be able to reach agreements concerning what music to play, how, when and where to rehearse or perform and a plethora of similar issues, otherwise they cannot produce any music at all. As Terry said:

Terry	I mean the thing that splits most bands up is personality clashes.
Rob	You can have a tiff at some point, but most of the time you don't think 'Oh, here he comes, I'll sit on the other side of the bus so I don't have to talk to him.' That's the death of a band.
Brent	The very first band or group of people I remember playing with I think was through an advert in the local music shop. And it was a keyboard player who lived just outside of Swansea and I called him up and my parents dropped me across to his house and there was a bass player there … and basically I kind of liked the bass player, but for whatever reason, I can't remember now, I didn't particularly gravitate towards the keyboard player.
	L: As a musician you mean? Or as a person?
	B: I think probably personally more than anything. I don't think I had too much to sort of judge him on [as a musician] at that point you know, because it was the first thing I'd done and stuff. I seem to remember that he kind of wanted to control everything.
Steve	If I went to join a band and they all had an attitude I would leave the band. Because I couldn't handle that – not for money, not for music or anything, I wouldn't, I couldn't sit there and play music with people like that.
Richard	L: So do you do any covers at all?
	R: We used to but we kind of – we disagreed on all the songs. One person wouldn't like it and then, so we just gave up doing that.
	L: You mean one person wanted to do one song, someone else wanted to do a different song –
	R: Yeah. We did that – at first, we started off, there was just me and a guy called Alex. There was just me and him started, so we recorded them in stereo, one track at a time and so we did covers then because we weren't – neither of us were good enough to write songs really, we were all rubbish. Then gradually we just got extra people and we stopped doing covers because we disagreed on everything.

I have already indicated that the prominent role of enculturation in popular music learning practices goes along with the fact that the musicians are bound to like and identify with the music they play. Therefore band members must either have shared musical tastes, which form a significant part of friendship relations especially amongst adolescents, or they must be able to tolerate differences in taste within a looser broad consensus. Three voices from Deepvoid:

Steve	Yeah, everyone likes a different sort of music so it's good. It's good because it all mixes up. So you've got a bit of rock, jazz, blues, funk in there, so it's all kind of – bit of grunge in there – so it's all, it's a complete mix of the whole lot …
	… I mean we sort of – we've got different tastes but they sort of merge as well, how we play, which is nice.
Simon	And we all had totally different tastes, I mean Illy [the singer] is into a load of funk and jazz sort of stuff, and Steve [bass player in this study] listens to more or less anything he likes and plays everything he likes. And Robin is more into the, I don't know, sort of alternative sort of music as well. Together we sort of do mix well.
	L: Do you feel that's a strength of the band?

S: Definitely.

Andy   There's a lot of really acoustic sort of pieces, very gentle, and I've been using that; I've been sneaking in an acoustic guitar. They don't realize what I'm doing. Not that they ever would object to it, but it's just – it's not what we usually play. Yeah. I'm playing with that. And I managed to get a Spanish guitar on the last recording we did – sneaked it in there. Because they tend to think that plastic strings sound a bit childish but – [trails off].

Deepvoid's musical identity is, of course, wrapped up with the eclectic (or 'post-modern') musical developments characteristic of much popular music in the late 1990s, in which it was quite normal to borrow and mix elements from a range of previously juxtaposed or even opposed musical styles and genres, all in one song. Such mixing is not, as many people seem to think, peculiar to late twentieth-century popular music but is a recurrent phenomenon throughout the entire history of music and is exemplified by composers as far apart as J. S. Bach and Debussy. However, that is another discussion. In the context of late twentieth-century popular music, as will be illustrated in more detail later in this chapter, it was not only members of Deepvoid, nor only musicians referring to the 1990s, who indicated broad tolerance. On the contrary, in all cases musical tastes were negotiable and crossed over several style boundaries.

Such consensus implies a willingness to listen to each other's ideas:

Richard   With my friends [what I value is] not being amazingly good – they've got to be you know, good enough to play, but with them it's listening to your ideas; and that's not just the musical side of it but that you've got to be part of the band.

Players must be able to share equipment and take turns:

Richard   Well we try and – there's three of us that play the guitar, one drummer and a singer, but the three guitarists, we swap round see, because none of us really likes playing the bass guitar, we prefer the lead guitar stuff, so we all swap round and stuff ...

    ... I've got to be part of a band – it's got to be all of us, not just one person writing the songs; so we've all got to listen and talk to each other and stuff and not just say 'No that's rubbish', you know. Just be nice about it. Get on.

The high value placed on friendship, shared taste, tolerance and the ability to listen to each others' ideas are necessary because the music being played is arrived at through choice, and the activities of the band are voluntary and unsupervised by adults or others in positions of authority.

The ideal of consensual, tolerant relationships and cooperation during rehearsals can bring along with it a deep commitment to the band.

Steve   I suppose punctuality, being there on time. You got to be committed. You got to turn up on time for gigs, you got to turn up on time for practices, you got to bring your money to practices, stuff like that.

Andy   Above competence, which I do regard highly, is dedication. I mean I've worked with some people who will talk one way and it will just not come out in their actions. Say you had to learn something, or you had to write something, and everyone's done everything for the next week and there's one person who's just – 'Oh , I forgot, sorry mate, I was out on the piss last night.' It's just – there's nothing worse than one person letting you all down, or if you're the only one who's trying.

L: So, if you had a break, like say there's an established, really successful or famous band and miraculously and wonderfully you happened to get a position in that band. Would you be prepared to take that?

A: And leave the band I'm in?

L: Yeah.

A: No. No, I've put too much of my energy and my life into this band. In some ways that's actually been detrimental to the role I play because when you're running a band, not just playing in it, when you're trying to promote them and manage them and so forth, it's a full-time job in itself and everyone's always saying to me 'You should get someone else to do it, it should be someone separate.' But it's a matter of finding someone you can trust. Your career, someone whose hands you can put the band into safely and believe they'll do something and that. But no, I wouldn't quit this band …

… I tend to value loyalty, actually, more than anything else.

Emily   And commitment as well, because I look forward – sometimes the band rehearsals are like the best thing in my week – I just really look forward to them so much, that if then somebody turns around on that day and says 'Oh, I really can't be bothered to rehearse today, let's call it off', that just really, really annoys me, because I've been looking forward to it … because I'm not forcing them to play and if they don't want to play they should say so.

Love, even passion for music were explicit in the words of all the interviewees, and they preferred to make music with other musicians who felt similarly.

Rob   I like other musicians to still be as passionate about what they do as I am. I'll never forget my first BBC session, for *Not the Nine O'clock News* [a mainstream TV programme], where we had a string section playing with us; and all the rhythm section, i.e. the young guys, dashed into the control room to hear what we'd just put down, and all the string players pulled out their *Guardians* and sat reading the paper. I thought, 'I never want to end up with that kind of "It's a job" attitude.' So I think it's like, if they still have a great enthusiasm, if it's still a passion.

Will   I don't think it's necessarily snobbish to enjoy people's company who are as passionate about something as you are, and to know that much about it.

Emily   I want someone to mind, I want someone to either – because I'm quite fiery – I want someone to either object or agree. I don't want someone who says ' I don't mind' because that, I don't know, that just really annoys me … I want people to share that same passion.

Just as the ability to play with 'feel' or 'spirit' was valued over and above technical prowess, so were friendship relations and commitment.

Steve   If they can play it and they can play the music they want to play and it sounds right, that's all that matters. I don't think – fair enough you got to look up to people that can play really well – but I think if you can play an instrument and you can play as good as the band you're in then ... that's fine, you're in the right band. I mean you got to be good enough to play in a band, but you haven't got to be brilliant. If you can play in a band and it works, then it works.

... As the band develops you got to, you got to develop with it. So I've just tried to add bits in, and as I've done that I've got better and better and I mean – I wouldn't say I'm the best bass player in the world, far from it – but I'm good enough for what we play. And that's all it needs to be, I suppose.

Not only are good relationships and commitment necessary for the survival of the band as a social unit, but most significantly in musicological terms they go further to affect the precise nature and feel of the music played.

Simon   A good sense of reading off, if you're in a band, you need a good sense of reading off people and how many times, or what they're playing, what's going on next and – definitely need that. You have to work with each other to be really tight, I think. I mean you don't have to play with the band for ages to be tight, you just have to, you know, click. I think you have to sort of you know, get on well with people, I think that definitely helps in a band. See, you come across all sorts of people I think in bands, and I think you have to have an understanding of other people's attitudes and their intentions of how the music should go as well. Definitely, it's always listen to other people, see what they want, yeah.

Michael I think, I think it's – the most important thing to me in, well in pop music certainly is empathy with the rest of the band. And my band I play in we're very empathetic, um whatever that word is. Having played with the guitarist for five years, of course, it helps that. Like occasionally from time to time I'll think 'Triplet run coming up here', and I'll play a triplet run and the guitarist will also play a triplet run without having communicated beforehand and that – I think that's absolutely excellent when that happens. And little things like that. Just having the bass part following the bass drum, and every so often the drummer will do a double bass drum bounce or something, and the bassist will also do a double thing – I think that, that really makes music for me, just the little attention to detail that will bring the music to life.

... But occasionally as with my band it just sort of happens because we feel that there needs to be a triplet run or a bit of syncopation there and we all do it together and I, I love it when that happens – that's really great.

This inter-musician contact is also a major part of the enjoyment of playing as a group experience.

Whilst bad relationships, in Rob's words cited earlier, mean 'the death of the band', good relationships and commitment mean that non-band members must be excluded from watching rehearsals. Cohen (1991) and Bennett (1980) lay considerable emphasis on this. Because the bands they observed were made up almost entirely of males, this meant that most of the significant others who were excluded were females – girlfriends and wives. Whilst the exclusion of women from rock bands is a historical outcome of centuries of circumscription concerning women's roles in music and is referable, amongst other things, to unequal relations between the sexes, the reasons for excluding females from rehearsals cannot be explained entirely as sexism. In the 1980s and 1990s, as all-female bands began to be more common in popular music, this meant that boyfriends and husbands had to be excluded (see Bayton 1997); and where the band is mixed, or where band members have same-sex relationships with non-band members, partners of either sex will be excluded. Another reason for the exclusion of outsiders is to do with the importance of talking about the music. I mentioned in Chapter 3 that talking to each other and to other musicians played a major part in learning. The presence of outsiders – of either sex – will obviously mitigate against the feasibility of such in-group interaction. Other reasons indicated by Bennett (1980, p. 67f.) are reluctance to allow outsiders to hear the band playing badly, making mistakes or attempting half-formulated ideas.

The oldest and most experienced musicians in this study made dark references to people they had met or worked with during their careers, for whom they had neither liking nor respect, and many famous musicians of all kinds are known as much for their less-than-loved personalities as for their musicianship. But the point that concerns me in the context of this book is that such a large number of the musicians were forthcoming in *placing explicit emphasis* on valuing empathetic personal qualities, loyalty and commitment in other musicians, and all in response to a question, not about personality, but musicianship. Regardless of the notoriety of individual musicians, and of the vagaries and legalized exploitation that can be laid at the door of the music industry, the suggestion is that the development of musicianship for many musicians such as those interviewed here appears to be inseparable from the development of respect for qualities which, as will be discussed in the final chapter, are close to the heart of many formal music educators.

Valuing oneself

As well as being fun, the musicians' activities raised their self-esteem and the esteem which they considered their peers had for them. This became apparent, despite the fact that I did not ask them any questions at all about self-esteem. (See especially Horn 1984 for a discussion of this area.)

Nanette   My earliest memories? Well, OK, I was actually born in Africa and I came to this country when I was 5, and – it's quite a funny story actually – I used to have a terrible lisp, so I was really shy and not very, um, not very confident. And I used to copy Shirley Bassey at home by myself watching the telly, which drove my family nuts. But one day I remember singing in the loo at my junior school, and I was just singing away and basically the kids gathered outside the door and they thought there was a tape machine on, OK. So they pulled me out of this loo and took me all the way round the school and stood me on tables and said 'Sing'. Because I'd copied it off pat and they just couldn't believe that it wasn't a record. I'd just copied it, it was 'The Minute you Walked in the Joint' ... Yeah, and I got all the hip movements and [laughs]. When I think about it now, before that day, every time I put my hand up to say 'Please Miss' to answer a question, the whole class would mimic me because I had such a bad lisp. It was terrible. And then I just suddenly discovered that singing was the one thing that I could do for which I was accepted, you know, because if you're foreign as well, you're slightly different, you're not, you're not accepted ... Yeah, so that's it, yeah – it's exactly that feeling. Suddenly you're accepted, you know, one day you aren't and it's [lisps] 'th th th' every time you said anything in class, but then the next day, it's fine. It's like you're one of the gang, do you know what I mean, it's strange.

Steve   ... you just want to learn a song and you just want to learn it so bad so you can play it, so when you go to school next day with your guitar you can show your mates – 'Oh guess what I can play!'

Andy   Yeah, I mean, first of all it was getting the right chord progressions – you'd walk into school, you'd just learnt 'Knocking on Heaven's Door' or something, sit in the music centre in front of everybody else and you'd play it and they'd be like 'Yeah, that's right, yeah.'

Emily   Well, it's really nice when someone says 'Oh that's really cool, did you write that?'

The only one of the interviewees whose self-esteem came across as low was Terry. This arose partly from his personal history of involvement with late hippy sub-cultural value systems.

Terry   When we were in Hawkwind, we used to, you know, put down pop stars as such, you know, 'Look at me' and you know what I mean. So I was never sort of pushy of myself.

He loves jazz, and I asked him:

Terry   L: Have you ever wanted to be a jazz drummer, or thought about it?
             T: Yeah, I have, yeah. But there again, I don't know, I think it's almost a self-depreciation thing that, you know, because jazz drummers technically, usually, are really good. I've never considered myself technical at all, really. You know, I had someone ask me if I was a basher and crasher, 'Yes', I said.

Later:

L: ... If you're out for a month and you go back into a band, you've got to do a bit of practice before you go to a rehearsal –
T: Well I never do. [Pause]
L: But you should do?
T: Well I should practise all the time. I'd be really shit hot if I had done.

Terry did not teach, because he thought it would not be 'fair to teach if you can't read notation'. As well as this, and as well as having voluntarily given up a career in a successful band with an impending charts hit when he was only 19 or 20, he continued to fail to 'push himself' in the present. At the time of the interviews he had a steady job as an assistant school grounds and buildings caretaker, he normally gigged only two or three times a month, he never practised apart from a couple of weeks when he was preparing for one exceptional concert, his drums were not kept at his house and although he would have liked to get more gigs, he never attempted to fix any for himself. As already mentioned, there was consensus amongst the musicologists, musicians and music educators to whom I played examples of his music that his self-depreciation was unfounded, and there was huge enthusiasm for his drumming amongst his listeners and fellow-musicians.

Popular music, especially in its highly commercial forms, is often associated with the idolization of stars by their fans. The difference between being a fan and being a musician is not cut and dried. On one hand, many fans habitually sing their favourite songs along with or separately from the recordings, and yet would not conceive of themselves as popular musicians engaged in informal learning practices. On the other hand, especially for younger musicians who are just starting out, the move from listener-fan-mode into musician-fan-mode is likely to fluctuate backwards and forwards for some time before they identify themselves as a musician at all. (See Bennett 1980, pp. 4–5 and Frith 1996, p. 55f. for discussions of this.) Either way, being a fan can provide a public or a private means of accruing kudos and constructing a positive personal identity through image-identification with the star. For the musician-fan such image-identification can translate into actions that produce the same or similar music to that of the star. In addition, as discussed at the end of Chapter 2, many of the musicians in this study had dreamt of stardom for themselves, although always with a touch of realism, when they were young. Being a fan, being able to imitate one or more stars and having ambitions of personal stardom can act as vivid motivating factors for young popular musicians.

Rob   Every Friday morning at school we'd either have a pupil doing a live performance, or we'd have a piece of music played on the tannoy in the hall; and again, I used to look at whoever was performing and think, 'Wow, it must be so cool to play in front of everybody.' I would certainly become slightly stage-struck as well … I won the verse-speaking contest several times and I used to absolutely panic before going on stage, I was just crippled by stage fright, and I'd go on stage and then recite. But once I was up there I thought, 'They're all listening to me, this is fantastic. I like this' …

                … And I held this thing [bass guitar, for the first time] and I just thought, 'Wow, this looks' – not sounds, or anything – 'this *looks* so cool. And this would improve my social status at school amazingly if I had one of these things'!

> ... As I said ... when I first started doing it, it was to improve my social stature, to meet members of the opposite sex, to, in a way I think, to annoy my parents.

Steve   When you got a guitar in front of you, you got your teenage idols there and you can copy them and do it how they do it, it just makes you feel good, doesn't it? ...

> ... A lot of people don't actually grow up, young people, listening to classical music. Because it doesn't interest them. There's no idols there or anything, it's just a sound, isn't it?

Leo   L: And then, what made you want to take up the sax?

> Leo: I just, I like the sound of the instrument, and it was, kind of it was cool, so, yeah, I wanted to play the saxophone.

Will revealed the seriousness and commitment that can lie behind what is sometimes dismissed as 'mindless' idolization. On one hand, he had clearly gone in for some of the trappings of fandom when at school. For this he was bullied by other boys (as mentioned earlier); but he was himself critical of those boys because they seemed to suffer from far more superficial, commercially-motivated constructions of musical taste than he did.

Will   I think a lot of it is to do with the age that you are. I remember when I was about 13 I was into the Beatles, Kiss and Elvis and I stuck with it, because I mean, I was bullied because of Elvis, pictures torn down, splattered with ink, etc. etc. Because it always seemed to me that the music that they [other boys in his school] were listening to, they didn't actually enjoy it. Anything that was in the charts, it was just popular and it was like getting a new pair of trainers or getting the right haircut, and it just didn't mean anything to me ... It wasn't cool to like [classical music] and they weren't willing to take that risk, and I always thought that – it just never occurred to me that you put something down because it's not seen by others to be the 'in thing'. It wasn't a concept I was very familiar with.

Rob described himself as

Rob   ... the biggest Beatles fan on the planet; as far as I'm concerned 'Sgt Pepper's' changed my life (there's another milestone).

For those musicians who pursue their music-making activities as a central and prolonged part of life, dreams of stardom will normally drop away: in some cases, this happens just as the dreams begin to be replaced by an increase of skill or versatility and, therefore, just at the point when they begin to be less far-fetched.

Rob   I think it only really dawned on me that I'd have to be very good at it when I saw what the competition was like professionally, and then it stopped being something that was just a bit of a local bass hero in Hemel Hempstead into 'You're going to really have to pull your socks up.'

Attitudes to 'other' music

I asked all the musicians the questions 'What do you feel about music other than your favourite style, or the style your band plays?' and 'Do you think your popular music skills and knowledge affect your ability to appreciate other styles of music?' In cases where classical music was not mentioned in the response, or had not already been mentioned in response to another question, I added an explicit query concerning what they felt about it. We saw in Chapter 3 that popular musicians' learning practices rely upon and thereby improve their aural skills. An off-shoot of the development of aural skills is that the skills extend beyond application to the styles of music being practised to also encompass other styles. I have already mentioned in this chapter that the musical tastes of the musicians in the study were eclectic, and it should also be clear that the older musicians were familiar with how to play a large number of sub-styles in popular music and in most cases jazz. Indeed, all the musicians' listening interests, tempered of course by their age and the sheer amount of years' listening experience they had behind them, were wide.

It is a common assumption that the musical tastes of adolescents tend to be narrower than those of young children and adults.[3] However, it is worth surmising that this might not necessarily be the case with adolescents who themselves take on the identity of being a musician, or that these adolescents might pass out of such a phase earlier than their non-musician peers. Two of the musicians in this study, aged 19 and 18 respectively – Andy and Michael – both referred to this syndrome in terms of their own experiences, but couched as having been mere phases that were now surpassed.

Andy I mean, when I was younger I was very much into heavy metal. I had a big biker jacket and long hair, which I shaved off a couple of months ago. I mean, I grew out of that with time and after you've sort of learnt how to play a certain style, I was looking around and I was listening and even though there were things that I shouldn't have liked – purely for the associations – I couldn't help but appreciate them. I did appreciate what was going on with the musical work there, the way it was produced, the layers, the rhythms, etc. So it widens with time – I believe the older you get, the types of music you can appreciate are a much wider variety.

Michael M: But, yes, I do listen to classical music.
   L: Have you always done so?
   M: No. Ten, er five years ago I would never ever listen to classical music ever. Couldn't – well, no I won't say I couldn't stand it but I was not a classical music fan. But now I appreciate a lot more the intricacies of the harmonies, the complicated nature of certain pieces.

Apart from these two references, there were few indications from either the older or the younger musicians, that they had ever been closed to styles with which they did not immediately identify.

Bernie   The great thing about the music I've always liked, it's never lost it, through time, it's always sounded – I still like it now, and I think I always will you know, it's an evergreen sort of thing, you know … So the thing is, my interests are very, you know, are quite broad, and that can be a problem as well as a benefit, because you know with broad interests there's so much you can learn, can find out.

Terry   I can remember being very young and listening to the, er, because we had a scrapyard where I grew up as a kid and they always had the light programme on which was great; you know they used to play jazz, you know what I mean, big band stuff. There was a radio on in the background all the time. You know I really remember from really young, all the jazz classics that I've you know, known for ages, and classical stuff as I say, you know.
            … I quite like big sounds you know … some classical pieces you know – the fullness.
            … I mean I'm really fortunate and I think, you know, it might be a lot to do with like the early light programme, that my musical tastes are huge and I, you know I'm really pleased about that and I always have been you know.

Steve   I like every type of music there is. The only thing I don't like is death metal – don't like that. But I like all the rest – anything classical – I listen to anything. If I like the sound of it I like it, if I don't like the sound of it, I don't like it – doesn't matter what sort of music it is.

Simon   I mean I enjoy all sorts of music.

When it came to classical music specifically – this being the music which is most obviously considered or most commonly assumed to be antipathetic to teenagers and popular musicians – the majority of the musicians were bursting with enthusiasm and no one showed the slightest disrespect for it. Only Brent was reserved about it but even then, without a trace of derision or antipathy:

Brent   I've never had a great interest in classical music, I suppose partly fuelled by ignorance. There's so much stuff out there I don't know. I've got a few classical CDs but it's just, I don't know what's out there, and I haven't taken the time to find out what I like.

Amongst the others, both older and younger alike, were those who expressed enthusiasm for classical music as well as playing a variety of classical and pre-classical pieces – especially Bach in the case of guitarists – to widen their knowledge and skills, or just for fun.

Bernie   [When I was at school] I was mad about Bach. I still am, I love J. S. Bach.
Rob (thinking back mainly to his teenage years)
            If you think about say the beginning of the 'Rite of Spring' [Stravinsky], that bassoon melody, when I found out that that was a bassoon *stretched* into its *highest* register, I thought (here's another sort of voice of realization) I thought to myself, 'Hang on, what happens if you take an instrument out of its usual sort of slot in music and start making it do things it's not supposed, well, people say it's not supposed to do?' What I mean is, it's not its accepted role. Well, I kind of look at the bass guitar like that.

... and my friend ... suggested reading up about the Bach cello suites so I had a crack at that, so it was like becoming sort of a voracious reader – anything I could get my hands on that might increase the power of my playing, I did.

... I'd also go and buy, I remember buying [J. S. Bach's] Brandenburg 3 [concerto] because I loved the bass line. This is how I got into prog rock because I used to listen to the Nice which became ELP and when I heard them doing the 'Karelia Suite' by Sibelius I went and bought the score for that, just to see how it – or 'Blue Rondo à la Turk' which was, you know, the Mozart rondo, and I became very adept at taking the bass lines out of those pieces of music and adapting them for bass guitar.

Andy   The rhythm guitar book was where I started – that was the first one – but there's a classical compilation, so I mean there's pieces by Mozart, Bach, there's 'Swan Lake' and so forth, and I go through at my own pace. There's no necessity to learn them thoroughly or anything, so that's the ease of it.

Will   I remember coming out of the music lessons [at school] and people laughing at the classical music saying, you know, 'It's just, so stupid.'
L: Mmm. But you didn't feel like that?
W: No, I thought it was a bit disrespectful to say that. Because you know, we had been told that – we hadn't been told, you could tell that they were playing this music for a reason, it was grand, majestic music, whatever it was and it just shouldn't be talked about like that.

Michael   I listen to more pop music than I do classical music but I still – I like classical music a lot, and what I really like is when I recognize a piece of classical music that's been used in pop music. My favourite band is Manfred Mann's Earth Band and they use lots and lots of bits of classical tunes – there's Jupiter from the 'Planet Suite' appears in 'Joybringer' and there's all sorts of other bits that appear here and there and I recognize them and that's good. But, yes, I do listen to classical music.

Emily took my question as an implicit putdown of popular music, as though I was rhetorically asking her if it had damaged her capacity to appreciate classical music:

Emily   L: Do you feel that your interest in popular music makes it easier for you, or more difficult for you, or neither, to appreciate classical music?
E: I think really it's, I think it doesn't make a difference, because kids are, like I say they are always going to like popular music because it's, like – popular! But it's not made it more difficult to like classical music. I've not found it boring. I mean it is like different, it's completely different to popular music. It's, I don't know. I think it's about tolerance really, because you have to, I mean, I don't know. I don't think it's affected how much I like classical music or not. Because there are some pieces of classical music which I really do like, I mean genuinely, not just because they've been played to me a lot or stuff. I think it's the actual piece of music. I like obviously the kind of famous ones like the 'Moonlight Sonata'; there is one piece, the first piece I remember actually really liking is, well 'The Planets' my Dad bought me, and the ballet 'Romeo and Juliet', and also there's this piece, I can't remember the composer but it's called 'Le Boeuf sur le Toit' [Milhaud]; my brother bought that and I really liked that one.

Richard   My Mum and Dad listen to quite a bit of classical music so it was always there. I can appreciate it more now that I play an instrument because, I'm not saying it's better but having all those instruments playing at once rather than just the guitar and the singing – I know it's not better either way but just, I don't know, I can appreciate it musically: as a musician if that makes sense.
L: Yeah, that does. So you mean you can hear more of what's going on?
R: Yeah, and I can – don't really know how to say it, sorry.
L: Just – just say the words, it doesn't matter if they make sense or not.
R: You've – before I started playing, it was just music, but now you can see how it's made up – things like that. And in that way you can appreciate it more. But I still feel it's lacking in some areas though.

Leo   L: And how about the composition, you know if you hear, say, a Beethoven symphony or something, do you think that you get an appreciation of what he's doing?
Leo: Definitely. I find that when I listen to classical, I feel very belittled.
L: Do you?
Leo: Because it's so big, there's like so much in it and it must be so hard to write a classical piece because, it's just so much more than what I, what I do. Like when I write a piece I just sit down at my keyboard or computer; but when I think about classical, sort of it, it's mostly in the head, and the parts are massive, the scores are huge, and that just sort of baffles me how people can do it, but it's amazing I guess.

In some cases, love of classical music had been fuelled by coming into contact with it through formal education, and one person, Rob, had been deeply impressed and influenced by his school music teacher.

Summary

I have suggested that popular musicians' attitudes towards music learning are quite far removed from any notion of being disciplined or requiring discipline, in so far as that concept is associated with something unpleasant or obligatory. By contrast, for them music learning is highly enjoyable and voluntary, with love, even passion for music and music-making being interwoven in all aspects. A few of them were prepared to describe their approaches as disciplined, with the proviso that this could include enjoyment; and the majority were prepared to describe their approaches as systematic. For most, the systematic nature of the learning had been difficult to organize or recognize in the early stages, but became increasingly controlled and apparent as time went by. Despite this, there was a tendency for the musicians to consider that they had not 'learnt' anything, unless they had also been 'taught' it.

The values which they place upon musicianship fall into two areas. One area concerns performance and creativity. Here they respect technical proficiency but their highest accolades are reserved for the ability to play with 'feel'. The other area concerns not musical matters so much as personal qualities. Here they emphasize the value of empathetic relationships involving cooperation, reliability, commitment, tolerance and shared tastes, along with a shared passion for music. Being a musician is felt to enhance self-esteem, and I suggested that being a fan and dreaming of stardom can also enhance motivation towards music learning. Finally, the musicians have respect for a wide range of musical styles, including in some cases a fervent love of classical music.

As with the discussion in Chapter 3 concerning the acquisition of skills and knowledge, there are signs that age and maturity, as is to be expected, tend to affect popular musicians' attitudes towards and values concerning music and music learning. But again, there are no grounds to suggest that social, musical or educational changes over the last forty years have had very much influence over the attitudes and values towards music learning of musicians in the Anglo-American guitar-based rock and popular fields.

Notes

1. For excellent illustrations of this from the point of view of young semi-professional rock musicians see Berkaak (1999) and Cohen (1991, pp. 140–43), and for the views of some famous musicians, Lilliestam (1996, p 201f.). For a theoretical discussion of the concept of authenticity see Fornäs (1995). In musicology this concept is discussed in relation to rock (for example, Moore 1998) and 'classical' music (for example, Kenyon 1988) although used in slightly, and fascinatingly, different ways.
2. See Chapter 3, pp. 74–5 for a previous discussion of related points. The musicians in the band which was the subject of Berkaak's study (1999) provide an illustration of a career trajectory along these lines. One of the musicians spent hours learning from copying recordings and later went on to be a full-time session musician; two others placed more value on unsullied individual expression and when the band folded were not able or willing to re-establish themselves in a satisfactory performing context. Also see many of the other texts cited, especially Cohen (1991) and Bennett (1980) for similar perspectives.
3. There is surprisingly little empirical research on this claim. For reviews of relevant literature in the psychology of music see Philip Russell (1997, pp. 145–7) with relation to musical taste and age in general; Zillman and Gan (1997) and Epstein (1995) with relation to adolescents' listening practices. For teachers' views on the matter, see Chapter 6, p. 138 below. Work on adolescents' and young peoples' musical reception practices in popular music studies and cultural studies is extensive. See, for example, Willis (1978), Frith (1983), Thornton (1995) or consult journals such as *Popular Music* and *Popular Music and Society*.

Chapter 5

Popular musicians in traditional music education

This chapter will consider the musicians' experiences of what I will refer to as 'traditional music education'. First I will examine *classical* instrumental tuition as it was experienced by nine of the musicians, including older and younger ones. Then I will look at classroom music in schools as it was experienced by the older musicians only, over the period from the 1960s to the end of the 1980s. The following chapter will look at the musicians' experiences of what I will term the 'new music education', including *popular* music instrumental tuition across the whole age span, then school class-teaching for the younger musicians from the early 1990s to the end of the century. I will also look briefly at experiences of popular music further and higher education courses in that chapter. There are three principle aims of the two chapters, taken together. One is to illuminate those learning experiences within formal music education that can reasonably be considered to have contributed, through either conscious or unconscious means, to the musicians' development of popular music skills and knowledge. The second is to examine the musicians' encounters with formal music education in general terms not necessarily tied to learning experiences, and the attitudes and values which marked these encounters. The third is to chart changes in formal music education as experienced by the musicians over the last forty years of the twentieth century. Each section begins with a brief historical account of the overall educational context within which the musicians' profiles are situated, paying particular attention where relevant to the incorporation of popular music into formal settings.

Classical instrumental tuition

An overall picture of ethos and provision

Since the mid-nineteenth century, Britain has seen the development of what has become an internationally renowned tradition of classical instrumental tuition, supported by youth orchestras and other ensembles, community music-making ventures, junior music schools, summer schools and many other activities. Private lessons are available either by personal arrangement with a teacher or through a school or other centre; funded lessons are provided in some schools and music centres by Local Education Authorities or are included as part of the overall fee by most further and higher education institutions. One-to-one tuition is the traditional norm, although small groups of three or more students per lesson are by no means uncommon, depending on the circumstances, especially in school provision at the more elementary levels.

Although there are enormous differences in the ways that individual teachers approach their work, it is possible to identify some fundamental principles, values and aims that are generally shared and that characterize British classical instrumental teaching overall. In some respects, instrumental teaching is often understood to take the form of 'training' as distinct from 'education'. This is the case in so far as emphasis is placed upon the rigorous development of technique and its application to the sensitive interpretation of a limited repertoire of pieces; pupils and students are expected to practise regularly; and tuition and practice regimes involve a balance of technical exercises – such as scales, arppeggios or studies – and pieces of music. Whilst teachers will, to varying degrees, educate their pupils and students in general matters such as musical form, music history, theory or the development of the relevant instrument and its repertoire, the central focus of lessons is on developing technique, expressivity and repertoire on the instrument itself.

British classical instrumental tuition has grown up in tandem with a highly influential system of grade exams which are developed, validated and overseen by conservatories and other bodies. Instrumental lessons are by no means necessarily geared to grade exam syllabi, but most teachers are willing to enter at least some of their pupils for the exams, many teachers intend to enter all of their pupils, and even teachers who shy away from entering their pupils are themselves likely to have been brought up through the grade system. Although instrumental teaching does not always involve an explicit curriculum, the widespread influence of the grades means that a great deal of teaching occurs with reference to a syllabus and therefore involves a high level of teacher direction. The grades are normally from I (the primary grade) to VIII, with the possibility of proceeding to a diploma or a degree afterwards. Candidates sit each grade regardless of their age, in accordance with their attainment, which is informally assessed by their teacher prior to entry. As well as practical exams, there are written theory exams, also arranged as Grades I to VIII and beyond. The grade system has a major presence within instrumental teaching in this country, and by virtue of direct exportation and of indirect influence, it also affects instrumental teaching in many other parts of the world today.[1]

The musicians taking classical instrumental tuition and grade exams

As mentioned at the beginning of Chapter 3, Terry was the only one of the musicians in this study who had received no instrumental tuition. Nine of the others had taken classical lessons, and a different nine, with five overlaps, had taken popular lessons (see Table 2 in the Appendix, p. 220 for a summary of who had taken what lessons). Here I will focus on the classical lessons. In all cases, except Nanette's singing lessons, these had occurred entirely when the musicians were children or young teenagers, and had nearly all lasted for very brief periods involving as little as three or four lessons, or even just one lesson. Only Emily had received sustained classical tuition lasting more than four years. She and Nanette were the only two interviewees who were taking classical lessons at the time of the interviews. Four of the musicians had taken practical classical grade exams, all to Grade IV or below, and two had taken theory grades.

Nanette had first gone to a teacher in her late teens, after having been singing professionally for a couple of years. Of all those who had taken classical lessons, she was the most ready and able to make connections between what she had learnt through the lessons and the skills and knowledge to which she had recourse as a popular musician. This was mainly facilitated because at her request the lessons had been explicitly geared to developing transferable techniques – especially diaphragm breathing – rather than to singing pieces of music. Describing her first singing teacher, Nanette said:

Nanette   ... she helped me to be able to sort of use my voice, not only correctly but also to be able to cope with the whole area that I hadn't worked on before, one I didn't even know existed.
L: So what sort of techniques did she give you to help you with that?
N: Well, breathing. You know, the whole thing about supporting the note on the breath and the whole thing about the diaphragm and deep breathing, and I got books and stuff like that ...
... I mean she was classically trained, she was quite an elderly lady, but she just had a knack of being able to bring what she'd learnt and the experience that she had to any kind of singer. So the basic foundations – she basically taught me the foundations. Because I was losing my voice like, every week, I was struggling. And then I started going to her and suddenly I was able to cope and I was able to get all those high notes, night after night.
... and I think that's why I've ended up after all these years not having any nodules or anything like that, which I've got to be thankful for really.

Later, at the age of 38, a couple of months before the interview, she had embarked upon a conservatory performance course in classical singing. I asked what had made her take the decision to enroll on the course. The response she gave demands some contextualization. I regard Nanette as a superior singer, both technically and musically (that is, in terms of 'feel'), and, as mentioned in previous chapters, such a view has been confirmed by everyone to whom I have played samples of her music, including classical singing teachers at various venues, many of whom have come up to me afterwards to ask who Nanette is, and say things like 'She's amazing.' The song I usually played them, which is also the one referred to in the quote below, is Nanette's own recording of one of her compositions, 'Always'. The vocal line begins on a rich but clear, sustained high G which gradually develops a vibrato. I would agree with her friend, referred to below, in saying that it is not an 'authentic classical' sound, but given that any intentions of the singer are not apparent in the recording, this does not detract from the perfect intonation, the controlled crescendo and vibrato, the commitment in the voice, or the generally authoritative way in which it demands the listener's attention. The voice then swoops down to middle register, still retaining the same tone quality, before switching to a contrasting husky, breathy tone in the low register. Shortly after that, there is a vocal lead with three-part vocal harmony behind it, all with Nanette's own over-dubbed voice.

Nanette   L: You decided to go and do a degree in music and get classical singing training. So what made you take that decision?
N: Well, I want to pursue a sort of popular/classical mix, and someone said to me whose opinion I really respect, after listening to my tape she said 'It's not authentic.' So that's what I'm aiming for – a pure, classical sound that's authentic ... Yeah, she's talking about the slightly operatic stuff that I'm doing. And I thought to myself 'I would really love to be able to master a classical aria', something, you know I'd love to be able to master one of those and maybe combine it with some sort of pop thing, do you know what I mean?
... My singing teacher now says that I have the potential to do something classical, but when you actually look at it, a lot of people start higher education when they're 18 and they're learning classical songs all those years and they can also sight-read – so, I'll just see how I get on. But I'll find a way of using it I know, what I'm learning now.
L: Are you finding it very, very different, learning to sing, say, classical operatic arias?
N: It's – you have to start totally from scratch. Because everything in pop is on the breath and in classical, there shouldn't be any breath with the note, it should just be a pure note. The principles are the same if you're singing correctly, you know, it's all to do with the diaphragm and deep breathing and everything. But to get that classical sound you've got to think the opposite. Everything to do with pop is like I say, the sound has got breath with it, and the shape of your mouth and the way you use your jaw is actually very important with pop music; whereas with classical, your jaw has got to be loose and in one position in order to free the larynx to get that sound. So it is totally different, which is quite a challenge.

About six months after the interview Nanette appeared as a soloist performing three songs on the famous BBC programme *Songs of Praise*. In sum, she was striving both to countenance differences and to make connections between the classical and popular spheres, and had always found tuition more than helpful – a necessity – in the realm of technique.

Two others amongst the musicians, Rob and Michael, also made connections between skills and knowledge acquired through classical tuition and their transference to the realm of popular music. In both cases this had occurred during their early teens rather than, as with Nanette, when they were mature musicians. Rob had been loaned a trumpet by his school when he was about 13, and his parents had arranged private lessons with

Rob   ... a trumpet player called Bernard Brown from the LSO [London Symphony Orchestra]. And he again was a fantastic teacher. I don't remember learning to read music, I just became aware through his teaching that I could. And then by this time music of *all* kinds had well and truly taken a hold of my imagination.

He took lessons for three years, as well as playing in the school orchestra, and 'loved it'. We have already seen (Chapter 3, p. 39) how the ability to read the treble clef fluently had stood him in good stead during one of his first professional engagements, albeit he had to teach himself to transpose for the bass clef on the spot. He also took 'a few' piano lessons in his early teens, in which the bass clef evidently did not impress itself upon him, but which provided him with the 'basic keyboard skills' that he was later to use in his composing/arranging company. At around 21 years of age, he took Grade VII theory, and found it

Rob   Great fun. That's where I learnt my initial arranging skills ... I later took a part-time course at the Guildhall [School of Music and Drama in London], so that was when I was 19, so I must have been about 21 by this time, so I knew how to arrange Beethoven piano sonatas for string quartet and stuff.

By comparison with Nanette, he had not made so immediate or direct a transfer from the formal classical tuition he had received to the informal popular music learning practices with which he was engaged. Transposing his knowledge of the treble clef to the bass clef was the first experience in which he had made any connection between the two musical spheres. Previously, for example

Rob   ... I hadn't even thought about the concept of scales and arpeggios, which I'd done on the trumpet – I never thought about adapting that for the bass, it was just a question of adapting my current repertoire.

When he did eventually start practising scales and arpeggios, it was...

Rob   ... unwittingly ... I didn't know – I was doing it again by ear and by sound ... It was like a kind of voyage of discovery. I'd done it all on the trumpet: I don't know why the two never tied up. I think it was partly to do with the fact that with the trumpet, I could read well, I could play it, but I could never improvise on it. Whereas with the bass guitar, because I hadn't done a standard structured way of learning, it was much freer.

In general, what he had learnt in the formal classical realm made itself apparent as potentially useful to him in the field of popular music, not whilst he was in the early stages of learning popular music, but much later, and after having become professional. This, of course, does not mean that it was not useful, but only that he was not aware of its being so. The likelihood is that his formal classical training entered his popular music learning in unconscious ways more akin to enculturation than formal tuition.

Michael, mainly a drummer, took piano lessons when he was aged 8 to 12, including passing Grades I to IV, but had 'never really got into the piano to the same degree as the drums' and had given up the lessons about three years before the interview. However, at the time of the interview he had

> *Michael*   ... started hooking myself up with some other bands, not to play long-term, just to sort of jam with them a bit. I'm starting to quite enjoy playing the keyboard instruments again now – because I didn't play for a long time after I stopped learning the piano. Um. But yes, about six months ago I started playing the keyboards. I make this distinction, being the difference between piano and keyboard, in that, piano I think there's equal emphasis on both hands and I think with the keyboard there's more emphasis on the right hand and that's my, my style of playing. So I'm doing that with bands now ... It took me quite a long time to remember everything that I'd learnt from the piano lessons but it did, it did come back after going at it for a little while.

It would not be quite accurate to say there is equal emphasis on both hands in all piano playing, as this would depend on the genre, style, historical era and composer of the music. However, classical piano teaching usually places equal emphasis on developing both hands so as to maximize technical proficiency and flexibility. Notice how Michael is interested in playing to the standard he requires, and how he adopts what he calls *his* style of playing. As with Rob, some skills and knowledge gained through classical lessons were entering his popular music learning practices, and were helping him to become more of an all-round musician, which was a stated ambition. But at this stage, the transfer occurred indirectly and in connection with a perception more atuned to the differences than to the similarities between the two.

Brent and Emily had not made many connections at all between their classical tuition and their popular music learning practices. In his late teens, Brent had taken piano lessons up to Grade III and had 'tried to study some tuned percussion' (which is essentially a classical music practice, as distinct from taking kit lessons), although he had experienced difficulty finding a teacher for the latter. He also took Grade VI theory and studied towards Grade VIII but never took the exam. One main reason for all these lessons and grades was that he was at the time attempting to gain entrance into a university music degree (to be discussed in Chapter 6), rather than because he felt any intrinsic lack of skills and knowledge needed to pursue his career as it was. I asked him how he had responded to the lessons:

Brent   I don't feel it was wasted because I did the theory and did some basic piano so – it was good fun.

Regarding preparation for the theory grades specifically:

Brent   Interesting. It was something that, at that point I needed to do, to try and get into the university course, and I was obviously aware that I didn't know much about anything other than rhythm and drums, so yes. It was generally fairly interesting.

However, as will be seen later, his application to university was unsuccessful and he did not make any direct use in his professional work of what he had learnt in his classical practical or theory lessons.

Emily had been having cello lessons since the age of 7, and had passed Grade IV. I asked her if she enjoyed playing the cello.

Emily   I do yeah. It's, um, it's different from the guitar. Because I don't write any of my own stuff. It's the complete opposite. Because it's very disciplined. I've got a teacher, do my scales, do grade exams, all of that. It's different. I'm not as likely to pick it up and practise it if I don't have anything to practise specifically. So I think it's more, with the cello it's more disciplined … I mean there are, I do, sometimes I think 'Hey I'd really like to go and play the cello for an hour', but it's not quite the same.

She was the youngest of the musicians to be so explicit in finding difference and contrast between formal classical approaches and informal popular music practices, whilst at the same time persisting with and enjoying both. She was conscious of transferring some skills:

Emily   I think the technique that you learn when you're playing a classical instrument or when you're having lessons has definitely helped because I know about rhythms, I know about structures and that sort of thing; and if I didn't learn any instrument I wouldn't know anything about that. And that's quite important.

The childhood or teenage experiences of the others who had experienced classical tuition were more negative, including those of Nanette at an earlier period of her life, and of Michael and Emily, with reference to the piano. Steve was the most forthcoming on this subject. His response represents the general feeling and also picks up a number of threads concerning informal learning practices discussed in previous chapters: the importance of liking and identifying with the music played and with the musicians who play it, the significance of the sound of the instrument, and the influence of such factors in enhancing enjoyment and motivation. He had taken trumpet lessons when he was 12 or 13:

Steve   It didn't go on for long. I didn't like it – it was boring. And I gave that one up.
L: And what was it that you didn't like about it, apart from being boring?
S: Well, it only had three things on it and it was just like, [sings] doo doo doo
tune like that. It wasn't worth playing. He used to get me to play the same
thing over and over again 'til I got it right and it was just getting so tedious.
And, er, I just didn't enjoy it. I had sore lips afterwards, I just couldn't really,
I didn't really get into it so I just gave it up because it was costing Mum and
Dad money …
      … I never really got into it or anything, it didn't really do anything for me.
Because he never really showed me – I think there was a few notes on the
thing, and he said 'That's that one, that's that one, that's that one', but I only
knew them three notes on the trumpet and that was it. Nothing else. So I was
just following these notes that didn't mean anything to me. With these three
fingers on the buttons.
L: When you started your bass guitar and you started playing along with
Nirvana, presumably to begin with you were only playing three notes, you
know at the very early stages? Obviously the guitar's a different instrument,
but you were playing quite simple things, so what was the difference, then, in
your motivation: I mean why did you feel motivated towards pursuing that
and not the trumpet?
S: Because I, I didn't, I don't enjoy trumpet music [laughs] if you know what
I mean, but I enjoyed listening to the guitar and if I could mimic the guitar and
it sounded good, then it made me feel good. But playing three notes on a
trumpet which is like some nursery rhyme or something, didn't give me
anything at all … And I could help myself better on the bass. It made, it
sounded good, and it was just enjoyable. You can pick a song you like. Well,
with the trumpet – you couldn't play a Nirvana song on the trumpet; well, you
probably could but it wouldn't sound anything like it. But then when you got
a guitar in front of you, you got your teenage idols there and you can copy
them and do it how they do it, it just makes you feel good, doesn't it?

Below are further snippets which share aspects in common with Steve's
perspectives – the sense of 'getting nowhere' and of alienation from the music
played or from the instrument itself – concerning classical lessons taken when
the speakers were all somewhere between the ages of 11 and 15, unless
otherwise stated.

Nanette (piano lessons)
      I gave up piano because I didn't want to practise and I thought 'Well I don't
know how this relates to me, at all.' It just didn't seem right; it was so alien.
Shame really …
      … It didn't relate to what I wanted to do. Even at that early age I suppose I
must have had the idea that I wanted to be doing some sort of pop stuff or
whatever … and you've really got to do the practice to make it worthwhile.
My Mum couldn't really afford lessons.
Will (violin lessons and piano lessons)
      But I didn't want to know: it was drums.

Andy (classical guitar lessons)
> ... and I just – the progression was so slow in getting somewhere, I just – I gave up on that idea for a while.

Simon (piano lessons)
> I wasn't too interested, I just thought it'd be nice to have it, you know. I mean I like the piano, I do like the sound, but I don't – I spent more time playing my drums than I did playing piano. I just didn't have the time to do that.

Michael (piano lessons, including taking Grades I to IV)
> But I never really got into that in the same level I got into the drums.

Emily (piano lessons)
> ... but I haven't really got that much out of it. I had lessons for about three years but I'm giving up because I just, I don't know, I just don't get much out of it, I don't practise it; so I figure if I have the book and I've got the piano at home, I might as well just do it when I want.

Leo (violin lessons aged c. *10 to 13, including taking Grade III)*
> Well, I play it, but I'm not actually doing lessons at the moment, and I don't really practise at all.
> L: And what made you give up the lessons?
> Leo: I wasn't really progressing anywhere.

These sentiments contrast sadly and starkly with the short quotes concerning the musicians' enjoyment of playing their popular music instruments in Chapter 4, pp. 104–6.

Traditional classroom music education

Music in the classroom is particularly important to the themes discussed in this book, because although only a minority of the population of any country is ever given the opportunity to take formal instrumental lessons, a much larger proportion of children and young people in many countries have music lessons in their school classrooms. It is in schools that the opportunities are given for the vast majority of the population to engage with music learning of a formal nature; and it is away from schools that so many vernacular musicians in the past have turned in search of other music learning experiences. As distinct from instrumental tuition, which provides a specialist training for a minority of the population, classroom music in schools is intended to provide a general, liberal music education for all. In some countries, including England where this research was carried out, music in school is now an entitlement and therefore affects, or should affect, the entire population.

The musicians' responses in this chapter mainly concern secondary rather than primary schooling. One reason for this is that most of the musicians over the age of 21 had virtually no primary school music lessons that they could remember, provision being quite sparse during the period when they were in attendance, and experiences evidently being relatively unmemorable. Another reason is that most British primary schools lack a specialist music teacher, so even the experiences of the younger musicians were very disparate. However, the primary music curriculum, in cases where music *has* been an active part of the life of a school, has in general terms developed along principles that are not dissimilar from those of the secondary sector, therefore many of the issues discussed here are relevant across the sectors. Clearly primary school classroom music is – or has the potential to be – of paramount importance in the musical development of children. Although the musicians' experiences here focus on the secondary classroom, their implications have much broader significance and in the final chapter of the book many of the discussions will apply specifically to the primary sector.

Forty or so years ago, when Bernie was at school, the music curriculum in Britain was built largely on class singing, music history and musical appreciation involving a mixture of mainly post-seventeenth-century Western classical music and settings of folk songs collected by early twentieth-century composers. Despite the existence of classroom instruments such as inexpensive glockenspiels, xylophones, chime bars and recorders, in most schools instrumental playing took place only outside the classroom during extra-curricular time. Many schools taught rudiments, and pupils over the age of about 14 studied harmony and counterpoint, but hardly anyone studied composition until they were in higher education. At the age of about 14, music became an optional subject. Pupils in the higher academic ability bracket were able to select a music Ordinary Level (O Level) course, and those on a less academic path could select the music Certificate of Secondary Education (CSE). From their inception in the 1950s and 1960s respectively, both the O Level and the CSE were based entirely on classical music, involving rudiments, harmony and counterpoint and music history. During the late 1960s teachers began to demand the addition of a performance exam, and this became the norm by the 1970s. However, only the performance of classical music on orchestral instruments, the piano or voice was acceptable. Furthermore, in order to achieve the greatest possible success in the higher-status O Level exam, it was necessary to have undertaken at least two years and more usually five or six years of specialist instrumental tuition, outside and in excess of the normal school curriculum.

During the 1970s radically new and highly influential approaches to music education in schools appeared. One such approach, spearheaded in Britain by the work of Paynter and Aston (1970), involved the introduction of composition in a free, experimental or 'creative' vein, for *all* pupils. (Also see Schafer 1967, Self 1967 and Dennis 1970.) The pedagogy espoused by this movement was progressive or radical in its inclusion of group-learning and child-centred methods, but as Vulliamy (1977b, p. 207f.) pointed out, it was conservative in that it advanced atonal, 'serious' or contemporary classical music and ignored popular culture. Another change was the development of an integrated approach to musical activities for all children, involving the combination of composition, performance and structured listening, supplemented by literature studies and the acquisition of technical skills. The strongest statement of this was Keith Swanwick's (1979) mnemonic C(L)A(S)P, standing for Composition, Audition and Performance, with (Literature) and (Skills) in supporting roles. Both these moves were later to have a major influence on the development of new syllabi and curricula in Britain, and attracted huge interest in many other countries (see for example, Her Majesty's Inspectorate 1985, Department of Education and Science 1986, 1992, Department for Education 1995).

A third major development was the introduction of popular music into the curriculum, supported by respected musicologists such as Wilfred Mellers (1976), and by a number of publications from music educators.[2] Growing numbers of teachers incorporated popular music into their general class lessons for ages 11 to 14. A very small number of schools incorporated it into the CSE exam for ages 14 to 16, by taking advantage of a ruling that individual schools could develop their own syllabi which were then validated by the Examinations Board. This ruling did not, however, apply to O Level, the upshot of which was that the higher-status O Level exam included only classical music, and the lower-status CSE exam included almost entirely classical music, with a few pockets where popular music was taught.

In 1982 I conducted a questionnaire in secondary schools, which included asking teachers whether they taught 'classical', 'popular', 'folk' and 'avant-garde' music, and to give reasons for their answers (see Green 1988). Out of the 61 teachers in 61 schools, 58 taught classical music, 46 taught popular music, 44 taught folk music and 34 taught avant-garde, or twentieth-century classical music. Twenty-one of the teachers taught all four styles. Although a space was given for them to add any further comments or styles, only one teacher mentioned jazz and no one mentioned world music. So classical music took clear precedence, but popular music also had a significant presence. However, the numbers of teachers who included each style is less interesting and informative than the prose responses giving rationales for the inclusion of the styles, as well as examples of teaching methods and curriculum content. Restricting the discussion here to classical and popular music only, in recognition of the prime place of classical music in education at that time, here are some responses to the question 'Do you teach classical music?':

Yes. It is part of our heritage. It contains valuable musical elements. It is essential for public examinations.

Yes. The heritage should be presented before young pupils since the opportunity would not otherwise exist. Seeds sown now may well bear fruit in later years.

Yes. It offers the widest field of musical discovery – affords the greatest satisfaction to sing, play and listen to. Any musician worth his/her salt must pass on the source of his/her lifetime enjoyment in the hope that others will derive the same pleasure from it.

Of course! The reasons should be obvious: basic grounding; techniques; standard background to any other musical developments.

Yes in so far as 'classical' = expressive, and in so far as it is an art form, and is the style of music that a) requires the greatest concentration and b) requires the greatest explanation and c) requires the greatest sensitivity.

Only three out of the 61 randomly selected teachers said they did not teach classical music, two without giving a reason and the other one on the grounds that the ethnicity and the 'low intelligence' of her pupils made it unsuitable.

Although popular music had a major presence in terms of curriculum time, it was approached in different ways to classical music. Teachers often used it at the end of the lesson as a 'treat', to entertain children, or to pacify 'low ability' pupils, rather than presenting it for serious study. (See Vulliamy 1977b on this.) Overall, their attitudes towards it contrasted starkly with those towards classical music. To illustrate this, here are some further examples of answers to the same question ('Do you teach classical music?'):

Yes. Since children have very little knowledge of any music apart from disco/pop etc. and therefore teaching classical music broadens their musical knowledge.

Yes. I introduce children to classical music. Pop music they listen to anyway, there seems little point in teaching it therefore.

Yes. Children have 'pop' thrust upon them every day and therefore we try to broaden their musical appreciation.

Yes … My 'boss' talks about 'the adolescent deviation around the arts'.

Yes. I think it important that children should hear music other than the pop diet that they have fed off since they were infants.

Yes. I introduce children to classical music. Pop music they listen to anyway, there seems little point in teaching it therefore.

And in response to 'Do you teach popular music?':

No. The pupils seem sufficiently saturated in this cultural area to warrant its exclusion from the curriculum.

No. Most teenagers surround themselves with pop music 24 hours a day. Music lessons give the opportunity to show other music exists.

The greatest emphasis was on the history of popular music (seventeen teachers mentioned it), some of it geared to studying links between popular music and society, with projects and written work of various kinds. Six teachers stated that pupils sang pop songs in class, with only three mentioning that pupils played instruments in connection with popular music, and two indicating some practical activity linked to popular music creativity. Teachers in only three schools mentioned that they possessed basic popular music instruments (electric guitar and/or drum kit.) Whilst teachers declared that they gave the highest priority to playing and singing, popular music occupied an area that was perceived as overall the least important – history – and included only a very small amount of singing and even less playing. In order to succeed at music in school – in terms of gaining praise, being given the opportunity to have extra-curricular instrumental lessons, passing exams and so on – it was normally necessary for pupils to accept the superiority of classical music; and in order to be in a position to opt for music at age 14, pupils were normally required to have already been taking classical instrumental tuition.

The musicians as pupils in traditional classrooms

The oldest nine musicians in this study started secondary school in the following years:

Bernie:	1960
Terry:	1963
Rob:	1964
Nanette:	1971
Brent:	1975
Peter:	1982
Will:	1986
Steve:	1988
Andy:	1990

The first six were therefore at school during the time that the curriculum was built on traditional principles as described above. Although the next three musicians were at school during or just after a time when major changes occurred in the curriculum, these changes had little or no effect on the music departments of their particular schools at that time. Therefore, with only one or two areas of exception, all these musicians experienced what can generally be referred to as traditional classroom music education. I will begin by considering their experiences of general class lessons for children mostly between the ages of 11 to 14; then I will examine the role of the specialist option (O Level/CSE, later GCSE), normally taken between the ages of 14 to 16. Finally I will consider their involvement in formally ratified, and informally tolerated, extra-curricular activities.

General class lessons Rob was the only one who had appreciated – and had indeed been inspired by – his school music teacher.

Rob   ... it got to the stage where I used to just talk to him a lot. I must have just badgered him, he was probably sick of the sight of me, but he didn't mind taking time out to show me all the little bits and pieces that I was curious about ...

           ... I would stay in and help him put away all the orchestral scores and he'd tell me about this, that and the other. I remember him once, during the lunch hour, working through 'All the little piggies', you know the Beatles song from the 'White Album', showing me how George Martin had used Mozart to do the string section. And he'd show me all sorts of things as an individual rather than in the class. Every time he showed me something, I wanted more ...

           ... Oh, he was a very fine pianist. He got me interested in looking at scores, so much so that I'd buy music just to look at it and see how it worked ...

           ... He was very pro-active. He really pushed it. If somebody was interested in music, he was interested in you.

           ... He wasn't a bigot – people who are only into one bag and that's it – he had ears for everything.

In the context of music education generally at that time, a teacher who could cross over different musical styles in the ways Rob describes was a rarity, and any truly inspirational teacher is always as rare as they are invaluable. This teacher had a major effect on Rob's future development as a musician – 'Definitely. Without a doubt ... He had a profound effect I think on the way my life has panned out' – his influence being discernible in Rob's eclecticism, wide range of musical skills and continuing interest in both the classical and the popular realms.

Rob   And I'd love to, if he's still alive, I'd love to talk to him ... He would obviously have known the kind of areas that I'm fascinated by now, which is where twentieth-century modernism meets rural folk – look at Delius and Grainger – and it would be wonderful to actually discuss those aspects with him now. But, you know, one loses touch. But, yes, to cut a long story short, he did influence all sorts of things.

However, as the reader may have observed, the inspiring teaching that Rob described occurred rather informally and outside of class lessons. Unfortunately, as regards the classroom, Rob could only remember one example of a lesson having seemed enlightening:

Rob   I remember him playing us Honegger's 'Pacific 231' and he was saying to us, 'What you can do here is listen to all the different layers in the composition', and he made me very aware at the time that I could actually listen to different structures. I didn't have to listen to a piece of music coming at me face on, but I could actually dissect the various bandwidths, the frequencies, layers of texture. I could listen to several pieces within one piece.

The majority of Rob's classroom experiences, as will be seen in due course, were less informative for him, and as such, corresponded sadly with those of all the other eight musicians considered in this section.

For Brent and Peter classroom music had been barely existent, for want of a specialist teacher. Others (including Peter) remembered music lessons more in terms of having 'skived' or 'bunked off' them than through having been present in them.

Peter   All I can remember about music lessons in my middle school was hiding in the toilets during one of the lessons.

Terry   He was very strict and nobody liked him much. I think he was quite a good teacher, but I didn't go very often, I hardly went, I was always bunking off.

The content of lessons as described by those who did attend them is broadly commensurate with the description of traditional classroom music education given earlier, as involving singing, music history, appreciation and rudiments, and covering both classical and popular music. For example:

Will   We learnt about different composers, classical music, what their dates were, listened to examples of their music, how they fitted in with each other, looked at – I remember one lesson on the Beatles, watching a video on them, taking part in musical activities like splitting the class up into say four or five different sections, someone sings something and the next group sings it, then carry on and everyone ends up together. I remember one lesson about, um, rhythm and notes, what the notes are called … 'Every Good Boy' etc.

Rob found the lessons too elementary, something which will have been familiar to many other pupils who, like him, were taking classical instrumental lessons:

Rob   Well, he taught us very elementary theory … but to be quite frank, the elementary theory lessons that we were having, I'd already surpassed on the trumpet, so I have to say I'd daydream. I think Mr Sanders understood. He was aware that only a few of us were becoming dedicated.

Memories of 'mucking around' were quite forthcoming:

Bernie   I was always getting into trouble, because I didn't take, I mean I just enjoyed playing the guitar, I wasn't interested in the school curriculum and I used to really mess around a lot, and I used to get myself into all sorts of trouble, and I used to upset her [the teacher] quite, I must admit, I used to upset her quite a bit, because she was trying her best to you know get things, do things, and I'm larking about …

      … It was, we're in class, we're listening to 'Die Fliedermaus', and I'm just not interested in the slightest bit you know, making paper aeroplanes, all this sort of business, doing funny drawings, you know.

Steve   Mainly keyboards and just mucking around really. [Laughs] That's what most music lessons are at school – mucking around – pressing all the keys in for sounds and stuff on the – that's mainly what we done. Banging on little tom-tom things and, I don't remember what I done at school in music, don't remember anything. Nothing at all.

Andy   But we never, when we were in music class which was compulsory up to the third year we never really paid attention to half the stuff, really … It was basic notation, singing … The lessons were just awkward. The teacher was – everyone thought he was a bit funny. Because if you couldn't play the recorder right, he'd make you put your hand under the boy next to you, under his seat, so he's sitting on your hand. And we had some strange ideas about him.

Terry and Nanette also found the lessons alienating and difficult to relate to:

Terry   L: And in the actual lessons, have you got any memory, you say you actually bunked off quite a lot of them. Can you remember anything you did in the ones you didn't bunk off?
             T: What, music?
             L: Yeah.
             T: Not really, I think he just used to sit us there and play tapes and that was pretty much it really.
Nanette   I remember going to one music lesson and sitting there, and they were playing classical music and I just had no affinity with it – I just thought 'No', and I gave it up in the third year …
             … I thought 'This is not for me at all'. Because it was, it was just sitting around listening to stuff.

As we have seen, many teachers did include popular music in their lessons, although, in ways that rendered it implicitly inferior. From the viewpoints of the pupils within this study it made little difference whether the music was classical or popular.

Nanette   … it was just sitting around listening to stuff.
             L: Listening to classical music?
             N: Um, I think they put one – I can remember a rock, some rock guitar thing as well. But I didn't see how that could relate to me at all. I just didn't see it.
Brent   The only thing I can remember at all about anything vaguely music-related, and I don't remember whether they were specifically music lessons or just general kind of lower school lessons, was in the other secondary school I went to. We had a teacher that used to play acoustic guitar and she'd bring the guitar and sing some songs, and I remember she brought in 'Sounds of Silence' by Simon and Garfunkel and played that, and I remember she used to bring in 'Joseph and the Amazing Technicolour Dreamcoat' and play that sometimes.
             L: And you would all sing? Or you would listen to her singing?
             B: Well, she'd – for the latter two she brought the records in, but I think maybe she might have played on the guitar, I can't remember.
Andy   … it was purely classical. The only thing he played that wasn't was a song by ELO [the rock group Electric Light Orchestra]. And none of us had heard of ELO – I didn't know who it was, so we didn't really take much interest in that. But at the time it was just things that we couldn't listen to really.

Post-14 option courses Of these nine musicians, highly motivated and committed as they were in the realms of informal learning and popular music –

from Bernie aged 50, to Andy aged 19 – only one had chosen to take music as an optional subject after the age of 14. This was Bernie, and his story provides a stark example of the failure of a formal music education system to recognize and reward musicianship. As we have seen, by the time he was 14 he could play a large number of covers, along with all the major, minor, modal and pentatonic scales and related arpeggios on the guitar at approximately 240 notes per minute; he had an understanding of triadic and tetrachordal harmony; he was able to notate entire lead guitar parts from slowed-down recordings and he had done several gigs with local bands. It was only three years later that he was to turn professional, when Caleb Kwaye and Reggie Dwight (later to become Elton John) left Long John Baldry's backing band Bluesology and Bernie was selected, over thirty contestants at an audition, to replace Kwaye. His music teacher at school had been aware that he had some performing skills and used to write what Bernie described as 'quasi-classical' pieces for him to play during school drama productions. However, as seen above, Bernie could not relate to the lessons, but 'messed around' and 'larked about' in them. When he announced to her that he wished to take music O Level

Bernie   ... she laughed in my face, she said 'What, you want to do O Level music? You must be joking.' She said 'You'll never pass' ... The reason why she said this was because you know, you had to write a paper about, you know on composers and pieces of music, operas and stuff, and of course I, you know ... It was, we're in class, we're listening to 'Die Fliedermaus', and I'm just not interested in the slightest bit you know, making paper aeroplanes, all this sort of business, doing funny drawings, you know.

L: But in the end you did the O Level.

B: And passed it.

L: Yeah.

B: With a grade 1. [The highest] You know.

L: Yeah. And how did you find doing, you had to do all that sort of music history?

B: I crammed. I crammed it all into a year. I apologised. You know, I apologised to her, first, I started off, I said, 'I'm really sorry', I said, you know 'I've been, I really haven't been any help to you at all, not only for myself, but I've made life difficult for you as well, and I'm really sorry. But I'd like to do music, and I'll come in after school, and do extra, voluntary detentions' you know, 'I'll do that willingly, if I can learn', you know. It was 'La Bohème', 'Die Fliedermaus', and it was the Baroque, the period I chose, because I was mad about Bach, I still am, I love J. S. Bach; so I did that, and of course, all the, all the rest of it, the theory side of it, I'd learnt it all from this other chap [the dance-band musician who taught him when he was 11 to 12] you see, the theory side of things, you know.

L: So you had to do what, you had to do a bit of four-part chorale writing –

B: Yeah, like, 'There's a part missing; write it in.' And like, 'Here's a, here's four bars of 3/8, what's wrong?', and there's four beats in one bar, there's a dotted note where there shouldn't be, things like that. Just generally, and then there's, you know, 'What is an anacrusis?', you know. Things like this. So,

> you know, I mean I, I didn't have any trouble with that at all I mean um –
> L: So it was really a matter of learning from books –
> B: The historical side of it yeah.

Like so many young, future popular musicians of the 1960s, Bernie left school at 15 and went to Art College to do a foundation course. We see here that even though he had already developed an appreciation for at least one 'classical' composer, J. S. Bach, this had not helped him to relate to the formal classroom music he was offered. Furthermore, the parts of the curriculum on which he needed to catch up were not those that required any specifically musical or musicological skills but rather the ability to read, understand, remember and write prose mainly relating to historical facts.

Although Rob did not opt for O Level, two years later he did opt for the Advanced, or A Level which followed straight on from O Level and is the precursor to university entrance. However, there was only one other pupil taking the course, and although at this stage it would not normally have been the case that pupils would find the theory easy, Rob was frustrated by the fact that his classmate – who *had* taken the O Level – was slow on the uptake and, he felt, held the lessons back.

Rob   ... it kind of petered out, not the passion for music but the study of it, because I felt I was getting nowhere fast, waiting for this other person to catch up. Very frustrating.

Clearly both he and Bernie found the technical, theoretical side of the work relatively easy.

Will was misinformed by his Head of Department, whose advice was in direct contradiction to government stipulations that GCSE music, which had by that time replaced the O Level, must be open to all pupils, including those who had no instrumental lessons, those whose reading abilities were minimal and those who played any instrument (Department of Education and Science 1986, p. 2). I asked Will why he had not chosen the GCSE:

Will   Because I was told that I didn't have piano skills. Wasn't able to read music. I couldn't play two instruments – guitar was not really regarded as an instrument – and I couldn't read music, that I wasn't allowed to do GCSE. It was really only for your trumpeters, your piano players, violin players.

Brent had also wanted to opt for music O Level, but as he was the only person in his school to choose it, the course did not run.

For others, opting for music was not even in the question. To Nanette, music had been 'not for me at all', the option did not occur to Steve, and Andy chose Art and Design instead.

Andy   I found out a couple of years later that you didn't have to choose between the two like I had thought, but I still wasn't that bothered. I was doing well enough with the band as it was. We were getting gigs, I mean people were hearing us and so forth, so I didn't see it as being of any consequence.

Many of these players later came to regret either the fact that a music option had not been open to them, or that they had avoided it when it was open. Apart from Bernie's O Level, none of the eleven professional or semi-professional popular musicians in this study had gained a single qualification in music before they became professional.

Formal and informal extra-curricular music activities within the school As we have seen, Rob played in the school symphonic wind band and the school orchestra, and 'loved it'. But he was exceptional in this, and was the only one of these older nine musicians who was committed to classical instrumental lessons. Some teachers had recognized the musical ability of the others, but rather than incorporating their skills into class lessons, appealing to and improving upon them, teachers employed them in the provision of music for extra-curricular performances, not in forms which the young musicians were developing themselves, but in adaptations to suit the traditional ethos of music in the school, and the needs of the teacher. Bernie's teacher

Bernie   … got me involved in playing the guitar for school plays and stuff; and she'd write the music for it. She'd write a little guitar part, sort of like a quasi-classical thing and I'd play that.

Nanette's teachers gave her lead singing roles.

Nanette   They just then put me in all the plays. As long as I was in the end-of-year production and doing well in that, then that was OK. That seemed to be the main interest they took in me.

Terry and Andy took part in a small number of classical concerts. Terry sang in the choir and especially remembered a performance of *Carmen*, which he enjoyed (not to mention 'some pretty duff things as well actually'). But when it came to a popular music item in an end-of-term lampoon, his role was to mime into a microphone, pretending to be Eric Burdon of The Animals. When I asked the (rhetorical) question whether his teacher had ever required him to play the drums in a school concert: 'No, no, oh no, no, no.' Andy also took part in a classical music concert, but clearly without having developed any appreciation for the music in question or any sense of having learnt anything:

Andy   We did a production of Benjamin Britten – I think it was Benjamin Britten – 'Noye's Fludde' I think it was. It was all very basic, it was designed for

someone who couldn't play music to be able to play. It was all on the open strings on violins and cellos and so forth. That was, that was good, that was a laugh but it was easy, there was nothing to learn really for that ...
... It wasn't something that many people took seriously.

Such extra-curricular experiences were appreciated by all those who had them, especially Nanette:

Nanette   All the schools that I've been to, they were really, really supportive, really, really good, you know. The teachers were excellent and the productions at my secondary school – well, the effort that they put in was incredible. They really were proper productions, you know, 'Fiddler on the Roof', things like that.

But they sidestepped rather than developed the skills, knowledge, attitudes and values of the young popular musicians involved, and except for Nanette's voice, the main instrument of each player was neither seen nor heard in a concert.

As mentioned in Chapter 3 (pp. 78–9) (and see Bennett 1980, pp. 24–5), schools have for a long time played a major role in the development of popular musicians, not through the formal music education they offer, but through the provision of resources such as rehearsal spaces and instruments, formal and informal performance opportunities and, most particularly, large numbers of young people with shared musical interests. In the case of the musicians in this study, even those who had attended schools with a very traditional outlook had in some cases been provided with access to instruments they did not possess at home (especially drum kits), rehearsal spaces and opportunities to play in concerts and, in most cases, to form bands with friends. Bernie, Rob, Will, Steve and Andy all formed their first bands with school-mates and rehearsed on school premises, and three of them were given opportunities to perform in school concerts with their bands.

However, this input by the school traditionally occurred almost entirely outside the classroom, was largely unsupervised and often flew in the face of the music department's ethos. The pupils often had to make do with getting instruments, as was the case for Andy, when the storeroom was unlocked and unguarded, and all their rehearsal activities occurred in the interstices of the curriculum, in rooms that could only occasionally be occupied without getting 'kicked out', during breaks and lunch hours, at times when lessons were being 'skived', or after school when no one else was around.

Andy   You'd walk into school, you'd just learnt 'Knocking on Heaven's Door' or something, sit in the music centre in front of everybody else and you'd play it and they'd be like, 'Yeah, that's right, yeah.' Then you'd get kicked out because you're not playing classical music ... And so you'd come out and next lunchtime you show everyone again.

Once, Steve's teacher organized a 'battle of the bands' outside of ordinary music lessons. Although the support of the school was fundamental to the performance opportunity, in which about four bands took part, the teacher made no input other than to allow the pupils to organize themselves. As will be discussed in Chapter 7, a balance between giving support and 'letting be' can have advantages where the development of young popular musicians is concerned. But Steve's account of the proceedings provides an example of one of the ways in which popular music is implicitly treated as inferior by traditional music departments (see Vulliamy 1977b, Green 1988). The concert took place at the end of the last day of term. Unlike a more formal school concert, which in most schools means that the performers have to wear the 'correct' uniform, this one took place on a 'mufti' day, meaning that pupils could wear ordinary clothes in return for a small payment for charity. It was thus leant connotations of holiday time and 'winding down' rather than of work and studious preparation for exams. Whilst a formal school concert usually requires that the audience remain seated and keep quiet, in this case the audience were allowed to come and go as they pleased – 'If they didn't like it they just walked out.' Rather than being presented as a concert for the sake of the music, or a competitive event with an experienced adjudicator present, as is common in British schools, the event was characterized as a 'battle' and the bands were left to fight it out between themselves. Since it took place during the school day, parents and other friends of the school were not invited. Overall, it served to entertain pupils, or to 'keep the troops happy' in the words of one teacher answering my questionnaire, and as a 'treat' at the end of term, rather than being presented as a serious educational or cultural undertaking of which the school could be proud.

Will's school afforded the greatest extra-curricular popular music opportunities, supported by his regular one-to-one electric guitar lessons which have already been noted. He was the only one of the interviewees who had attended a private school, or what is known in England as a 'public school', and it was a very famous and prestigious one with ample resources.

Will   We were very lucky. We had something called 'Rock Soc' which was designed for any band that wanted to rehearse. You went to the music school, there was a booking sheet, you booked it, just wrote the name of the band in, in one hour slots. And it was a large sound-proofed room miles from anywhere so you could play as hard as you liked. The school bought a really nice drum kit, two great guitar amps, brand new PA, so you just took your instruments and everything was there. And at the end of every term they held an enormous rock concert. Thousands was spent on an enormous PA, lights, smoke machine. They had it done the proper way. TV screens at the back and catwalk, it was like, you know, the event of the term.

But it was all done without the blessing or support of the Music Department, the Head of which had

Will   ... nothing to do with it. He didn't like it that much. Because it was always getting us into trouble, because it was miles away, people were always smoking, etc. etc.

Apart from Rob's out-of-class contact with his teacher, Will was the only other of these older musicians who felt he had benefited as a rock musician from the input of the school. In his case, this occurred through both the peripatetic teaching and the extra-curricular activities described above.

Will   L: And if that hadn't been there in your education, do you think you would have still become a musician?
          W: No. I think I might have strummed a few chords and still be listening to Kiss regularly but no. We were always encouraged to do something. We were always, even at the junior level, putting on little concerts ... I'm sure it made a world of difference.

Summary

Seven out of the nine musicians in the sample who took classical instrumental lessons got little out of them, finding the lessons boring, the progress slow and the music difficult to relate to. Most of them had not made any links between those lessons and their informal popular music learning practices. Only Rob and Emily had positive experiences of instrumental tuition, but Rob had not made any links across the formal and informal spheres until after becoming a fully professional session musician, and Emily saw her cello lessons as the 'complete opposite' of her popular music practices. The oldest nine musicians, all of whom had experience of traditional classroom music education, almost without exception felt alienated during their class lessons. Although the resources and the presence of other young people in schools made it possible for many of them to set up and even perform in their first bands, the school had in general not recognized, rewarded or helped them to pursue the popular music skills and knowledge that they were developing outside the boundaries of formal education; nor had their teachers apparently been aware of, or interested in, their high levels of enthusiasm and commitment to music.

Notes

1.   The main boards in Britain are the Associated Board of the Royal Schools of Music, and boards representing the Guildhall School of Music and Drama, Trinity College of Music and the London College of Music. All these boards export their grades to many countries overseas. There are also hundreds of locally managed boards under the auspices of Education Authorities and other funded and private concerns.

2. The first monograph supporting popular music in schools was Swanwick (1968). Work on the exclusion and downgrading of popular music in schools was conducted in the sociology of education by Vulliamy (1977a and b). This lead to a heated debate between Swanwick (1984a and b), and Vulliamy and Shepherd (1984a, 1984b, 1985). Also see Green (1988) for a critique of the pop/classical split in education at that time. Influential texts designed for teachers and classroom use were Vulliamy and Lee (1976, 1982), Burnett (1972), Farmer (1976). In the USA the central forum, the Music Educators' National Conference, staged a major discussion of popular music and education in 1969. See *Music Educators' Journal* (1969, 1991), especially Cutietta (1991); also see Nettl (1995), Newsom (1998), Volk (1998), Herbert and Campbell (2000) for discussions of how popular music has fared there since, which, it seems feasible to suggest, has been less well than in Britain, Australia, Hong Kong, Thailand and Japan amongst other countries. See, for example, *Research Studies in Music Education* (1999), the *International Journal of Music Education* (2000), no. 36, Ho (1996), Koizumi (1998, 2002), Maryprasith (1999).

Chapter 6

Popular musicians in the new music education

This chapter will first examine the experiences of those musicians who took instrumental tuition in popular music, dating back to Bernie's lessons in the early 1960s and going up to the end of the century. Then I will look at the younger musicians' experiences of what I will refer to as the 'new classroom music education', in which a vast increase in the diversity of curriculum content, along with a broadening of teachers' perspectives, occurred during the 1990s. This will be followed by a brief discussion of some aspects of the musicians' encounters with post-schooling courses in popular music. At the end of the chapter I will consider the musicians' stated views of the advantages and disadvantages of including popular music in formal education.

Popular music instrumental tuition

An overall picture of ethos and provision

As well as informal learning practices, formal tuition has been available to popular musicians for many years. In the past some professional and amateur popular musicians would teach on a casual basis; others turned their hand to teaching either part-time or full-time in order to supplement or replace their performance careers; and in recent years, popular musicians are increasingly setting out to gain qualifications and make a career of teaching. In support of this growth area, new instrumental grade exams were developed during the 1990s, specifically dedicated to popular music as well as jazz and various traditional, folk and 'light' popular styles.[1] As will be indicated later, large numbers of post-schooling courses are also now available, which include popular music instrumental tuition in various forms from individual lessons to relatively large groups of around fifteen students to one teacher.

The musicians taking popular instrumental tuition and popular music grade exams

Table 2 in the Appendix (p. 220) provides a résumé of which musicians took lessons and grades in both classical and popular spheres, showing that nine of the fourteen had taken popular instrumental lessons. Most of the lessons had occurred during their teenage years, the main exception to this being Brent, who had lessons over a longer time span but with gaps, sometimes of several years between teachers. Only Will had received sustained popular instrumental tuition lasting more than four years. In his case, as well as those of Simon and Michael, lessons had been provided by a peripatetic teacher at their schools, a situation which could not have occurred, except under very unusual circumstances, before the mid-1970s, and was still rare in the mid-1980s. At the time of the interviews, only one of the musicians had availed himself of the new popular music grade exam system, and this was not one of the younger musicians who might be expected to have been 'brought up' in line with the new syllabi, but Rob, who had put himself in for the Rock School Grade VIII bass guitar exam at the age of 41, in order to enhance his paper qualifications for university entrance. This was the only practical grade above grade IV in either classical or popular music to have been taken by any of the musicians. About eighteen months after the interviews Richard Dowdall took the Rock School Grade IV electric guitar exam, passing with Distinction.

As with the classical sphere, the interviewees' responses to popular music tuition were both positive and negative. First, I will consider the more positive experiences. Notice that, as with classical tuition, their memories of popular music lessons centred around acquiring technique, partly through exercises such as scales and learning to read notation. Bernie taught himself from the age of 6, then took lessons for a year, aged 11 or 12, from a workmate of his father's who was a guitarist in the factory dance band.

Bernie   So he played stuff they do at tea dances or the Christmas party for the works. Basically, we did all the major and minor scales, arpeggios, chord inversions, and then I'd learnt several tunes, and I'd learnt also, he did actually get me into sight-reading, reading melodies written out in notation.

Brent started drum lessons when he was 9. Notation reading was central, and although Brent felt in retrospect that his teacher had not emphasized technique, it had obviously had a major presence in the lessons:

Brent   … he didn't emphasize technique too much, certainly for me, although I suspect that might have been to do with the age I was at and he probably thought that if he had me there doing repetitive single stroke rolls or whatever it would bore me …
          … Well, when I first started with him it wasn't that he didn't teach technique because he did, but it wasn't like he really focused on it particularly. You know when I first went to him I think within the first few lessons at least, if not the first lesson he talked about double stroke rolls, single stroke rolls, paradiddles at some point, press rolls. But there are a whole bunch of thirty or more drum rudiments, and certainly we didn't go through all of those. I mean not that they're absolutely necessary to play anyway but they are a good bunch

of things to work on just to develop the technique. However poor the technique may have been, the stage I was at then was actually getting to play some things at all, whereas as you get older, although there are still things that you're still struggling to play, you're also refining things, where the technique tends to become more important to a degree.

Although their memories of lessons were positive, and the tuition clearly made a major contribution to their overall development, both Bernie's and Brent's early lessons were short-lived. At the end of a year, Bernie's teacher said he had nothing else to teach him, and Bernie has not had a lesson since. Brent's early tuition was sporadic, partly because he moved to a different town where he never acquired a new teacher, and partly because

Brent   … I remember I had a period of studying with him and then it tailed off for a while. I think I actually went through short periods of losing interest for whatever reason and then rekindled my interest and studied with him a bit longer.

In his mid-twenties after having played professionally for some time, he went to two different teachers for advanced lessons, Joel Rothman and Bob Armstrong.

Brent   Bob was the best teacher I ever had … He certainly turned several things around for me, certainly technically: how my hands were actually working and stuff.
L: How did he go about doing that?
B: Just by refining the technique and particularly in terms of double stroke rolls. I'd never really thought too much about how I was doing things until I went to Bob. You know it was just like, you would hopefully arrive at being able to do something just by keeping trying to do it but without actually analysing it too much. But with Bob he would say 'Well, move your finger slightly here' and 'Use this finger' and you know – it was much more specific. And he was really good at breaking things down so that if you wanted to get from A to C he could get you there via point B.

Three others – Will, Simon and Michael – benefited from more extended periods of lessons during their teenage years. Will got his first electric guitar when he was 14. I asked him how he felt about it.

Will   Um. Yeah. It was a big disappointment because I only knew how to play chords – not very well either – and I was expecting this massive sort of distorted rock guitar sound and it sounded awful, so I thought I had to go and buy lots of effects. [Laughing] Lots of effects – it didn't sound any better. So I thought, 'I'd better learn how to play this', so I started having lessons.

The lessons began about a year after having first got the instrument, continuing until he left school at 18.

> I could take tunes I liked and say 'How do you do this?' And he would show
> me, teach me about music theory as well as guitar techniques …
>   … Having lessons gave me the confidence to get my own band together, to
> join the big band, the blues band, the small jazz band, the house band, just
> every band there was.

He then took a two-year diploma course in popular music performance, one of
the first of its kind in Britain, which included group guitar lessons, before going
on to study for a general humanities degree.

Simon had kit as well as percussion lessons for four years and took the Grade
IV practical percussion exam. He spent his first year on the snare drum only:

Simon   … which is all, you know, marches and stuff. I think that was the best way to
learn anyway, so you get the coordination right, so you get how to move your
hands and stuff. And from there I moved on through that. And as I got better
I've – well he started off doing the rock beat and then you're down to more
Latin, more jazz and then; but you get to the stage, like when I was in the fifth
year he'd taught me more or less all he knew, well the teacher I had then, so I
just jammed with him 'til I got a new teacher.

Michael originally took lessons with

Michael   … the other drummer at church because I used to admire him very much. I
used to like his drum kit and he sometimes let me play it and that was always
good fun. I was quite impressed by him and he actually gave me a few lessons
before I got the drum kit. This was on his drum kit and I really enjoyed that,
but my parents decided not to give me a whole drum kit at once in case I got
it and then wasn't interested in it – that's when I just got the, the one drum to
start with.

He then took drum lessons with a peripatetic teacher at his school, for three
years up until the interview.

Peter, Emily and Richard had relatively few lessons, partly because in the
latter two cases their experiences tended to have been more negative than those
described above. Peter had taken one early lesson which 'got my fingers
working', then in the months just before the interview he 'tracked down a teacher
and had a few lessons from my friends'. Emily had three acoustic guitar lessons
from a private teacher.

Emily   Well, he said 'What do you want to learn?', and I said 'Oasis' because I was
like a really big fan of theirs at the time, and because that was the time we
were covering 'Don't Look Back in Anger' and so he like went through that
with me; he taught me how to strum properly, which I was like doing really
badly, and he was going to start teaching me lead guitar. He taught me all the
pentatonic scales and then, I don't know, I went away and stopped having
lessons so I didn't actually get to learn lead guitar.

Richard   For the first, the summer holidays afterwards I kind of went at it myself but it wasn't quite working because, I knew about music, it's just I couldn't, I wasn't doing it right with the guitar.

L: Yeah, what sort of things were you not doing right?

R: I was playing too high up and stuff, but I just didn't realize that, and my hand was out here and that sort of thing. I was playing bar chords wrong – all these, just little things – and I just thought I'd better have a few lessons to get it sorted out ... and that helped but he didn't seem to be teaching me that much afterwards. It was just 'OK let's practise some more scales', so – that was the only teacher I had and I didn't know whether he was a good teacher or anything – so I stopped. So I just started playing by myself and practising and doing stuff ... I was only having lessons for about two terms or something.

Leo had been taking saxophone lessons ever since starting the instrument.

Leo   The guy I've got teaching me he's actually, he plays, I think he's got a quartet, and, yeah, he's a jazz musician, so he teaches me jazz; but he's more interested in my technique, the way I'm playing the saxophone rather than what I'm actually playing.

L: Right. Can you describe what sort of things you do in your lessons with him?

Leo: Well, usually, at the beginning, we do, we just do like, when I'm setting up, I have to practise my breathing, and then when I start off with a couple of scales and maybe practise a piece, and go over timing, and that kind of stuff, and a little bit of theory; he teaches me about different modes and scales and all that kind of thing.

As mentioned in Chapter 3, p. 90, 'my Mum and Dad get a bit annoyed with me because I don't practise enough'. In most respects his saxophone lessons could more appropriately be considered under the title of formal jazz or classical tuition than popular tuition.

The new classroom music education

The 'new classroom music education' took hold during the second half of the 1980s and through the 1990s. In the mid-1980s the British government developed a new exam system for 14 to 16 year olds in England and Wales, and the first cohort of pupils started the course in September 1986. This was called the General Certificate of Secondary Education (GCSE), and one of its main aims was to get rid of the previous divide between the O Level and the CSE, mentioned in the previous chapter. The GCSE involved all pupils in working to the same syllabus and taking the same exam at the end (see Department of Education and Science 1986). It had a major effect on music education in England and Wales, where the curriculum underwent radical transformation. With impetus from primary schooling, increasing demands from government inspectors (see Her Majesty's

Inspectorate 1985), researchers (especially Payntor and Aston 1970, Vulliamy and Lee 1976, 1982, Swanwick 1979) and many teachers, the previous, virtually hegemonic position of classical music, history and singing in the classroom crumbled. (For more details also see Green 1988, pp. 74–9.)

The new syllabus included the stipulation that pupils should study various styles of music including folk and popular music, jazz, contemporary classical music and perhaps the most innovatory aspect, that misnamed 'world music'. All pupils, for the first time, were required to demonstrate ability in three areas: music listening to a wide variety of styles; performance on any instrument from the sitar to the electric keyboard; and composition, including original composition, improvisation and/or arrangement, in any musical style or sub-style. It was possible to submit performance in an ensemble, to be assessed in rehearsing and directing an ensemble and to replace the traditional sight-reading test with improvisation. Own compositions could double up as performances. Notation was not compulsory, although this depended on the particular board and syllabus. GCSE swept away the old division of the 14 to 16 age range curriculum into two mutually exclusive courses, and at the same time opened the way for any pupil to follow the course and sit the exam, submitting performances and compositions in any musical style on any instrument, and being required to recognize and comment on a wide variety of music from many historical eras and geographical regions.

Five years after the GCSE was implemented, the government introduced another radical change: for the first time in British history, a National Curriculum (Department of Education and Science 1992, Department for Education 1995). The contents and activities originally proposed by the Music Working Party largely reflected the Music GCSE syllabus. However, whereas the latter had not attracted a huge amount of interest from the public at large, the development of the Music National Curriculum was accompanied by high levels of controversy over what music was considered valuable enough to be included and what music was considered inferior or even harmful or pernicious enough to be excluded, as well as wrangles over what musical activities were suitable for the classroom. The variety of styles and the equal emphasis which the original Working Party had placed on composing alongside listening and performing caused consternation amongst traditionalists who believed that pupils ought to use their time in being introduced to the cultural heritage, rather than studying popular and world music, or making up their own music in any style whatsoever. Angry articles appeared in the national press, tempers ran high and large-scale cultural battles over the value of the British national heritage and the (lack of) value of popular music raged. (See Swanwick (1992), Shepherd and Vulliamy (1994) and Gammon (1999) for discussions and illustrations of the debacle.)

In general, the critical reception of the proposals went against the sentiments of music teachers, teacher-educators, music lecturers and many others, including well-known musical figures in both the classical and popular fields, who were vociferous in defending the original, more far-reaching proposals. To cut a long story short, a compromise was eventually reached when the proposals were toned down to decrease the emphasis on performing and composing, and on popular and world music, whilst still allowing them all a place. As is evident in the literature on British music education since, and as I will briefly illustrate with reference to my own research below, it is reasonable to suggest that the majority of schools did include a large amount of classroom performance and composition as well as a wide variety of music, at least as wide, and probably even wider than that implied by the final National Curriculum document.

As well as the above changes in exam syllabi and curricula, the development of cheap electric instruments and music information technology had a major impact on classroom practices. Electric keyboards became very common. They were often deployed in the form of a 'keyboard lab' in which pupils could work individually on set tasks and the teacher could 'listen in' from a central console. They could also be taken, along with other classroom instruments, into practice rooms or other available spaces for small-group work. In addition, increasing numbers of schools purchased recording equipment and computers with music hardware and software; and the presence of a dedicated recording studio in a school, although not common, was far from a rarity.

We have seen that until the mid-1980s and in some cases beyond, school music classrooms were characterized by quite traditional music teaching methods and content, despite the influence of progressive approaches related to the 'avant-garde', the incorporation of composing activities and the entrance of popular music into the curriculum. By contrast, the period from 1986 onwards involved an indisputably noteworthy amount of innovation. The basic form and content of the GCSE music syllabus and the National Curriculum for music as described here (necessarily in general terms) were largely unchanged by the time of the interviews with the musicians in 1998–9.

In 1998 I also issued a questionnaire which was as close as possible to the questionnaire of 1982 discussed in the previous chapter (pp. 137–9), and received replies from the same number of teachers (sixty-one). The data from the two questionnaires illuminates the general shifts in teachers' views and uses of music in the classroom at two points in time sixteen years apart, showing enormous changes in their 'common-sense' attitudes to many aspects of music and music education, not least of which is popular music, its educational value and its role in practical classroom work. A detailed examination and comparison of the two sets of data is available in Green (2002), but in the present context I will restrict myself to some brief general observations.

First, it is helpful to compare the overall picture of whether or not teachers included each of the four styles – 'classical', 'popular', 'folk' and 'avant-garde' music – from the 1982 data (see Chapter 5, pp. 137–9), with the data collected in 1998. In the latter questionnaire I added two styles, 'jazz' and 'world music', and used the term 'twentieth-century classical music' instead of 'avant-garde music', to reflect the expansion of curriculum content and a change in the usage of terminology that had taken place in the years between the two questionnaires. An alteration to the phrasing of each question was also required. By 1998 it would have been compromising to ask teachers *whether or not* they included a particular style of music in their curricula, as the law stated that they *should* include all the styles mentioned. Instead I asked them to rate the styles 'in terms of how important they are for your particular pupils'. A score of 3 was given for 'most important', 2 for 'of moderate importance', 1 for 'of some use' and 0 for 'not included at all' (just in case some teachers wished to be honest about this!). The total scores for relative emphasis for each style were:

Popular music:	145
Classical music:	134
World music:	134
Jazz:	114
Twentieth-century classical:	107
Folk music:	87

The overriding change suggested by these results, combined with an analysis of the prose responses, is that by 1998 classical music had lost its previously hegemonic position. Not only do the above scores put popular music higher in teachers' estimations of importance than classical music, but remarkably, world music, which was not apparently even a part of teachers' consciousness in 1982, had risen to a position on a par with classical music. This latter development in the role of world music in schools is obviously of major significance, forming a vast subject and demanding full examination in its own right. I have therefore been forced to leave out any discussion of it here.[2] It is, however, worth noting that many comments from teachers answering additional questions on the advantages and disadvantages of teaching world music included ditto signs to the same questions on popular music, or comments such as 'Same as with popular music'. Indeed, much of what is called 'world music' falls under the category of popular music and shares with it a vernacular character (see Manuel 1988). This is one of the reasons why in Chapter 1 I suggested that many of the findings and suggestions in this book are generalizable beyond the field of popular music, which is the object of concern here.

To focus on popular music: by the end of the century, teachers' prose responses indicated massive shifts in their attitudes towards popular music as well as radical changes in the ways they used it in classrooms and extra-curricular activities. This point can be illustrated in conjunction with a further point: that not only were the styles of classical music, popular music and 'world music' generally regarded as more equal, but there was far more emphasis on classroom performance and composition, integrated with listening. In particular it was notable what a strong emphasis large numbers of teachers placed upon common musical elements, or universals, that cut across musical styles. (For a discussion of which concerning school classrooms, see Stock 1996.) Here, for example, is a representative selection of responses to the question concerning how much emphasis is placed on teaching popular music:

> Excellent vehicle for teaching many – all musical elements. It ... has many examples of varied and interesting textures, timbres, structures etc.

> I cover all the styles below in the course of every year and make every effort not only to demonstrate the special qualities of each but also to draw out connections especially with current examples in popular music. E.g. Guantanamera has recently been produced by Fugees fused with rap.

> [The curriculum in Year 9 is] based on less familiar styles such as blues and reggae. These are then discussed in relation to more current styles. At all stages there is an attempt to relate concepts from any style of music to other styles they are more familiar with.

> All these areas come through different projects that we do, e.g. we don't teach popular music separately but as part of projects on ostinato/music with a story/instruments ... Eg I would choose Coolio "I'll C U when U get there" rather than Pachelbel's Canon in D or I would play both versions when teaching ostinato.

> I don't teach popular music – or any other sort. This sounds glib, but I teach pupils to listen and compose music in broadest sense. How one approaches that has to remain flexible and varied. There would always be reference to aspects of 'pop' music – e.g. chord structures, style of singing, improvisation, verse/chorus form, style etc. etc. But this would apply equally to music from India, China, African Continent, Far Eastern etc. etc. 'If it fits, use it! I draw attention to, and give credence to, whatever it happens to be, but this is secondary to the musical content and method of composition.

> I teach 'concepts', elements through pop music.

Overall, attitudes could hardly have been more different from those in 1982.

Popular music in the new classrooms

There are, of course, many problems involved in teaching popular music in schools, not necessarily related to specifically musical knowledge, skills, attitudes or values. Popular music has often been cast in antipathy to education, a classic expression of which is Pink Floyd's hit, 'Brick in the Wall', which reached Number 1 in the British charts in 1982. The song puts anti-educational sentiments ('We don't need no education') into the mouths of a chorus of children, suggests that schools engage in 'thought control' and implies that teachers bully children. It sustained some criticism at the time, and many teachers felt that it was damaging. There are several other anti-school popular songs, urging pupils to truant or misbehave in the classroom, glorifying them for doing so, or representing them, especially uniformed girls, in ways that either gain sexual heat or ideological 'cool' precisely by their connotations of 'sacrilege' or disobedience. Some lyrics, visual associations or other connotations of popular music are often unsuitable for classrooms, especially where younger children are concerned, or require a great deal of sensitivity and understanding on the part of teachers in leading discussions about social issues with older pupils.

As many teachers in both questionnaires pointed out, other problems arise because pupils can be divided amongst themselves over popular music, narrow and partisan in their tastes, and over-influenced by the charts, especially when younger, or fiercely defensive over rapidly changing musical sub-cultures as they get older. Many teachers noted that they found it difficult to keep their knowledge and resources up to date with musical trends, which change rapidly, and several feared being seen as cultural intruders if they introduced popular music into the classroom. Problems of this nature are by no means insignificant, and some of them are addressed in a different context in the next chapter.[3] But in the context of the present chapter, my main aim is to examine the classroom experiences of young popular musicians who were on the receiving end of the new music education. This involves attempting to ascertain the nature of their experiences, considering whether these experiences were significantly different from those of the musicians' older colleagues in more traditional music classrooms, and assessing to what extent the experiences contributed to the development of the musicians' popular music skills and knowledge.

The musicians as pupils in the new classrooms

The five youngest musicians in this study started secondary school in the following years:

Simon: 1990
Michael: 1991
Emily: 1994
Richard   1994
Leo: 1994

Although to a lesser extent in Michael's case, all of them experienced classrooms in which the official changes were having an impact, where the teaching and learning practices included classroom performance and composition as well as listening and appraising work, and covered a wide range of musical styles including popular and world musics. Overall the influence of the classroom on these younger musicians' acquisition of popular music skills and knowledge, as well as their attitudes towards formal music education, represent a striking contrast with those of the older musicians.

General class lessons An experience of Emily's is helpful in illustrating the bridge between the traditional and the new classroom approaches, in that her school underwent a change from one teacher who practised the former, to a different teacher who practised the latter.

Emily	Before Mr. C. came to my school, in my first year, we had this really bad teacher. She was like, she'd had a classical training, obviously, and she was just like, we were doing projects. If he hadn't come along – we did a blues project with him, the first thing he did with us – but if he hadn't come along we'd have done a project on medieval instruments; and I'm sorry but that really doesn't interest me. Blues is just so much more interesting. I don't know, my friends, some of my friends don't like blues, but most people prefer it to medieval instruments; and it was actually *music* we were learning about, not like, how the instruments are made and that; that's just boring. I think, like one of my friends in another school doesn't; they're not allowed to have any rock music at all in their GCSE and that, and it's just so backward I think, because it's – it's all music.

Simon, Michael and Richard (the latter in relation to his primary school) had some memories of general class lessons that were akin to those of the older musicians in traditional contexts, although with differences particularly concerning equipment. One area that came across rather negatively concerned the overuse of electric keyboards, in which context it is also worth re-quoting Steve, whose experiences were discussed in the previous chapter under the topic of traditional music education, but whose school stepped out of traditional practices in so far as to use keyboards.

Steve	Mainly keyboards and just mucking around really. (Laughs) That's what most music lessons are at school – mucking around – pressing all the keys in for sounds and stuff – that's mainly what we done. Banging on little tom-tom things and, I don't remember what I done at school in music, don't remember anything. Nothing at all.
Richard	… we were all confined to keyboards – we didn't, there was nothing else much you could use.
Simon	Not much to be quite honest. We were doing sort of learning the keyboard – sit around and you had your earphones on; you'd have a sheet and that was it really. You had a sheet in front of you and then the music teacher would listen in to you. Had to always have a sheet. Once you'd passed that you go on to the next one. We'd do a bit of history, music history – only a little bit – and the main part of it was theory, but nothing too much though in those – can't remember now. I didn't learn too much in those years of the music – didn't learn anything really.

Michael also felt he had not gained a lot, and had memories of lessons consisting mainly of

Michael   … music appreciation. We did a bit of composition and things but it was quite, quite simple really.
           L: Was it mainly classical music or a mixture of styles?
           M: Mostly classical – I don't think we've ever done any pop music in school.

However, Emily, Richard and Leo had experienced general class lessons where a much greater mixture of musical styles and practices was the norm. African, Latin American and Indian music, jazz, the blues and reggae were all described as involving practical activities, mixed in with references to music history, the Baroque, classical music generally, theory, notation reading and small-group composition work. Lessons on world music had made a particular impression on Emily and Leo, although without having given rise to any conscious direct influence on their popular music skills and knowledge. For example:

Leo   We had to learn Indian ragas … I found it quite interesting. I liked the sound, but it's not actually relevant to what I'm doing … I don't actually use it.

The one area that came across strongly as having made a particular impression on these three pupils, and which did appear to have fed directly into their informal learning practices, was practical lessons on the blues. Emily's feelings about blues lessons were cited at the beginning of this section. Concerning the other two:

Richard   I actually quite liked doing the blues stuff at school. We got told the blues rhythm – it was kind of handed to us on a plate basically. You had to use the blues scale, and it was just how people interpreted it, what melody you came up with.
           L: And did you, was it just melody, what about chord progressions?
           R: Yeah, the blues chords. It was keyboards touch-chord single-finger thing – someone did that, someone hit a cymbal and someone else, I played melody.

He had enjoyed a reggae project, but when it came to asking for details:

Richard   R: Can't remember it.
           L: You can't remember anything.
           R: Blues sticks in my head.

I asked the musicians whether they felt any of the things they had learnt in class music lessons had helped or were helping them in their development as popular musicians:

Richard   The blues did, because you know with some songs you can see a bit of blues in it, and the song that we wrote – I actually really liked it, I can remember it and it was really good fun playing it; but the other stuff, it, it just wasn't my style of music.

Leo   The blues stuff was quite useful for my saxophone playing, because it helped me, it helped me to hear chord changes and stuff, and just learn the 12-bar sequence of it. So it was quite useful.

The post-14 option course (GCSE) Despite not having been particularly enamoured of general class music lessons, but mainly because he had been given drum lessons by the school, Simon opted for the GCSE, as did all the others considered here except Richard, who regretted it very shortly afterwards. All the GCSE lessons were portrayed in terms that were very much in line with the content and activities of the new music classroom described from the perspectives of teachers earlier. Furthermore, as distinct from the O Level course which Bernie had followed, all four candidates were able to submit, as a formal part of their exam work, tape recordings of their own popular compositions and/or performances with their bands.

Simon had given in one recording on which he had over-dubbed himself on guitar, bass and drums using a TASCAM portastudio. He did the work both during class, 'So I was lucky in lessons', and during other times, 'Whenever I could really. It's getting in there, sort of trying to get the parts down, which was nice.' For part of Simon's performance exam, Andy and other members of Deepvoid who were at a different school to Simon came in and played whilst he was assessed. Leo's school also had a four-track tape recorder on which he laid down his pieces during music lessons. Although Michael's teacher did not include any popular music in the lessons, he was open to the pupils' own popular music submissions.

Michael   You had to submit your solo performance and ensemble performance recorded on a tape for the GCSE course, and you could do whatever you wanted. Most people did classical pieces; I chose to do a pop piece and Mr R. said that wasn't a problem, although I never was taught popular music in the lessons.

Pupils submitted not only popular music compositions and performances, but an eclectic mixture. For example, Michael's compositions included a solo drum piece called 'Chukkabilly Choo Choo' in a 1950s popular style, a 'Passacaglia for harpsichord' and a 'classical duet for flute and piano'. Emily submitted a rock piece played by her band, with the addition of a cello, and a neo-classical duet for violin and cello.

Formal education provided them with many analytic and notation skills which were additional to their informally acquired knowledge and skills. For example, after Simon had over-dubbed himself playing guitar, bass and drums on the TASCAM, he had to write down what he had played in conventional notation. Emily's piece for her band was written out in full score, 'like all the parts and all the chords and all the tab for guitarists and stuff'.

Emily's words below can sum up the generally positive attitudes expressed about the GCSE course:

Emily   L: Did you enjoy learning about all those different kinds of music?
E: Some of it I liked more than others, because I just have an interest in it. Like jazz music, for example, that was nice, learning about it because you have to obviously listen to a lot of the music that you're learning about and if it's just endless stuff like – I don't know, I can't remember the one I hated the most – but I did like, really like learning about jazz and world music and stuff, because we'd all sit there going like this [moves around] along to the music. But, yeah, I liked it, it's been an interesting two years I think.

Crossing styles and transferring from the formal to the informal Of the musicians who had experienced traditional classroom music, only Rob had expressed any respect for his class teacher or had made any indications of a class teacher having helped him to acquire musical skills and knowledge which he valued. Whilst his experiences differed from those of the younger musicians in that they occurred mainly outside the classroom, they were similar in one significant respect: they concerned his teacher showing him how music worked in a variety of styles, often pointing out crossovers between popular and classical music. As discussed earlier (pp. 158–9), such eclecticism, and with it explicit attention to musical 'universals' or elements that cross over many styles, has become increasingly common and is today of major significance in the music classroom in Britain. As well as crossing over between musical styles, such an approach could also be expected to aid in the transfer of musical skills and knowledge from formal music education to informal learning practices. Unlike the older musicians, none of whom felt that their classroom experiences had helped their development as popular musicians, the younger ones were often able to relate their formal education to their informal learning practices. This is already apparent to a large extent in the above discussion of their GCSE work. Below are some further perspectives on it.

I asked them whether they felt that their formal classroom music education had helped their informal development as popular musicians.

Simon   Definitely. Yeah, definitely. I mean just through music, music history and through the theory as well and how the songs are, I learnt like loads. And what has happened now, is what you're listening for in it, you know, dynamics and things, you can sort of see how it works, you know, like in the classical music, see how that works and try to put it – not, you know, I'm not going to try and perform Deepvoid in a classical way, you know – but you can see their ideas and how they're using their ideas and trying to, well if it works, use it you know, use some of their ideas in what you're doing.
L: So you feel – are you saying you feel that you appreciate and understand more about classical music than you would have done if you hadn't –
S: Oh, definitely, definitely, yeah. If I hadn't done that then, well, I probably wouldn't be able to listen to it at all.

Michael and Emily were glad to be able to put names to different musical elements.

Michael   It's certainly made me able to communicate with the rest of the band in a different way, because if I'd just learnt the drums without doing the music course I would still be able to play the drums, but I wouldn't be able to say things like 'We need a syncopated bit here or a triplet run' or – well I might be able to use those – but the more complicated things, I might not be able to communicate to the band what I can hear and what I want them to play ...

... But I've also got the more theoretical knowledge, you know. Doing the pop things with bands and stuff is very much practical, just playing – very rarely involves even reading music. And what I learnt at school concentrates on the reading music, looking at the theory side of music. And not just music in performance either – music in music appreciation and things like that.

L: Yeah and you learnt about, er, presumably expressions [which he had already used] like suspended fourths and seconds – that comes from the work you did?

M: Yes. Although I knew about using them from what my Dad had said, but I never would have known what to call them.

Emily   God, I don't know ... I mean I don't want to be one of those – I think the term is 'muso' or something – I don't want to be one of the people who are always talking about the technical, theory side of music; but it's good to say, you know – because Ruth and Vicky [other members of her band] are also in my GCSE class, Ruth plays sax as well, and Vicky plays piano – it's quite good to be able to talk about musical terms with them without saying, you know 'That thingy there.' It's nice to know the terms and that.

L: And you get those terms from –

E: From the GCSE lessons, some of the theory lessons.

It was this side of musical knowledge that caused both Steve and Richard to regret not having taken the GCSE music option.

Steve   Yeah. I could've learned how to read music properly. That's what I've always wanted to do, I've always wanted to be able to read music. But I can't really afford lessons now, and I'm trying to save for a mortgage and stuff like that. I can't, if I can play that's good enough for me, I don't need to know how to read music.

L: Sure, you don't need it but you feel if you'd been given that in your lessons that it would've helped?

S: Yeah, yeah. Would have helped a lot.

L: Anything else that you could've gained from that?

S: Um. Timing and stuff like that, different types of timing, going half time, double time, missing beats and stuff like that and getting the timing in your hands if you're playing the guitar. When you miss a step and stuff like that. You've got to, I mean normally you can sense it anyway but if I'd learnt it properly – there's no harm in learning more, is there? If you knew it to start with then you can just carry on from there, but I just learnt it all myself really – no one's taught me anything apart from my Dad. He taught me the basics and I carried on from there ...

... I'd like to get better at what I'm playing, I want to have bass lessons, proper bass lessons, just to make myself that much better. But I can't really afford that at the moment ...

... Because when someone's showing you how to do it, it makes life a whole lot easier doesn't it?

L: Yeah, that's right.

S: How to get, not necessarily how to do it, but how to go about doing it. Once you know how to go about doing it you can practise it and learn it yourself. First of all you think 'How the hell do you do that?' You've got to have someone to teach you. Which is why I want lessons. I can't afford them.

Richard   I'd know what things were called in music rather than – because now it's mostly by ear and I know a few names – and in A Level I think they do how they composed it and stuff, and like how or what note they used to get this certain effect, and I've never been taught any of that. I've been taught the basics and that's it, and I feel that I want to know that, to sort of help me to play and write songs and stuff.

Leo found the school encouraging, partly because of his teacher's willingness to countenance any kind of music and musical experimentation.

Leo   L: ... do you feel that this input from the school, do you think that will help you to improve as a musician?

Leo: I think it will because it's like, it's very, it's very encouraging. And basically we're, we can compose whatever we want, however we want to do it; there's no restrictions on us as to what we do, so I think, I think it will help a lot, because sort of, we've been told to experiment as much as possible and so, and we've been taught that way, and I think that's good, useful, it will be helpful I hope.

Emily and Leo both expressed appreciation of their music teachers: Mr. C was 'generally very supportive' and 'encouraging' for Emily and her friends, and Leo's teacher was 'a good guy'.

Despite the help gained from GCSE music, Michael was the only one who went on to the next stage, the A Level. He was in the throes of applying for a university course in music and technology when I interviewed him. None of the others were planning to go on to music A Level, including Emily, even though her cello playing would have made it a distinct possibility and she was being encouraged to take the course by both her cello teacher and her GCSE teacher.

Emily   Not really interested in that. Because I do, I don't mind listening to other pieces, like learning about other styles and stuff but, no, it's just not really – and it gets quite academic as well, which is really what I want to get away from with music.

L: In favour of?

E: In favour of it being completely separate. Like I said, like I look forward to the band; it's kind of a release from the normal stuff.

Formal and informal extra-curricular music activities within the school The younger pupils were given more opportunities to use school resources in the production of popular music than their older colleagues, and received more encouragement and recognition for doing so. Emily's school, although state-funded, was a highly selective girls' school offering places on the basis of academic ability. The school put on two musical events each year, both adjudicated concerts in which the girls presented solo and ensemble performances which they had worked up on their own, outside curricular time. One event was dedicated to classical music and the other to popular music, both being given the same status and taking place in the same week. I had the great pleasure of adjudicating the popular music event the year after Emily had left the school, and found the standards remarkably high. Here, the principle of allowing pupils to organize themselves, albeit in a selective school, was applied to both musical areas, and achieved results that were equally appreciated by one and all (except that the popular music event attracted a far larger audience).

Richard, the only one of the five who had not opted for GCSE music, was in a position akin to some of the older musicians in that his band used school resources in unsupervised time, and were given performance opportunities in school concerts. But unlike his older colleagues, he did not have to 'sneak into' practice rooms or fear getting 'kicked out' of them.

Richard   What we'd do, we'd go into school and use the keyboards to record the drumbeats, then put them on a tape, bring it home, then do all the chords, then the lead guitar and bass and then we'd sing over it.

When I interviewed him they were still a rehearsal band ...

... but there was a school concert that we did where all the bands in the school could come and play and all the jugglers and people like that can perform and stuff.

Regarding more formal, traditional or classical extra-curricular activities, both of the younger drummers, Simon and Michael, were given percussion lessons as well as kit lessons to help them with GCSE, and played in the school orchestra, which they enjoyed although not as much as they enjoyed playing with their bands. Emily played the cello in a variety of school classical music ensembles, and Leo played in the school jazz band.

Popular music in further and higher education

Especially for students aged 14 and over, it is necessary to distinguish between the treatment of popular music in two broad fields of education. One of these fields includes cultural studies and media studies courses, in which popular music is considered from sociological, historical or otherwise critical intellectual angles.[4] The other field concerns *music* courses that are either entirely dedicated to popular music or include modules on popular music. Such courses may incorporate similarly critical approaches, but they usually also place emphasis on specifically musical and musicological skills including instrumental performance, composition and improvisation, musical analysis, notation, style history and aural skills. The comments here are directed to this latter field – that is, music courses – although overlaps occur and many issues are pertinent across the fields. At post-schooling level, including community provision, further and higher education or their equivalents in many countries, popular music courses are so diverse as to warrant a whole book about them.[5] But since some of the interviewees had encountered such courses either as students or applicants, I will include here a brief general discussion of some aspects of provision and of the musicians' experiences in this area.

Post-compulsory popular music courses first started up in voluntary and self-financed programmes, subsidised community programmes and further, rather than higher education spheres.[6] In the United States of the early 1990s, Walser (1993, p. ix) described the 'catacombs of a nineteenth-century warehouse' behind whose closed doors, along winding passageways, musicians practised heavy rock music 'through all hours of the day and night'; and he compares the scenario with that of a conservatory in many ways, except that 'this music does not enjoy institutional prestige or receive governmental subsidy' (p. ix). That last exception seems set to change. The availability of popular music courses and modules at further education level in many countries since the early 1990s has increased rapidly. In Britain this process can be described as nothing short of an explosion, as by the middle of the decade there were over 500 FE popular music courses on offer (Norton York: private correspondence; also see Drumbreck 2000, *British Music Education Yearbook* 2000).

It is characteristic of the entrance of popular music into formal education that the above courses lead to qualifications of a lower status than higher education courses, that is university or conservatory degrees. Although higher education has been slower to recognize popular music, increasing numbers of traditional music degrees are currently incorporating modules on popular music, and growing numbers of dedicated HE popular music courses are being developed. Currently the offer is by no means sufficient to meet the demand. Whilst some traditional music degrees in Britain are under-recruiting, applications for the few dedicated popular music degrees that do exist are overflowing. For example, at the time of writing there are approximately 800 applications for every 40 places at Salford University and about 500 for every 30 places at the University of Westminster (information from the Heads of Departments, Derek Scott and Norton York). Again, this situation is changing rapidly and (not surprisingly with recruitment figures like these) increasing numbers of HE popular music courses are being developed in many countries.

Aspects of the musicians' experiences of FE and HE popular music courses

Of the ten older musicians, all of whom had left school before the interviews reported in this book, everyone except Terry, Steve and Simon had gone on to take, or apply to, either a community course, a short FE course, a full-time diploma or a degree in or involving music. As has already been mentioned, Nanette was unique amongst the interviewees in registering for a conservatory training in classical singing. Rob took a joint honours in music and business studies as a mature student, mainly to help him change career in setting up his own composition and arranging company. Later he registered for a Ph.D., which he was engaged in at the time of the interview, and he also entered HE as a lecturer and Head of Bass Guitar in one of the first dedicated popular music performance degree courses in Britain (the Guitar Institute and Drum Tech, Acton, London).

Three others had attempted to re-enter education as mature students, only to find their way into music degrees blocked. For example, at the time of the interviews, Andy was taking a media studies degree:

Andy   I'm not doing a degree in media studies because I *wanted* to.
L: You're doing it for what reason?
A: I tried getting into music everywhere. They won't take you though – you need the academic qualifications.

Before registering for his media degree, he had approached a music department in a British university where he had done a summer course. It may be remembered that Brent would have liked to do music O Level but that the choice was not available in his school. He was then also denied access to the next rung, A Level, and with it, to university. He tried to compensate for this by taking a year out, which is when he took his grade exams, then attempted to get into university to study music. But like Andy with his media studies degree, he ended up doing a degree in another subject, in his case, computer science. Both he and Andy had similar experiences of rejection:

Andy   I did a course over the summer at X University – this was a music course. There were about five different short day courses. I spoke to the Head of Music there and – it's just the contempt that some people look at you with. It's, I don't know, it's not disheartening, it just, it just makes you frustrated, gets you angry. And he was just saying, 'Look if you want to do music here, go back to college, do music A Level and then we'll see.' I was like – I heard the words and I left.

Brent   When I was first applying to university I wasn't sure what I was going to do, so I started off looking at maths courses and then I stumbled across something in the UCCA [University entrance] handbook saying X University were doing a music degree that was quite modern; it wasn't all classical stuff – there were probably elements of that but they had a fair amount of other stuff which was at the time state-of-the-art. And it said that you didn't have to have A Level music necessarily, so I did actually apply to try and get in there. I called them up and said that I didn't play anything other than drums, could only read drum music. And basically they said 'Oh that's fine just come and see us, we'll interview you, audition you.' And I felt they kind of strung me along a bit because I told them originally that all I could do was play drums and read drum music and they said 'That's fine come along'; and they sent me this stuff to go up to the interview and when I got there they said 'Oh there'll be pieces to harmonise and essay questions to write' and it was like, you know I can't do that. So I basically I then took a year out, I finished my A Levels, I took a year out and I stayed on at college, the sixth form college I was at and that's when I did the Grade III piano and I tried to study some tuned percussion … my initial thought I suppose at the back of my mind was maybe if I go to [the same university] and do something else, then I might be able to transfer across at some point, but that never happened.

Bernie could not get onto a music degree either, but attended university as a mature student reading for a Humanities degree and then became eligible for acceptance onto a post-graduate teacher training course in secondary music (PGCE), which he completed successfully. The year after I interviewed him, Andy transferred to a music degree at a different university, from where he wrote me an enthusiastic letter with a list and description of the new skills and knowledge he was acquiring, including analytic and notation skills, harmony and counterpoint.

One of Peter's first bands was formed during a 'Training for Work' National Vocational Qualification FE course in variety entertainment. It included a music module in which performances were prepared, and during one of the rehearsals for this, 'a group of us realized that we were playing really well together'. But, like so many of the musicians' experiences at school, and despite the fact that this was a vocational FE course specifically designed to include popular music, 'for the rest of the course, we skipped lectures and rehearsed together'. The course somehow did not reach the parts that informal peer-group practices were reaching. Andy also had a negative experience, in his case of a community-based popular music course:

Andy   The first lesson was covering everything that we could do – it was intermediate rock guitar – and the second lesson was again the same thing. I just gave up after that, that was it.
        L: Why did you give up?
        A: I didn't feel that it had anything to offer. There was nothing new, nothing – I don't know, it just, it didn't help at all.

Will was another musician with experience of a dedicated FE course in popular music performance (a course which was awarded degree status two years after Will had finished it). His experiences again do not seem far removed from the way he had felt at school, and there were aspects of the group instrumental teaching approach that he found problematic:

Will	You've got all the other students widdling away on electric guitar. Sometimes I didn't have a clue what they [the tutors] were talking about; other times I just about got it … I think that if you're going to learn about something like music the questions you want to ask are as important as what you're being told. If there's something that you're not sure about – to be uncertain about music, where it comes from – you need to ask questions, rather than just feel terrified …
	… I had a dreadful, one of the teachers at the [FE college] – an absolutely awful teacher – ask a question and he said, you know, 'If you don't understand it you're an idiot', sort of thing! [Laughs] Feel confident to go out tonight and play? Didn't help me. Actually I went back to my school – to my old guitar teacher – because I felt so unconfident about this question about modes, and asked him to explain it to me.
	L: Right. Was it an idiotic question?
	W: No, well, no. I told people afterwards. No one else had understood what he was going on about. He obviously didn't appreciate that.

He then went to university to take a humanities degree, but was able to sit a module on popular music. Andy also took one module on popular music, taught by the music department, which was open to him during his media degree. Here, their experiences were less negative:

Will	At X university we had lessons in the second year which was about the history of rock and pop … We were looking at how the music developed … I think what it comes down to is the teacher. I had no problem in the second year understanding what he said.
Andy	The amount of classical music involved is very minimal and – that's not to say it's a good thing or a bad thing – but it's more to do with modern music. He deals with music, he explains it in a comprehensible way, you can understand him, it's enough. And the terms he comes out with, I mean I've come across them before, not in popular music texts or books, but in classical texts and so forth. That's the only place I've seen them before. But he explains it in such a way that it relates to popular music. There's a lot of terms that I've heard that I've never understood, but now I can work them out.

Disappointingly, some of the musicians' experiences of applying to post-schooling popular music courses led to rejection, apparently without any recognition of their skills and knowledge; and some of their experiences of practical aspects of courses once they had been accepted were quite often reminiscent of the kinds of alienation they had felt in class lessons at school.

The musicians' views of popular music in formal education

Many of the musicians who had opted out of music or who had never felt it was an option in the first place later regretted it.

Nanette   I just thought 'No', and I gave it up in the third year – I had an option to give it up. I gave it up! I can't believe it! Now! Think!

Steve   I could've learned how to read music properly. That's what I've always wanted to do, I've always wanted to be able to read music …

    … I'd like to get better at what I'm playing. I want to have bass lessons, proper bass lessons, just to make myself that much better. But I can't really afford that at the moment.

Andy   … and I just – the progression was so slow in getting somewhere, I just – I gave up on that idea for a while. Which was something – looking back now, I wish I hadn't given up.

Richard   I just wish I'd done music instead of history really.

I asked all the musicians if they thought the incorporation of popular music into contemporary education, especially school classrooms, was a good or a bad thing. The response indicated some anxieties about analysing popular music and/or studying its history. Rob, Andy and Will had reservations about 'losing soul' or 'killing' music with too much analysis or history, and expressed doubts about the suitability of popular music for these approaches.

Rob   We start to analyse, pull it apart, I mean what is there to analyse? It's – pop music in a lot of respects is a disposable item …

    … when people actually start pulling the stuff apart and trying to put some sort of importance into something that: I mean Lennon and McCartney, two guys who are musically untrained (and I am the biggest Beatles fan on the planet, as far as I'm concerned 'Sgt Pepper's' changed my life), but two guys sat together with a guitar apiece and saying, 'What do you think about this?', 'Well what will we do with this idea I've got?', 'Oh that's a good song isn't it?'

Andy   Music history and analysis are like a revelation but at the same time I often feel that you lose some soul …

    … I like to think of it as a puzzle, and if you start unravelling puzzles for people then the pleasure of it is often taken away. The joy is just gone.

Will   … if you attach the word 'history' to popular music you're creating the greatest sin of all. But then how else do you teach it? I mean firstly it's not designed to be taught in the classroom. I think it – you know at the time, in the sixties, if you approached Mick Jagger and said to him, 'Oh, what you doing there with Keith? Great stuff, I can't wait to teach that!' I mean, you can't! I don't know.

Some of the musicians were explicit in valuing the fact that they, and in Andy's case other members of his band, were self-taught.

Terry   I know some people who have been taught music, not drummers, and, er, they're stuck in those confines, do you know what I mean; they can't improvise and things like that; so, you know, it could have also been a hindrance. So I, because of that I've really quite shied away from it, you know.

Peter   I regard myself as being self-taught and I think that's been the best really, rather than being taught by someone.

Andy   I mean again, the singer of our band: to my knowledge he doesn't have such an understanding of music, and I think that's what makes him such a good songwriter. I mean amongst the rest of the band, we'll often come along with songs and we won't want to do them because we think, 'No, no'; it's just, 'You've worked that out too much, it's just too [pause] produced.' But with his stuff we know how raw it is, I mean, unintentional; and for that reason it's excusable and you can use it and it'll sound good.

Berkaak (1999), Lilliestam (1996), Cohen (1991) and Bennett (1980), amongst other sources, all quote similar views expressed by famous and non-famous rock musicians.

Brent was concerned about standards:

Brent   One of my overriding thoughts about the music education that I see [as a peripatatic drum teacher in three London schools] is, I think it's great that they expose the kids to music and they get them involved, but I get some kids come in and I say 'Well can you play? Have you played drums before? Can you play any other instruments?' And they say, 'Yeah I can play the keyboard' and I say 'Well, play me something', just to see what they can do. And they use two fingers and they think they can play. I mean that kind of thing concerns me a little bit ... I suppose it depends on the quality of the teaching as well and how rowdy the kids are. I mean you can't address the finer points of technique if the kids are running riot round the classroom.

However, all the musicians in this study, including those cited above, vigorously supported popular music as a *practical* classroom subject. Here are some short extracts from their responses, to give an idea of the warmth of the response.

Terry   A good thing, definitely. Oh, definitely a good thing, yeah.
          L: In what way?
          T: I mean it's, um, it's like it's the same as having art classes, you know with people painting and drawing and creating like that; it's exactly the same you know, being able to play music – you obviously need the instruments there to do it but you know – it can give you insights into all sorts of things ... music's a whole world in itself, you know.

Rob   L: So when you were saying classrooms can ruin popular music you're talking about an analytic approach, but would you say the same thing about encouraging creativity in the classroom?
          R: Certainly not, no.
          L: You would view that differently. Right, yeah. And performance as well, presumably?
          R: Oh, definitely, definitely, yeah.

Andy   Oh, yeah, definitely. Simon – well he's basically been my best friend since I was 5 years old. There was, um, two nearby schools – there was my school and his, another Catholic school – and they did pop and rock programmes in music education and he was a drummer so that is what he centred on mainly, and I remember going in there to see like – it was for a piece he had to hand in for his GCSE and I was playing accompaniment on it, playing the guitar – and the equipment they had was brilliant, and the whole attitude from the music staff was really good as well. I was dead impressed.
Simon   Oh, definitely, yeah.
Michael   That may well be a good thing because it means that the musicians of tomorrow, the famous pop stars, the rock stars, would have or might have a good musical training and would be able to play their instruments better. That would be a good thing.
Emily   Oh, I definitely think it's a good thing.
Leo   I think it's a good thing … I think it's a good thing that it's being done, definitely.

At the same time, the feeling was expressed that classical music should not be swamped by popular music. From the oldest to the youngest:

Terry   Yeah, but it's good to, it is good to have you know, the more influences the better. I mean ideally it would be best to mix it all up, you know.
Richard   I think it's a good thing but they should keep the other stuff as well. Because you want to have a choice of things I think.
            L: Yeah. So you mean when you say 'the other stuff', you mean they should keep the classical music as well?
            R: Yeah.

In Chapter 4 I thematized the importance for learners of liking and identifying with the music being played. This view came out explicitly in several of the musicians' responses concerning the place of popular music in education.

Terry   Well, music's music isn't it really. I mean any music. But then you can't make people sit down and do or enjoy what they don't like or what they don't enjoy. You can try, but I don't think it works that well …
            … You can't force people to enjoy something that they don't enjoy; you know you can get them into, if they like popular music, get them listening to pop music, like you said, and then take them into classical, you know; but the other way around, it won't work. It's like giving kids piano lessons; that's fine if they want them; if they don't, just forget about it, you know what I mean. If you have a piano there, they can muck about and find their own way; and then give them lessons if they want. But you can't, it's the horse to water thing, you know.
Simon   Oh, definitely, yeah. Because people are interested in it … You know popular music is just everywhere basically and people are interested in it, people do – they buy the records, they want to learn how to play them. [Laughs]
Emily   Oh, I definitely think it's a good thing. I think a lot of kids are like, I mean loads of kids have visions of being in bands and stuff; I suppose it's the most accessible music for them, because they hear it, you know. I don't know that many kids who listen to classical records.

Richard   You enjoy playing something more if you like it, I've found.
Leo   I think it's a good thing, because it's what we're listening to, so it's what we
           want to do, I would think, it's what people of our age wish to create and wish
           to make, so I think it's a good thing that it's being done, definitely.

Bernie expressed his support in ways that were in such fundamental agreement with the others, as well as picking up threads mentioned in earlier parts of this book, that I quote him in full.

Bernie   I think it's great, I think it's vital, I don't think it's good, I think it's vital, it's
          absolutely vital that kids in this very, very strange 'fin de siècle' that we are
          experiencing at the moment, where we have now got the task of throwing off
          the mantle of Thatcherism, of that thinking; we've got to get people, before
          it's too late, we've got to get people believing that there is such a thing as
          society, alright, and believing that it's good to share, that it's not a bad thing,
          and believing that it's not a right thing to want everything for yourself, and not
          to share with others, you know; and I think that through music, through the
          creative arts, they are very much a sharing experience, you know, the whole
          basis of it is interacting with other people, you need other people, you can't do
          it on your own. That's why I think that music education, we need to open it up
          more and more you know, and I think it's great that school – there's nothing
          wrong with the word 'school'; people think [in a drear voice] 'Oh school ' you
          know, but [in an enthusiastic voice] 'Great!' – teaching, education: open it up,
          find out; the kids want to know, the kids are inquisitive, the kids are searching,
          the kids are hungry and you know, that's great. I love these kids, I mean, they
          just want to know, they genuinely want to know, and when you're presented
          with somebody like that, you can't help it, that, anything you know about,
          you'll respond to them.

Summary

In general the experiences of the nine musicians who had taken popular music instrumental tuition were much more positive than those concerning classical tuition, not necessarily because the approaches of the teachers appear to have been particularly different so much as because the learners liked and identified with the music and the instrument being played. Nonetheless, the young players had not necessarily stuck with their lessons. Of these nine, for various reasons, Bernie, Brent, Peter, Emily and Richard had all quit lessons after a year or considerably less, and only Brent had returned to lessons, much later in life. At school, the younger musicians were far more appreciative of the music course than their older colleagues had been. Teachers' attitudes towards popular music were generally positive by the end of the century and had largely lost the implicit denigration of earlier times. Teaching strategies had also undergone radical changes, emphasizing classroom performance, composition and links between different musical styles from around the world and across the vernacular/art music divide. Young popular musicians were able to make connections between many of the skills and knowledge they were acquiring through formal and informal means. In spite of this, from all the evidence so far, their informal learning practices continued unabated.

At post-schooling levels, entry to music courses was blocked for some of the musicians even in the early 1990s, and those who did gain places had experiences which were not always dissimilar to some of the negative aspects of their schooling. Despite this, and notwithstanding some doubts about killing spontaneity, the musicians overwhelmingly supported the inclusion of practical popular music in education.

Notes

1. In Britain, Rock School's grade system for electric guitar, bass guitar and drum kit emerged and gained an increasing presence (see York 1993). The Associated Board of the Royal Schools of Music started up their first jazz syllabus in 1999 (see Beale 2001).
2. See Campbell (1991b), Dunbar-Hall (2000), Elliott (1989, 1990, 1995), Farrell (1990), Floyd (1996), Kwami (1989, 1996), Lundquist and Szego (1998), McCarthy (1997, 1999), Nwezi (1999), Oerhle (1991), Small (1980, 1983, 1987), Stock (1991, 1996), Volk (1998), Westerlund (1999) and Wiggins (1996) for some examples.
3. Some of the most helpful books continue to be Vulliamy and Lee (1976, 1982). For a good discussion relating to a rock programme in a USA middle school, see Newsom (1998). Also see the texts in Chapter 5, note 2.
4. For some good examples of cultural studies approaches to popular music see Swiss *et al.* (1998); for a consideration of the different perspectives offered by ethnographic and theoretical studies of popular music from the point of view of a sociologist see Frith (1992); and for a cultural studies approach to the interface between youth, popular music and education, McCarthy *et al.* (1999).
5. For some excellent discussions of a variety of problems and possibilities presented by the inclusion of popular music in further and higher education in a range of countries see Byrne and Sheridan (2000), Björnberg (1993), Downes (2000), Horn (1984), Isherwood (2000), Jones (2000), Lilliestam (1996), Scott *et al.* (2000), Tagg (1998), York (1992) and York and Pitts (1992).
6. People often use the expressions 'further' and 'higher education' interchangeably. However, technically they represent two quite distinct areas in British education, and this distinction is particularly significant in terms of course provision in popular music. Further education, also known as 'tertiary education', is for students of 16 and over, who are normally following vocational training courses or diploma-level liberal education courses. A few FE colleges run degrees. Higher education refers to the university sector, including music conservatories, and is normally for students aged 18 or over. Higher education courses in music may be vocational or liberal, or include a mixture of both. The conservatories are basically vocational, and the universities offer a more liberal education although specialization in performance at a university can tend towards the vocational.

Chapter 7

The formal and the informal: mutual reciprocity or a contradiction in terms?

The neglect of informal learning practices in formal music education

The examination of popular musicians' informal learning practices, attitudes and values in Chapters 3 and 4 considered some of the ways in which young musicians teach themselves to play music into which they are encultured and with which they identify, through listening and copying recordings, alongside an exchange of knowledge and skills with peers. Enjoyment, commitment, even passion for a wide variety of music run high. In Chapters 5 and 6 I looked into the musicians' experiences of formal music education. These were both negative and positive. On the negative side, the musicians were largely alienated by having to study music or engage in musical practices to which they could not relate and through which they felt unable to progress. On the positive side, they benefited from the acquisition of skills related to notation and technique, familiarity with musical terms and an understanding of theory and the forms and processes of a range of classical and vernacular musics. Whilst the informal learning practices, attitudes and values of young popular musicians do not appear to have undergone any radical changes, their formal music education experiences do seem to have significantly altered, mainly in positive directions, over the forty-year time span represented by the musicians in this study.

To what extent do the formal and the informal spheres of music education and learning exist in isolation from and ignorance of each other? Do the two spheres involve approaches that are irreconcilable, or do they complement each other? If the latter, could they be developed in tandem, without riding roughshod over the nature of either, in ways that would benefit a larger proportion of children and young people? These are the main questions I address in this final chapter.

Informal learning practices and popular music instrumental tuition

Bennett (1980) suggests that popular music instrumental tuition is never far away from the informal learning practice of listening and copying recordings, on the grounds that the teachers will have undoubtedly initially acquired their own skills and knowledge through this means.

> The point is that whether or not the initiate learns from a recording or from a teacher
> who has learned from a recording, the ability to get songs from records is the
> essential process for the transmission of rock music.
>
> (Bennett 1980, p. 138)

Finnegan (1989, p. 138) suggests that learning by listening and copying recordings 'has given the opportunity for a revolution in music-learning processes'. However, it is doubtful that such an opportunity is yet being seized, either by popular musician-teachers or by teachers in other formal settings.

It is not necessarily the case that just because a person learnt to play by informal means, they will then translate their informal *learning* practices into their formal teaching practices. It is one thing to experience a way of learning, and another thing to recognize its feasibility as a teaching method. Indeed, from initial findings in this study, it is reasonable to hypothesize that formal popular music instrumental tuition methods have much in common with formal classical instrumental tuition, and relatively little in common with informal music learning practices. A few popular musicians have come to talk to me after I have given presentations on the research for this book in Britain and other countries. One of their messages can be encapsulated in the following comment made by a British popular musician-teacher. I wrote it down as accurately as I could immediately after the conversation had taken place:

> I sat there listening to your descriptions of how popular musicians learn, and I felt
> like my whole life was passing before my eyes! ... And at first I thought, well,
> what's all the fuss about? At the time it had just seemed so natural. But I teach
> guitar and drums now, and you're right ... yes, that is how I learnt, but it's *not* how
> I teach.

Another said that he did emphasize informal practices, such as listening and copying recordings brought in by the pupil, but felt he was in a minority in doing so.

Five of the older musicians in this study – Bernie, Rob, Nanette, Brent and Will – were themselves instrumental teachers. Bernie and Brent worked as peripatetic teachers in a number of London schools; they, Nanette and Will all had private pupils; and Rob was in charge of bass tuition in his higher education popular music performance course. Whereas the interviews had been designed mainly to elicit an understanding of the musicians' experiences as learners, at the same time issues concerning their teaching came into all the discussions. In addition I had occasion to observe some of the teaching approaches of all of these five, except Brent, in a variety of ways. I attended a conference presentation by Rob on assessment and progression including videos of performances by his undergraduate students, Nanette taught my daughter singing for nearly a year; and Will gave me a two-hour lesson to show me around an electric guitar. I also observed Bernie teaching in classrooms on three occasions.

The dedication, preparation, follow-up and general standard of professionalism in all cases was very high, and commensurate with, or above, what I would expect from instrumental teachers trained entirely within formal music education spheres. But more significantly, not only their standards, but their teaching approaches in general also came across as fundamentally very similar to those of their classical colleagues, in so far as they included an understanding of technique as the necessary basis for musical interpretation and expression; an assumption that the student will practise regularly if progression is to occur; some emphasis on theory, notation, scales and/or other technical exercises; and a teacher–student relationship which is mainly teacher-directed. Some mention was made of allowing students to play pieces they liked, and of incorporating improvisation into the lessons, but these were not explicitly stressed.[1]

From the previous chapter, it seems that in their roles as learners rather than as teachers, some of the musicians in this study also responded to popular music instrumental tuition in ways which were similar to how they responded to classical instrumental tuition. For example, they found the lessons boring, could not relate to the music or the exercises they were given, and had no sense of 'getting anywhere'. Others had more positive responses, but these tended to differ from their responses to classical pedagogy, not so much as a result of any corresponding differences in approach on the part of the teacher, but as a result of several factors that I have already emphasized as having primary importance in learning to play popular music generally. Most importantly, the lessons were not the main means or motivation for learning the instrument, but were undertaken after the pupils had been self-motivated enough to procure for themselves an instrument whose associated music, sound or image they liked, and had already taken steps – a few in some cases, very many in others – along the paths afforded by informal learning practices. Formal tuition only contributed to a relatively small part of the musicians' overall development and was always a supplement to informal learning practices, such as enculturation, listening, copying and working with peers, all of which continued separately throughout the periods of tuition.

During the writing of this book I had an unsought and itself informal opportunity directly to compare two approaches to an instrumental teaching situation: one by a formal music educator and the other by a musician who provides an extreme example of immersion in informal learning practices and who had virtually no experience of formal music education as either a learner or a teacher. I had just bought a second-hand three-piece drum kit for my daughter Sophie, then aged 9. A friend came to call who was an experienced formal music educator, and who had played the drums as a second instrument many years previously. I asked him if he would 'just give Sophie ten minutes' on the kit to show her something basic and help her along a bit. Very kindly, he demonstrated how to hold the sticks, which, seeming to be fairly complex, took up most of the time. At the end of the ten minutes, no music had been made, and Sophie appeared to have gone back a few paces as she found herself unable to hold a twelve-inch length of tapered wood in each hand, something which had previously seemed natural and simple to her. A week or so later Terry called round. With Sophie's agreement, I made the same request of him. The first thing he said to her was 'Well, show me what you can do.' After she had played a simple pattern for a minute or so, he showed her a little up-beat stroke on the bass drum, which was perfectly judged in that it advanced what she was doing to great effect, lifting the beat and giving it more 'feel', at the same time stretching her technically just enough for her to strive, but not enough to put her off. Music-making, enjoyment and a sense of identity with the music all occurred, and progression and achievement were gained. Terry's final salvo was 'Yeah, that's it! Just keep going, and do *loads and loads* of playing. That's how I did it!' Despite his virtually complete lack of experience as either a teacher or a student in formal music education, such a cameo could appear in many books on good teaching approaches. However, even in this case, any suggestion of the informal practices of listening, copying or playing along to recordings was missing.

I mentioned in Chapter 3 (pp. 65–8) that the musicians in this study did not appear to have been particularly conscious of their listening and copying practices as learners, and in Chapter 4 (pp. 103–4) I noted a disjunction between their concepts of learning and teaching, such that something was not considered to have been *learnt* unless it had been formally *taught*. Thus the potential value in a vast range of informal learning practices is liable to be overlooked. It seems reasonable to suggest that many popular musicians, even those who are by and large informally self-taught, tend to adopt teaching methods quite similar to traditional formal pedagogical conventions when they become teachers. Thus many of the central informal learning practices by which these musicians mainly acquired their own skills and knowledge, including purposive, attentive and distracted listening and copying, unconscious learning, peer-directed and group learning may be overlooked by much popular music instrumental tuition. At the very least, formal popular music instrumental teachers cannot be *assumed* to teach their students in the ways that they themselves learned.

Informal learning practices and classroom music education

A similar situation to that described above is perhaps even more readily discernible in school classrooms. Whilst popular music and 'world music' in general have risen to a high status on a par with classical music in the curriculum of many countries, teachers are tending to adopt formal educational approaches towards these musics which hardly differ from their approaches towards Western classical music. This is particularly well illustrated by the use of notation in secondary classrooms. Although the younger musicians in this study found the classroom introduction to notation very helpful in many ways, at the same time, when using notation they often had to *compromise* rather than develop their normal musical approaches or activities, in order to fit in with the expectations of the teacher or the demands of the exam syllabus.

For example, Richard described general class lessons where pupils learnt blues progressions using the single-finger touch function on electric keyboards.

Richard   L: Did you improvise a bit with that melody or [pause]?
             R: No, because it was – you mean improvise on the spot, or [pause]?
             L: Yeah.
             R: No, we, we were taught to go and work it all out beforehand and write it
             down and stuff so we could say 'Look, this is what we've got.'

Michael felt it incumbent upon him to reproduce what he knew were inaccuracies in relation to the original recording of a song, but which were written into the printed notation (as is often the case in popular sheet music). Otherwise, he would have appeared to have been making mistakes.

Michael   The performance in our ensemble was a piece by the Beatles called 'The End'
             off the 'Abbey Road' album which has a little drum solo in it, and I happened
             to have the music for that. So I learnt it by, well from listening to it and the
             notation. And I think the notation disagreed with the music slightly but I played
             what it said on the music.
             L: Because?
             M: Because that's what I was giving in to be marked and Mr R. who would be
             marking, or whoever marked it probably may not know the song and would
             have the music and if I was playing differently to the music I might have lost
             marks.

In order to ascertain how far classroom teachers were conscious of any disjunction between formal and informal teaching and learning practices, and how far they did recognize any distinct characteristics in learning practices related to popular music, in my questionnaire of 1998 I asked 'Do you use the same techniques for teaching popular music as you use for teaching classical music?' Forty out of the total sixty-one said 'yes'. Here are a few examples:

Very similar. As with any project it is devised to develop understanding of something to do with music itself and incorporate listening/appraising, performing and/or composing.

Similar techniques. Lessons usually begin with some listening and appraising, discussion of techniques, whole class practice and small group work.

Similar techniques. I try not to make too many distinctions between stylistic preferences but always aim to get the students to appreciate the different styles and see them in their historical context.

Similar – I teach the way I teach!

I employ similar techniques. Looking at the structure of a popular piece. Listening and appraising a popular piece. Composing using a popular technique.

Same techniques. Following National Curriculum. Anxious to blur any notion of distinction in quality. Only difference is that it is easier to mobilise class performances with 31 in a class – but I think I will try and change this. Tend to be less chronological with pop music but still insist on same high standards.

The same. Music is music!

Same. In fact every effort is made not to distinguish between music types.

Similar techniques – aim to show that there are underlying similarities e.g. tonality, structures etc.

I basically use the same techniques – listen, sing/play, analyse, do. It doesn't particularly matter in the basic outline whether it's classical/pop.

Employ similar techniques. Important for students to see both are of equal importance and worth!

Though not 'modern' we use Elvis Presley's 'Love Me Tender' in Year 7. Taught through listening, notating and performing in a similar way to other more classical topics.

There were three examples of teachers employing notation with relation to popular music, in ways that went very much against the grain of informal popular music learning practices and are comparable with the descriptions of such usages by Richard and Michael above. This was in response to the question 'Do you experience any problems in using popular music in the classroom?':

Yes, sometimes. I find that whatever the compositions, pupils want to add a drum/percussion track (though I don't know if this is a correct procedure or not). At the moment I decided to perform a Sheryl Crow piece 'All I want to do' [*sic*] with the junior 'symphony orchestra' as they were moaning about always doing 'classical' or 'Beatles'. The syncopated rhythms that they 'hear' are difficult now they see them visually. I am struggling with the performance of the music although they want to continue with it!

Yes. Printed sheet music often (1) too high (2) not exactly as pupils know songs from recordings!

Yes. Students will perform by ear rather than by reading music.

Six teachers indicated that they did approach certain aspects of popular music teaching in a different way from classical music. But the differences only occasionally corresponded with any of the informal learning practices that have been considered in this book.

My basic approach/method is constant [regardless of the style of music]. However, teaching different musical styles must take account of particular qualities which define that style. Specific forms of activities may vary accordingly. For example certain styles of popular music lend themselves readily to forms of improvisation, however this does not mean teaching classical music cannot involve improvisation.

I employ similar techniques – although automatic and pre-set rhythms and chords on electronic keyboards sometimes make a difference – because I do not wish any particular kind of music to appear more or less important than any other.

Music is music! Rehearsal techniques for pop/classical music are the same – for performance. For analysis classical music can be/often is different. Perhaps because of the structure of a movement.

Method of analysis is very similar – looking at structure/form, rhythm, texture, etc. Notation different – use of chord symbols easier to understand. More use of keyboard rhythms etc. for pop music.

There were very few teachers who stated explicitly that they *do not* use similar techniques for teaching classical music as they use for popular music. Of the first three below, again, the differences in their approaches to popular music barely correspond with informal learning practices.

Different range of instruments – use of percussion/electronic percussion – sound effects, etc.

Different. Use of IT.

The advantage of pop is that you can teach a lot of musical techniques through it, vocal ensemble, harmony, descant singing, also composition through African techniques which are easier to handle for most pupils – the cell rather than the line.

The next two comments are perhaps more sensitive to some of the practices and values which I would suggest lie at the heart of informal music learning:

The music exists in the memory before any other process – that's a good thing because that's where it can be personally meaningful.

Similar. Very much practical-based activities. Use of improvisation which I use less with the classical work we do. Greater emphasis on experimentation.

Overall, there are grounds for suggesting – always with the recognition of the need for further research – that teachers' classroom approaches are closer to the conventional pedagogy associated with Western classical music than the wide variety of musics in the curriculum might seem to imply, and are generally very different indeed from the self-teaching and group informal learning practices of popular and other vernacular musicians. Whilst mixing up styles and showing cross-fertilization between them can be considered a great strength of the contemporary music classroom, it may nonetheless be overriding many helpful learning practices that are habitually employed outside the formal educational institution.

The neglect of informal learning practices in formal music education

In summary, despite the fact that many popular musicians are now becoming formal instrumental teachers, and despite formal music education's recent inclusion of popular music in schools and other institutions, there are grounds to suggest that the formal and the informal spheres of music learning and teaching continue to exist quite independently of each other, running along separate tracks which may occasionally cross, but rarely coincide to pursue a direction together. Whilst formal music education has welcomed popular *music* into its ranks, this is by no means the same thing as welcoming or even recognizing *informal learning practices* related to the acquisition of the relevant musical skills and knowledge. Rather, the inclusion of popular, as well as jazz and other world musics in both instrumental tuition and school curricula represents the addition of new educational content, but has not necessarily been accompanied by any corresponding changes in teaching strategy.

Several reasons for this situation can be surmised. With relation to popular, jazz and other vernacular world musics, clearly, it would be impossible and in many cases undesirable for music teachers to attempt an exact emulation of informal music learning practices. Formal teaching situations place all sorts of responsibilities on both teachers and learners, which necessitate the adoption of teaching and learning methods that are essentially similar to those that already exist in the formal education systems recognized by the culture, regardless of the style of music being taught. In both instrumental and classroom contexts, unlike in informal learning practices, one or more competent professionals are present and are in authority. These persons are expected to introduce learners to new, relevant skills and knowledge through structured activities. Progression and achievement are supposed to be demonstrable, one of the most convenient methods of realizing which is through tests and exam results. In school classrooms, until a certain age, children and young people are present by compulsion, in large numbers in relation to a teacher, and they all have to work together and follow the same curriculum to some extent or other. Teachers' own backgrounds also provide reasons why informal learning practices tend to be overlooked in the formal realm. On one hand, in the case of popular instrumental teachers, there is perhaps a tendency to undervalue how they themselves had learnt: as discussed above and in Chapter 4 (pp. 103–4) some of the musicians in this study did not consider their own informal acquisition of musical skills and knowledge to even 'count' as learning at all. Also, such teachers can reasonably assume that informal learning is anyway ongoing on the part of their students, making any intervention in it unnecessary. On the other hand, the majority of classical instrumental teachers and classroom music teachers are formally trained and many have never engaged in informal learning practices at all. For all such reasons, formal music education, instrumental and classroom programmes alike, is bound to involve practices that are very different from and even quite foreign to those we have seen adopted in the informal sphere.

In the case of many vernacular and art 'world musics', and much jazz, there are also other reasons why it is difficult or even impossible for Western formal music educators to bring into their studios and classrooms accurate replications of the learning practices associated with many such musics. For these learning practices often rely on the presence of an adult 'community of practice' (Lave and Wenger (1991), and Chapter 1, p. 16) that is steeped in the relevant musical tradition, or that offers apprenticeship training to young musicians, often through a guru but such musical communities and apprenticeships are increasingly rare. The relevant learning practices are also deeply interwoven with the cultural roots of the societies and communities in which the musics have developed, roots that are often very different from those of Western music education contexts and Western societies.[2]

But when it comes to bringing informal Western *popular* music learning practices into formal education, despite the obstacles and difficulties mentioned above, perhaps more opportunities than we realize are already present in the environment. For young popular musicians, rather than relying on an adult 'community of practice' for their musical enculturation and training, rely on two other main resources, both of which are readily available to young people in many countries. One involves their solitary, close attention to recordings of music that they like and identify with; the other involves interacting with their friends and peers. On top of these learning practices, popular music learners have a number of attitudes and values which are not far removed from some of those that are already recognized by several formal music educators. Finally, I am sure that many musicians and music teachers would agree, there are factors in informal popular music learning practices, attitudes and values which have considerable potential to bring about musical and social benefits. An examination of the extent to which these practices, attitudes and values could be incorporated and adapted within formal music education is the next, and the main, aim of this chapter.[3]

Informal learning practices, attitudes and values: their potential for the formal sphere

The suggestions that follow are in most cases *purely* suggestions which I feel it would be justifiable and worthwhile to try out. Many of them arise from a combination of the research and arguments put forward in this book so far with my own experiences as a classical instrumental teacher, school teacher and lecturer, but they have not been formally trialled. I would like to have the opportunity to put some of them into practice and evaluate them in one or more future research projects. For now, they are offered as humble suggestions in the hope that some educators may find them constructive points of departure or discussion.

In some ways the introduction and adaptation of informal learning practices would require teachers and lecturers to be *inactive* rather than proactive, which might be found unusual and difficult to justify; and for many formal music educators, making way for informal learning would take a considerable amount of courage, or even a leap of faith. However, if being less proactive than usual means that educators feel they are learning alongside their students, this amounts to a near-replication of many aspects of informal learning practices which we have seen are habitually employed by young popular musicians.[4] Courage and faith develop with knowledge and understanding, so that the more formal educators are able to observe and join in informal music learning practices, the better we can judge their value and suitability for the formal sphere.

Enculturation, listening and copying

In Chapters 2 to 4 I suggested that whilst musical enculturation is experienced by everyone to some extent, in informal learning practices it is closely interwoven with the acquisition of skills and knowledge involved in making music. Like a central trunk which is always present, it also branches out to affect both conscious and unconscious learning practices, from the earliest experimentation with musical performance and composition, through loose imitation, to close copying and the improvisatory adaptation of music with which learners identify. In this section I will consider the role of enculturation alongside the practice of learning by listening and copying in relation to formal music education.

The principle of learning by listening and copying does not in itself, of course, necessarily rely on the availability of *recorded* music. This practice, combined with close watching, has always been the main means of learning in all folk and traditional musics and many art musics undoubtedly since the dawn of humanity. However, in the present day in many Western contexts, the relative lack of communal music-making in the home and other places where people meet casually, and the loss of the habit of music-making as an activity in which anyone and everyone can join, mean that the circumstances which once provided the grounds on which such live listening, copying and watching activities could take place have been swept away. Recorded music has replaced live music in many contexts, and an increasing distance has opened up between musicians and listeners. For nearly a century, formal music education has turned its back upon the learning practices of the musicians who produce most of the music that comes out of loudspeakers. But perhaps by constructively embracing those same technological developments which many people consider to have alienated music-making, and noticing *how they are used* as one of the main means of self-education for popular musicians, we can find one key to the re-invigoration of music-making in general.

Classical instrumental tuition The nature of the contemporary musical soundscape means that most music which people hear, whether by choice or by default, is popular music of many kinds. Relatively few people, especially children and young people, *choose* to listen to classical music (see the figures for album sales on p. 4). People are not usually encultured into classical music with anything like the same intensity as they are into popular music, and this includes children who are taking classical instrumental lessons. Yet, classical instrumental teachers have not tended to compensate for this situation, and in general the importance of musical enculturation seems to be overlooked. Some teachers rarely or never demonstrate the pieces which their students are learning to play, and even in the case of those who do, the demonstration will often comprise only a fleeting rendition or two, sometimes of no more than a phrase or a few bars at a time. (See Lennon 1996 for research on classical piano teachers' views of and approaches to demonstration amongst other things.) Listening attentively, let alone purposively to one or more recordings of the music being learnt has never been a part of classical instrumental tuition.

From beginner to advanced standard, it is therefore often the case that students will work at a piece, either at an elementary or an advanced level, without ever having heard that piece being played in its entirety by anyone else. How can they be confident in knowing what it should sound like? Not only instrumental lessons, but related activities such as orchestral and other ensemble rehearsals are characterized by the same lack of attention to such listening. Recently I went to a primary school concert in which the orchestra, with very audible support from one of the teachers on the piano, attempted a virtually unrecognizable and exceedingly out-of-tune and out-of-time rendition of Gershwin's 'Summertime', which is in a musical style that is as foreign to children in this country as is any classical music. It was quite obvious that the players had no idea of how the music should *go*.

Many classically trained and formally educated musicians are likely to frown upon any suggestion of using recordings as a central teaching aid in musical performance contexts. The idea would have been anathema to some schools of thought in the past, when it was not uncommon for instrumental teachers to even forbid their students from listening to recordings or live performances of the music that they were learning, for fear that this would destroy their personal, individual interpretation of the piece. Such assumptions, which still exist in a few pockets of formal music education today, are really no different from the 'ideology of authenticity' which was discussed earlier (pp. 66, 103–4) in relation to rock music, and as is also the case in that sphere, they do not appear to be supported by any grounds. On the contrary, an apprenticeship involving exposure to a number of different ways of playing a particular piece, or of a variety of playing styles in general, is just as likely – or surely, more likely – to equip learners with the wider understanding necessary for the development of their own, 'individual' expression. No musical expression can result from unsullied individualism: if it did, it would replicate the primal musical cries of prehistoric humanity and would be unlikely to be counted as music today at all, least of all as Western classical music. Nowadays advanced classical musicians are regularly building programmes of listening to recordings into their regime, in preparation for a performance. Similar activities for beginners might bring many benefits.

Why not spend a few minutes as a regular part of otherwise traditional instrumental lessons, or during school and other youth ensemble rehearsals, listening to a recording or two of the pieces being learnt? Why not set up listening tasks as part of the practice and preparation routine? Why not tape record all or part of the lesson or rehearsal, so that in the event of no recording being available, the young instrumentalist can take home a recording of the teacher playing the piece and perhaps of themselves playing it too? Where no recordings are available, students could listen to other music of a similar style and genre instead, and where recordings are available, they could listen to additional similar music as well. Learners could be encouraged to listen not only as a formal part of their practice regime, but rather to 'have the music on' so that its 'feel' (including classical 'feel') emerges from the background of the home's soundscape from time to time and becomes a part of the child's musical enculturation. Whereas children and young people do not usually choose to listen to classical music, surely, if presented with recordings of the very same pieces which they are learning to play, and with which they therefore have an immediate point of identification, not much persuasion would be needed? Many parents spend hours encouraging their children to practise, but perhaps hours spent with a recording of the music, or of similar music, in the background would have more beneficial effects. (See Davidson *et al.* 1996 for psychological research to support this view.)

Steve could not relate to his classical trumpet lessons at all, it may be recalled:

Steve   Well, it only had three things on it and it was just like, [sings] doo doo doo tune like that, it wasn't worth playing.

But:

Steve   I like every type of music there is ... anything classical – I listen to anything. If I like the sound of it I like it, if I don't like the sound of it, I don't like it – doesn't matter what sort of music it is.

Building into classical instrumental lessons and home environments a habit of listening purposively, attentively and even distractedly to music that is either exactly the same as or similar to that being learnt could perhaps not only enhance children's knowledge and appreciation of a wider range of music than at present, but also engender their own playing with more 'feel'.

Not only could such listening enhance pupils' levels of enculturation into the music they are learning to play, but some classical teachers may be willing to get their students involved in attentive and even purposive listening geared to *aurally copying* the music, as in informal learning practices. For example, teachers could make a recording of themselves playing a piece suited to the ability of the student, and request that the student makes an attempt to either copy it exactly or imitate it loosely, by ear. For pieces that have been originally learnt either by notation or by ear, playing along *with* home-made or professional recordings could be another step. Such approaches could be combined with the imitation of different performances, until the learner finds that socialized and encultured individuality which we call 'their own voice'. In Chapters 3 and 4, I explored the notion that popular performers find 'their own voices', not as a result of some mysterious authenticity or ungrounded originality, but *after* an apprenticeship of close copying or covering existing recordings. Why should not the same happen for classical musicians? If looked at from another less romanticized and individualistic angle than has sometimes been the case, the practice of learning by listening and closely copying recordings can be seen, rather ironically, to replicate a highly traditional and formal pedagogic method, in that it involves obedience to the authority of a 'master'. Similarities between copying recordings and traditional pedagogy are also pointed out by Campbell (1995, p. 20) and Lilliestam (1996, pp. 206–7).

The notion of building listening and copying tasks into instrumental music teaching has been propounded before, perhaps most particularly by exponents of the famous Suzuki method of instrumental teaching. This method stems from the observation of parallels between the natural way in which children pick up their first language and the way in which they can acquire musical skills if introduced to them at a very early age. Attention is paid to touch, intonation, or 'feel', and imitation rather than notation from the beginning. As such, Suzuki principles have certain aspects in common with those arising from the consideration of popular musicians' informal learning practices here. Some of the main differences are that Suzuki and Suzuki-related methods arise from the comparison of music learning with *language* learning, that they relate mostly to the classical field, and that they require high levels of teacher-direction and parental supervision; whereas here I am suggesting comparisons between different approaches to *music* learning across styles, focusing on popular music and with high levels of learner autonomy, peer-directed learning, group learning and choice.

Popular instrumental tuition Children and young people taking instrumental lessons in popular music are far more likely than their colleagues in the classical field to be already encultured into the music they are learning, and to be engaged in a variety of informal learning practices running alongside their formal lessons. However, neither of these conditions can be taken for granted. More time than is possibly the case at present could beneficially be spent during popular instrumental lessons in listening to recorded music brought in by the student or provided by the teacher, loosely imitating and closing copying it, and generally attending to and perhaps giving some guidance concerning whatever informal practices learners describe themselves as being engaged upon. In such ways, links can be forged between the skills and knowledge that are acquired mainly informally and those that are acquired through formal tuition. As the discussion in previous chapters suggests, such links are not always obvious to the learners themselves, who can later feel frustrated by this fact. In short, many of the suggestions concerning the classical instrumental field above could apply also to the popular instrumental field.

Classroom music Listening to music has been emphasized to varying degrees in the history of classroom music education. In the context of the present discussion, it is perhaps ironic that listening is less central nowadays than it was at the height of the 'musical appreciation movement' during the 1940s and 1950s (Rainbow 1989, pp. 74–5, 310ff.), when pupils such as some of the older musicians in this study were required, in a misuse of recommended procedures, to do little else in lessons than sit quietly and listen to 'the classics'. Today, such practices have shifted in order to make room for listening to a much wider range of music and, of course, for engaging in a variety of performance and composition activities as well. However, only in the best practice at any stage in the history of classroom music education has listening to music been integrated with playing and composing (see e.g. Swanwick 1979). Even then, the integration of these three activities has not always meant playing the *same* music as that which is listened to, or even composing music in the *same* styles as those which are being listened to. On the contrary, as Chapter 6 shows (pp. 158–9, 164), the emphasis is more on showing musical universals, common characteristics or processes that occur across *different* styles. Attentive and purposive listening geared specifically to the precise copying, the loose imitation, the improvisatory adaptation or the composition of stylistically similar music by ear, such as popular music learners engage in, do not seem to have featured very much at all in classrooms.

In primary schools in most countries, if music is provided at all, it is largely taught by what are known as 'generalists', who have little or no specialist music training. In Britain and many other countries most primary schools also have a Music Coordinator, whose remit includes the encouragement and guidance of other staff, the development of teaching strategies and curriculum materials, the formation of a Music Policy and Scheme of Work for music in the school and other related tasks. Quite often, however, even Music Coordinators have themselves received little formal music education and, like their generalist colleagues, also feel 'unskilled' when it comes to music. Published research, as well as numerous unpublished MA and Ph.D. dissertations, have repeatedly shown that the majority of primary teachers openly declare a lack of confidence to take classes through even the simplest musical tasks (see Hennessy 2000). Even more worryingly, Hennessy found that those trainee primary teachers who *had* taken instrumental lessons when they were children, but had given them up in the early stages, expressed even more anxiety about teaching music in the classroom than did their colleagues who had *not* had instrumental lessons! Such a situation makes it difficult or impossible for most primary teachers to play an instrument in class, and makes many of them self-avowedly timid or even terrified of singing in front of a class. Small also bemoaned the fact that primary teachers felt they could not teach music because they were not 'trained musicians'.

> The untrained artist has elicited from his pupils art works of all kinds, the untrained writer has had them writing poems, projects, assorted writings, but the untrained musician has been convinced … that he can do nothing to help his children develop that musicality which is just as powerful as the other artistic impulses he has so generously released in his pupils.
>
> (Small 1980, p. 214)

Primary teachers, especially during the period from the 1950s up to the 1970s, regularly used to get children singing along with recordings and broadcasts, but the practice has been frowned upon by trained music educators more recently and is less common at the present time. It does have some disadvantages. For example, because the voices are massed, children are inclined to 'hide' behind the recording so that groaning, singing out of tune, failure to memorize the words, never mind the melody, and other problems can go undetected, whilst the ability to 'sing out' confidently can remain undeveloped. Where materials that have not been designed for children are used, teachers may choose recordings in unsuitable keys (too high or too low for the children's voices). It is particularly problematic to have massed voices in classes of thirty or more children attempting to sing along with a solo recorded voice, most especially where that voice is highly individual or idiosyncratic, thus making most popular music even less suitable for this practice than much classical music. However, if used judicially there are no reasons why copying and singing-along to a recording should not be incorporated into some class singing lessons. It could provide one means for generalist teachers to demonstrate a variety of vocal techniques, whilst dynamics, tempo or metric changes and the general 'feel' of the music will all enter into the children's enculturation experiences.

Copying recordings could possibly be used more effectively for small-group classroom instrumental and vocal work in primary and secondary schools. If a limited number of portable cassette or CD players were available, then many of those schools which already have the benefit of practice rooms, corridors and understairs cupboards where pupils habitually do group work would be equipped with the necessary resources. Those schools that possess popular music instruments, especially drum kits and electric and bass guitars, would be well catered for, but even schools which currently lack such instruments could go a long way with the ubiquitous electric keyboards, as well as a variety of tuned and untuned classroom percussion and, where possible, orchestral instruments brought in by some of the pupils.

As mentioned in Chapter 1, the learning practices considered in this book focus on the field of Anglo-American guitar-based rock and popular music and are not necessarily the same as learning practices in other areas of popular music such as rap and sub-styles, with strong emphases on synthesized and sampled sounds. However, whilst further research is called for, many fundamental aspects of the informal learning practices in such fields are likely to be similar to those of guitar-based popular music. These include, especially, the high degree of enculturation, listening, imitation and experimentation (see, for example, Stolzoff 2000), and in most cases the fact that the learning activities are largely unsupervised by adults. Also, although it is likely that the skills and knowledge needed in many forms of such music are acquired in more solitary conditions than rock, it is unlikely that the learning practices occur without a considerable input from peer-interaction, influencing a variety of factors from matters of taste to types of equipment. For classroom work in which school pupils can engage with such music, therefore, many of the suggestions in this chapter could be adapted. The necessary synthesized and sampled sounds can in most cases be readily supplied by even quite cheap keyboards. A large number of secondary schools now have advanced music information technology, which is already being employed in the creation of various sub-styles of popular music, classical music and many other musics, and could readily be geared to include a listening and copying programme if desired. Scratching and mixing with the use of two turntables would also not present resource problems beyond the bounds of possibility, and would undoubtedly inspire a great deal of motivation amongst pupils in many schools.

The proposal I will make here presupposes that the teacher has already done sufficient rhythmic work for all pupils in the class to be able to play simple riffs, melodies or chords in time with each other. This is not difficult and has been done many times with mixed ability general classes, including ones where none of the pupils take instrumental lessons outside the curriculum. However, I never cease to be amazed when visiting schools in London that this basic, fundamental and virtually universal practice of keeping a beat in a group seems to be overlooked by some teachers – including a few of those with music degrees and years of teaching experience – whose otherwise imaginative projects are ruined by the fact that the pupils cannot execute them in time together. There is very little music from any time or place in the world that does not have a pulse or beat, and in almost all the exceptional cases, whether it is a free improvisation in Indian classical music or an apparently chaotic passage in atonal twentieth-century classical music, the musicians are nonetheless likely to be *counting* in their heads, in time with each other, maintained by eye contact and other means, with exceeding accuracy.

Some children, especially those under the age of 11 or 12, do have great difficulty in keeping a beat, presumably because in most cases they have not been encultured into this practice. However, I have always found in working with children that if such individuals are given a very quiet instrument, or if during clapping exercises they are advised to clap with just two fingers instead of their whole hand, they lose their embarrassment and pick up the feel of the beat within at most three or four lessons. By far the majority of children have rhythmic abilities that all too frequently surpass the exercises that formal music educators introduce to them, a factor which is graphically illustrated time and again by Campbell (1998). She describes the covert music-making that went on during class music lessons in the USA, as children added complex improvised riffs and ostinati to the exercises they had been given, only to be told off by the teacher for doing so! (See Campbell 1998, especially pp. 46–56; also Harwood 1998a and b; Marsh 1995, 1999; Wemyss 1999; and Glover 2000 for similar discussions below. All these writers make pleas for music educators to pay more attention to children's playground games and the musicality they evidence.)

Having established a basic whole-group skill of being able to play or sing to a shared pulse, even in very elementary ways, pupils would then get into small groups and choose a short piece of music for their group (which might take some time and is likely to focus on pop songs but need not). They would then bring a cassette or CD of the music into school for approval by the teacher. In the next lesson or lessons, depending on the precise organization of the project, each piece would be listened to and discussed by the whole class, guided by the teacher. Suggestions, such as how to adapt school instruments or the pupils' voices to approximate those on the recording, which parts are most likely to be difficult to execute, which parts would be the best to start with and so on, would be proffered, thus involving the whole class in purposive listening. The small groups would then disperse into practice spaces, where available, with some appropriate instruments to *copy the recording* as best they could. Plenary sessions and a variety of follow-up work would ensue. Clearly, a practical research project is waiting to be done there. The results are by no means predictable, but I think it is fair to say that indications suggest it would be worth an attempt.[5]

I have engaged on various occasions in a similar activity with MA students of music education, except that it was all done in the space of two hours. For the minority of the students who were already popular or jazz musicians the exercise was merely intended to act as a window on possibilities for working with children. But the majority of the students were classically trained, and nearly all of them, including young, new music graduates from universities in many parts of the world, had never touched a drum kit, electric guitar or bass guitar in their lives, and had never before attempted to copy music from a recording, least of all in a small-group situation. After the exercise on one occasion, Katy Gainham, a distinguished concert flautist and Professor of Flute at the Guildhall School of Music in London, who was a student on the course, commented on her experience of playing the drum kit in her group's cover of Willie Mitchell's '30-60-909':

> It requires a suspension of one's usual thinking. It's the sort of experience I have with any music that is outside my usual sphere of knowledge, such as African music. If I thought too hard about what I was doing I didn't have enough concentration to do it, to keep three things going at once. It's a matter of letting go. It's different to the usual mentality of the classical musician. Nothing can replace the actual experience of participating in it.

Evaluations by other classically trained students have in general suggested that they find this exercise opens their ears and minds to dimensions of musicianship otherwise unknown and unappreciated.

Not only attempts at *exact* copying through purposive listening, but looser imitation through attentive and even distracted listening could also be incorporated into lessons and workshops. For example, the teacher could play a recording, perhaps once, perhaps several times over a span of weeks, depending on the precise aims of the exercise, and ask pupils to then work in small groups at making a piece of music that *sounds like*, but that does not exactly replicate, the one on the recording. Particular features could be picked out, such as helping pupils to notice and imitate a prominent bass-line, an angular melody, the rate of harmonic change, the mode or a huge variety of other characteristics, depending on the piece in question and the ability and prior experience of the teachers and learners involved. At the most extreme, pupils could be simply asked to make up a piece of music that sounds like a sub-style which they identify with. Such exercises could involve any kind of music.

Resourcing The listening and copying activities suggested above obviously have some implications for resourcing. Regarding the listening side, with the facility to record music played by the teacher in his or her own home as well as in institutions, to make recordings from the radio and increasingly, to download music from the Internet or use information technology programmes, the implications for building up supplies of recordings to support teaching programmes of this nature are surely not insurmountable. Once made, the recordings can be stored, used again and again, and are appropriate for individual, small-group and large-group work. Nor is the teacher necessarily the only or the best provider of recordings, for pupils' own recordings can be brought in to supply the most up-to-date material.

Regarding the copying side, as already implied, most schools in this country and many others have a selection of instruments, and although undoubtedly the majority of music teachers would like to have more, current levels would not in most cases absolutely demand enhancement for many of the suggestions above to be adapted and tried out. The main small-scale necessity, which many schools may not posses, would be enough portable cassette/CD players to resource the small-group work. The main large-scale necessity involves architecture, which would be virtually prohibitive where small rooms or other spaces and an amount of sound-proofing away from other classes could not be provided. In such situations whole-group work is the only feasibility, and though not desirable, it is not impossible (I say this from my own experience of working full-time in such a school for three years). Such architectural problems will affect all classroom music teaching in those schools that suffer from them, and really ought to be a thing of the past although, sadly, they are not.

Developing the ear

I suggested in Chapter 3 that the informal learning practices of popular musicians, especially listening, copying and improvising, can lead to the development of what can be called very 'good ears'. Although their aural abilities are not necessarily any better than those of classical musicians, they are likely to be better *sooner* and, moreover, to be possessed by the vast majority of the players involved, rather than the few. The aural work of vernacular musicians in general is meaningful in that it forms an intrinsic part of the 'real life' practices of both reproducing existing music and creating original music, alone and with others. As such, it contrasts with the traditional aural tests of formal music education, which despite changes in the last few decades still tend to involve an isolated individual in describing, analysing, notating or otherwise responding to music which is being used for the sake of the exercise. Improvisation, which is an aural activity *par excellence*, is by no means totally lacking from formal music education and is recognized today in many instrumental programmes, youth orchestras, classrooms and post-compulsory contexts. But students of classical music both in specialist instrumental programmes and general programmes must surely benefit by taking part in a variety of 'real life' aural copying, as well as experimental and improvisatory activities more frequently than they tend to at present.

Practice and technique, discipline and 'osmosis' in instrumental tuition

Whilst a few 'top' classical performers tend to engage in less practice than their peers, in general a high degree of regular, committed practice is accepted by instrumental teachers and other practitioners as being a necessary condition for technical and musical development to take place.[6] Most advice to learners and their parents is that practice is essential, particularly in the form of short regular sessions preferably every day, rather than sporadic sessions with long intervals in-between. For children, parental encouragement and the overseeing of practice is also considered to be of enormous benefit, whether or not the parents play instruments themselves.

Unfortunately in some cases over-zealousness in following such advice can result in scenarios such as those that were examined by Pitts *et al.* (2000). For example, one of their three video-taped case studies involved a 10-year-old saxophone pupil who was more or less forced to practise scales and pieces she hated, including the Christmas carol 'Good King Wenceslas' even though the month was May, for reasons she could not understand, and all under the watchful eye of her mother (see pp. 49–51).

> Singing is an important feature of her practise sessions; after playing a piece in the second session, she begins to sing far more fluently, moving her saxophone with a jazzy swing and pretending to play. It seems that her image of playing the saxophone is conflicting with the immediate difficulties of making a sound and reading notation, and so adding to her frustration with the task of practising.
>
> (p. 51)

Conversations such as the following are reported:

> Mother: Have you done your new scale?
> Daughter: Yes.
> Mother: Have you done it twice?
> Daughter: Yes.
> Mother: And you've done all your pieces?
> Daughter: Yes – twice.   (p. 50)

To which the authors comment:

> Throughout this conversation, the daughter has been shuffling uncomfortably with her back to the camera: hardly surprising as her description of her practise bears little resemblance to the reality.
>
> (p. 50)

Virtually no improvement took place during the periods of observation, but this did not prevent conversations such as:

Daughter: Now have I done enough, Mum?
Mother: Well do you think you've done enough?
Daughter: Yes, I think I'm pretty good at it.
Mother: Okay, that was great. (p. 51)

Pitts et al. comment:

> She is clearly practising under duress, and although her parents are supportive, their exaggerated praise and attempts at monitoring do little to lift the gloomy mood that pervades the practise sessions ... This girl is indicative of the potentially damaging effect of externally imposed practising strategies ...
>
> (p. 51)

By contrast to such scenes, the musicians I interviewed had taken a much less rigorous and more sporadic approach to practice sessions, usually with parental approval but in no cases with parental supervision. Practice sessions would vary from a solid five hours to ten minutes here and ten minutes there, and in most cases a player would go in for different levels of practice depending not only on their life-circumstances at the time but on how they felt. Practice was seen as a highly enjoyable or 'fun' activity and had no negative associations with any notions of imposed discipline. Many of the musicians saw no particular distinction between practising and playing. In some cases this was because their favourite way of 'practising' was to perform in public, on stage, even at quite early phases of the learning process; in others, it was because they preferred to practise real pieces rather than scales and other technical exercises. Some players took a more systematic approach to practice, such as Peter who set himself specific targets. Within one popular music band, there are likely to be as many different approaches to practice as there are players. Cope (1999, p. 68) found a similar variety of practice patterns amongst the primary school children who took part in his very successful project combining informal Scottish traditional fiddle playing with formal music education in a small community.

The development of technique is also placed at a very high premium in instrumental teaching programmes: a foundation stone really, which often forms a focus of attention from the very first lesson. Here, for example, is an expression of a fairly typical attitude, from two classical piano teachers in Greece:

[Teacher 1]
I always use technical exercises: scales, arpeggios and exercises from Hanon or Degliatelle with younger children. I show them several techniques to apply while practising. I insist on their doing them. You see, if you don't have a good technical basis you can't play well. Technique is the basis of good, successful playing. You may love playing a musical piece, you may want to express yourself through playing it, but if your technique doesn't help you, then – Of course, I always keep in mind that children may get bored with all these exercises; so I try to combine them with many other pieces and also I try to make breaks after finishing each

part of technical exercises. For instance, after having taught the major scales, I ask them to stop bringing their Hanon to the lesson for a week or two. Of course during these two weeks, I always try to keep a Czerny or something of the kind in our programme. Generally, I find technical exercises essential, but at the same time I try not to bombard my students with them; I try to keep a balance ... On many occasions I talk to them about technique and I try to explain its importance to them.

[Teacher 2]
As I expected, my students don't want to do their technical exercises. They find them boring! So, I talk to them and I explain to them that technical exercises are the 'medicine' for successful playing.

(Cited in Alevisopolou 1999, pp. 56–7)

The same researcher found that even teachers who explicitly declared that they avoided emphasizing technique, on the grounds that their students found it boring, nonetheless placed a great deal of emphasis upon it during lessons. I have already suggested that popular music instrumental teachers are just as likely to value technique as are classical instrumental teachers.

By contrast, popular music *learners* who are engaged in informal learning practices tend to acquire conscious concepts of technique and to become aware of accepted technical conventions at relatively late stages, if at all, and almost certainly after having already played with a band. We saw in Chapter 3 how some of the players in the present study, of which Rob was perhaps the most extreme example (pp. 84–6), had unconsciously taught themselves enough, or nearly enough technique to become freelance professionals; and had only afterwards discovered or been introduced to the notion that there might be other, more effective ways of doing things – in other words, conventional technique – through watching and interacting with other musicians. Such conventional technique was in several cases associated with classical music, not surprisingly given the longer history of formal music education in relation to that music.

I am sure that many formally trained classical instrumental teachers would share the presupposition – indeed the fear – that having gone a long way down the road of self-styled technique for even a short period of perhaps a year or so, musicians would then find it was too late to change, too difficult to get out of old, bad habits. The fear of this difficulty may be one of the main reasons for the emphasis placed upon developing good technique right from the start in classical practices. But on the contrary, the musicians in this study found it 'easy', to use Rob's word, to convert to a newly discovered conventional technique derived from classical music pedagogy, even at a late, advanced stage of playing. Such openness to and facility with what may be radical changes of technique may arise from the more flexible and less emotionally alienated approaches to practice associated with informal music learning, since learners are less inclined to struggle with activities and habits that have been formed on the basis of volunteerism and enjoyment, than those that have been developed in response to obligation. Cope's project (1999) produced a number of players who were acclaimed both in the local community and in competitions, without their necessarily having paid attention to conventional technique.

All but the most exceptional professional classical musician needs to follow a rigorous practice routine and to concentrate on the acquisition of conventionally tried-and-tested techniques; but the findings in this book and in projects such as Cope's suggest that it may be worth recognizing other approaches to practice and the acquisition of technique as well, approaches which could attract and sustain much larger numbers of people in being musically active and fulfilled than at present. As Cope says:

> Much of the research on practice is concerned with the development of expertise in instrument playing. The problem is that expertise does not represent a realistic goal for most children, not because they are not capable but because they do not wish to commit such a significant amount of their lives to music. The development of competence, on the other hand, is a realistic goal which can be achieved with modest amounts of practice.
>
> (1999, p. 72)

Not only might rigorous attention to practice and technique be unnecessary for the development of such musical facility, but as already indicated to some extent, it can be damaging. O'Neill's work (1997a, forthcoming a) in the psychology of music suggests that children who give up formal instrumental lessons do so not necessarily because they are either 'unmusical' or disinterested, but also as a result of a personality disposition which finds the emphasis on practice and technique, and the continuous assessment regime, punishing and demotivating. Indeed, a number of the musicians in this study, who are clearly highly musically motivated and able, quite exceptionally so in many cases, had given up instrumental lessons for just such reasons.

Strategies to combat such negative results of instrumental tuition could include recognizing that musicians taking instrumental lessons *can* develop to a level where they gain personal and musical fulfilment without necessarily engaging in regular, short, daily practice, and that some of them, such as the older musicians in this study, can go beyond that to develop superlative technique; countenancing the possibility that for some learners, spells of long, uninterrupted or intense practice with intervals of days, weeks or even months between them, might be the best way to proceed; being sensitive to the fact that practice routines and diaries, especially those that have to be filled in by parents and/or displayed to teachers every week, may not be an aid to every learner; being lenient in enforcing scales and technical exercises upon students whose response appears to be negative; and allowing students to play in ways that they find physically comfortable without getting over-concerned that their technique will thereby be 'ruined for ever'.

Liking and identifying with music and musicians: valuing one's 'own' music, valuing 'other' music

I have suggested throughout this book that liking and identifying with the music and/or the instrument being learnt are of deep importance to informal music learners, and many of the interviewees pointed to the importance of teaching music that children like, not only in order to provide what they saw as intrinsically worthwhile learning experiences, but also to motivate learners. Sloboda (1999, p. 451) hints at the possibility of new psychological research demonstrating that the freedom to choose what music one listens to has particularly noticeable beneficial effects on the individual's sense of well-being, and many popular music educators stress the importance of taking students' tastes in popular music seriously (see for example Björnberg 1993, Newsom 1998, also Marsh 1999 and many other texts cited in this chapter).

Introducing popular music into schools is no easy matter (see e.g. pp. 159–60), and when it is supposed to be music that children like and identify with the problems are multiplied by tensions over the ownership of 'sub-cultural capital' (Thornton 1995). Many of the teachers who answered my questionnaires in both 1982 and 1998 pointed out that pupils can view the introduction of popular music as an unwelcome intrusion by an outsider into their culture (see Newsom 1998 for a good discussion of this). Two said that pupils are so partisan in their musical tastes, that whereas they accept music in styles which are distant from them, they cannot tolerate any but 'their own' music when it comes to popular idioms. To make matters worse, arguments over musical sub-styles break out between different 'factions', to use a word employed by three teachers. Even the task of discovering what music it is that pupils like and identify with is not as straightforward as might be expected, especially given the unwillingness of many young people to divulge their private musical tastes (see Koizumi, forthcoming). For the teacher who can nonetheless cope with all the above, there remains the problem of keeping sufficiently informed, resourced and up to date in a fast-changing musical culture which is aggressively marketed at a generation of which teachers are themselves not a part.

What is the point, many people also feel, of teaching music with which pupils already identify and which they already like: surely music education should be about leading pupils beyond their pre-existing parochial tastes into a broader musical world? There is a further assumption that studying popular music in schools will deafen pupils to musical quality. Influential right-wing British critics such as Roger Scruton and Anthony O'Hear argue against popular music in education, on grounds of the music's postulated mechanism, mass production, commercialism or downright crudeness.[7] Nicholas Tate, Chief Curriculum Adviser to the British government at the turn of the twentieth century, implied that including popular music in the curriculum will lead to a degradation of the ability to tell 'good' from 'bad' music. For example:

Schools must introduce their pupils to high culture and help them to escape the growing creed that sees no difference between Schubert and Blur ... A fundamental purpose of the school curriculum is to transmit an appreciation of and commitment to the best of the culture we have inherited. We need a more active sense of education as preserving and transmitting, but in a way that is forward looking, the best of what we have inherited from the past ... we should aim to develop in young people a sense that some works of art, music, literature or architecture are more valuable than others.

(Nicholas Tate, cited in *The Times*, 8 February, 1996, p. 18)

Contrary to such fears and assumptions, from this study of popular musicians' learning practices, attitudes and values, it seems that knowledge and skill of a committed sort in one type of music into which musicians are encultured, and with which they identify, go hand in hand with an enhanced appreciation of musical sensitivity or feel and a capacity to appreciate a wide variety of musical styles (to a degree above and beyond that apparently enjoyed by Messrs Scruton, O'Hear and Tate). There are no good reasons to be afraid of listening to pupils' interests or to prevent them selecting songs with which they identify, so long as *what is done* with those songs gives pupils the opportunity to 'get inside' the music itself through practical music-making activities.

Many music teachers know from their own classroom work that if pupils become involved in the nuts and bolts, the bricks and mortar of music – music of any kind – partisanship begins to fall away and appreciation is enhanced. I have experienced, for example, classes of up to thirty mixed race and mixed sex, 'cool', 'hip' teenagers in an inner London school, rapt in listening to the fourth movement of Beethoven's Ninth Symphony, simply because they had all played the 'joy' theme themselves, together in class, on glockenspiels and other instruments! Such practical musical involvement, when related to music into which pupils are already encultured, with which they identify and which they like, gives them a musically informed ground from which they are more rather than less able to defend themselves from delusion by the machinations of the mass media, from uncritically embracing mechanical commercialism, from being so partisan that they cannot listen to any music but their 'own', or from lacking discrimination in taste. At university level, Björnberg makes the point that even in 'poor music' a certain quality, or what he refers to as 'musicness' (citing Brooks 1982), may be 'discovered precisely through the act of *playing* the "poor" music in question' (Björnberg 1993, p. 21; my italics). Nicholls was also convinced that if popular music is used creatively and practically in schools

... children will find that they are capable of producing more interesting pop music than is sold to them ... This could provide a formidable rival to the 'establishment pop' of the mass media!'

(1976, p. 121)

Finally, listening to and copying recordings chosen by pupils themselves, with the recording as the main musical authority, challenges the dichotomy between pupil-centred and authority-centred education, leaving music itself as the only 'leader'.[8]

Not only is pupils' identification with *music* at issue, but many formal music educators have tended to frown on pupils' 'idolization' of pop stars, and have discouraged 'fandom' from taking up time in the business of education. However as discussed in Chapter 4 (pp. 119–21), the admiration of stars, or the ambition to become a star, could help to motivate music learning. As Campbell says, 'instrumental performance may be linked to particular performers whose appearances and lifestyles children admire; the visual image as much as the sound of the instruments are often motivation for study' (1998, p. 189). Such a view is reinforced by Cohen's observation that for young rock musicians in Liverpool:

> Instruments were valued not only for their sound but for their visual qualities, particularly in relation to the image the band members wanted to present ... The importance attached to them and the dependence and affection bestowed upon them gave rise to a personalization of instruments, each being seen as having its own particular sound and identity.
>
> (Cohen 1991, p. 135)

It is often assumed that children and teenagers accept mass-mediated popular music uncritically and entirely passively. For a powerful counter to such a view see Middleton (1990), who provides a substantial argument as to why it is more reasonable to understand the consumption of popular music as a creative act (a position which is examined in much other writing in popular music studies; see especially Frith 1996). From the educationalists' point of view, Marsh's research on young children's culture leads her to say:

> The impact of popular music on children's musical play in the playground is clearly evident. However, its influence is not entirely hegemonic, but can be seen to be accommodated by children in a variety of ways. These include the interpolation of musical, textual or movement formulae derived from popular music performances into playground games; the parodying of popular music icons in game texts and movements; the adaptation of popular song texts and melodies accompanied by new game movements; the permeation of syncopated rhythmic patterns into game performances and the emulation of popular personae as embodiments of power in new playground games.
>
> (Marsh 1999, p. 9)

(Also see Campbell 1998, p. 186 where a similar point is made.)

For the child and young teenager, the adoption of some imaginary semblance of stardom could turn into increased respect and liking for oneself. Children and teenagers who idolize pop stars are not necessarily poor dupes, but may be going through normal healthy processes of development, in which children's imagination is naturally fired by role models. Stifling and disapproval of such processes by parents and teachers could stunt children's musical creativity, and in turn their ability to discriminate in musical quality and in the personal qualities of stars.

Friendship, taste and peer-directed learning in the classroom

In Chapter 4 I discussed the importance of friendship and shared taste in informal popular music learning practices. Newsom (1998) also emphasizes the importance of friendship and taste in the organization of his middle school rock programme in Los Angeles, and MacDonald and Miell (2000) report research which suggests that pupils' group compositions are judged more successful when the pupils were allowed to work in friendship groups. By contrast to the informal learning environment, teachers and pupils in formal settings are not usually in positions to select the make-up of the teaching group according to friendship or taste. Logically, one could go down a radical road and suggest that, just as some school subjects are once again being 'set' or 'streamed' by ability, so in the case of music we could instigate setting or streaming by friendship and musical taste! So we would have one class for pupils who are wedded to the latest charts vocal groups, another for those whose tastes are more cult-orientated, and so on. In reality, such a proposition could have undesirable results. For example, some groups in otherwise ethnically diverse schools would be likely to end up consisting of only Asian students, whilst others consist of white students and others of black students in a replication of segregation; and undoubtedly in mixed schools many of the groups would end up as single sex into the bargain. However, with sensitive handling, some flexibility of scheduling and a certain amount of compulsion whereby friendship and interest groups had to inter-mix for certain periods of time, such a proposal could bear fruit. Clearly, there is little to prevent extra-curricular groups from being mounted on such terms. Ensembles and choirs characterized by the style of music they perform, and into which pupils can opt if they wish, have existed for centuries outside the curriculum.

Group composition for all pupils, not only those taking specialist instrumental lessons, has become a regular occurrence in British music classrooms and in many other parts of the world during the last twenty years or so. Typically, students from the age of 5 right up to 16 and often beyond will be given a group composition task, sometimes of a thematic or programmatic nature such as 'The Storm', to use a hackneyed example; sometimes of a structural nature such as 'fast-slow-fast' or 'fugue'; or the task will combine these two paradigms. Pupils then work at their composition in pairs, or more typically in groups of three to six, usually returning for one or more plenary sessions at various stages when groups perform their work (thus integrating composition with performance), whilst their peers listen attentively to it (thus integrating listening). Sometimes recordings are made of the pieces and further follow-up work is undertaken, which in the best practice might link features of the pupils' compositions to those of some pre-existing music of a known composer or group.[9]

In the peer-directed and group learning music-making activities of young popular musicians, there is usually no adult cajoling or enforcing the activities, so the musicians have to be individually committed and able to negotiate leadership. There is no significantly more competent musician present who can give instructions and demonstrations of what is needed or tell people how or what to play, so the learners have to provide peer-role models, teach each other and learn by watching, listening to and imitating each other. The nature of the exercise and the choice of music to rehearse are agreed upon, with or without argument, by the members of the group. It is also up to them to choose whether or not they will make their work public, and at what stage to do so. No formal assessment is taking place, although the potential public display of the work and interaction within and between groups mean that informal peer assessment is of major significance. Failure to cooperate is likely to result in the disintegration of the group activities, either temporarily or permanently.

By contrast, group work in the school has a number of characteristics that set it apart from informal learning practices. For example, it is necessarily supervised to some degree by a teacher; the nature of the exercise is nearly always pre-designated, perhaps with some choice between tasks, by the teacher; the students are aware that at some stage they will be requested, often whether they like it or not, to demonstrate their work to others of their peer group, or in a more public context; in many cases, they are aware of being assessed; any misbehaviour or failure to cooperate can become the business of the teacher, either at the request of other members of the group or by accident. In a formal music education setting, it would be impossible to entirely replicate informal peer-directed and group learning practices, nor would it necessarily be in the best interests of the learners to do so. If such replication were taken to extremes, on one hand teachers themselves would become redundant and, on the other hand, riotous behaviour could ensue. Many teachers would feel guilty and irresponsible if they found themselves sitting for even ten minutes outside the classroom whilst pupils worked at copying their favourite recordings through peer interaction and without any intervention on teachers' parts! However, this is how young popular musicians have acquired their skills and knowledge for decades. Perhaps schoolteachers could bring about worthwhile results by standing back a little more than we do in many countries at present.

I mentioned in Chapter 5 how important and helpful it was for many of the older musicians in this study, when their schools, who were otherwise antipathetic to or disinterested in the pupils' popular music activities, made resources, space and time available for them to form bands and even give concerts. Chapter 6 also mentioned some of the positive benefits which can accrue when teachers give opportunities for pupils to 'get on with it' by themselves. Often a sensitive balance here may give the impression that the teacher is not 'doing much', whilst the input is actually crucial.

Emily   Mr C. is generally very supportive of us, he's always been quite encouraging and that. He's always been on at me not to give up the cello as well. But, our music's punk, but punk started up with people rebelling and stuff; but because Mr. C. allows us to play it, then we haven't got anything to rebel against. We don't need to – you know, he's always been, like 'Oh that's really good' and 'You're writing your own stuff' and that.

Every teacher and parent knows that children and young people respond well to praise and encouragement. Perhaps we should not be too afraid to give it, even when we ourselves have not been instrumental in the development of the work that is praised, or when we do not necessarily share the musical tastes and cultural values that go along with it.

Music theory and music practice

Notation has nearly always been at the forefront of classical instrumental teaching programmes, and from the explorations in this book it seems likely that it is also given a prominent position in popular instrumental tuition. Conventional notation is absent from most primary children's classroom education, whilst various types of graphic notation are often used. In secondary school classrooms conventional notation is introduced to many children up to the age of about 14, but in different ways and to different degrees. Most music syllabi and curricula for the 14 to 16 age range require basic notation skills. At post-16 levels any musician studying classical music for a nationally recognized exam is most likely to be expected to read and write notation, whereas those taking popular music courses will be required to read and write notation to varying extents depending on the course they are taking.

Music theory also features to various extents in both instrumental programmes and classrooms. Within the former, theory is often equatable with the sorts of rudiments required by grade syllabi (see p. 128) and, indeed, most British boards assessing instrumental performance require a pass in one of their intermediate theory grades before candidates are qualified to proceed onto the higher practical grades. In classrooms, theory might include the naming of what several curricula, including the English National Curriculum, refer to as musical 'elements'. These include concepts such as 'high', 'low', 'fast', 'slow', 'pitch', 'rhythm' and such like for the youngest children, to the naming of chord and note functions, keys, modes or structural components for older pupils. (See Hanley and Montgomery (forthcoming) for a critical exploration of concept-based curricula in Australia, Canada, the UK and the USA, and Dunbar-Hall (2000) in relation to Australia.)

A frequent cry of teacher-educators is that beginner music teachers (and unfortunately some experienced ones too) engage in far too much 'chalk and talk' related to notation and theory, when they could instead just walk over to an instrument and *play* an example of what they are talking about. A typical instance of such an approach that happens to have stuck in my mind is of observing a secondary school student teacher some years ago, who intended to get a class of 11 and 12-year-old pupils to work at group compositions using intervals of major and minor thirds. As she attempted to explain what a third is, by suggesting that 'you count up from the note you are playing on the keyboard, miss a note, and then play the next note', pupils' eyes began to glaze over; but when she got onto the difference between the major and the minor versions, as relating to 'whether or not another note intervenes, regardless of whether it is black or white, and that when it does the interval between the notes is called a tone, and when it doesn't the interval is called a semi-tone', the class were lost to her for ever more. Why did she not walk over to the piano and play some major and minor thirds; ask pupils to recognize and distinguish them aurally from other intervals; organize pupils into small groups with an instrument per person and the instruction to find some thirds intervals of their own, using their ears, before attempting to make up a piece involving these intervals? It could also have been helpful to supply each group with a recording of some two-part musical phrases using only thirds intervals, and request that these be copied aurally. Listening to music with melodies in strings of thirds would be another step.

The result of an overload on notation and theory divorced from listening and practical application is the likelihood that learners will end up knowing how to name notes on the stave or on an instrument, or knowing the names of musical procedures and elements, but not knowing what to *do* with them independently of any written or verbal instructions. At worst, pupils will learn very little that is meaningful or useful to them, or in Steve's words, they will learn 'nothing at all' (p. 141 above).

For popular and other vernacular musicians, notation is used only as a means to an end, never for its own sake, rarely to analyse music, for that is done aurally, and rarely to learn a new piece, for that is also done, first and foremost, aurally. Even those musicians in this study who used notation as part of their learning practices, put it after the aural experience and as a supplement to listening and copying. Rather than knowing the names of notes and technical terms without being able to use them creatively, as is so often the case for young formally educated musicians, for the self-taught popular musicians in this study, the situation tended to be the other way around: they knew how to put notes together, and how to use a number of technical musical elements including scales, modes, chords, rhythmic patterns, metric changes and such like, but in many cases, especially in the first few years, without knowing what to call them, or being able to discourse about or conceptualize them (as discussed in Chapter 4, pp. 93–6). But what is the point of knowing the names of musical procedures and elements if you can't use them? Surely this is the way around that notation and theory should be introduced in formal environments too: first learners should use musical elements and procedures in ways that are meaningful to them in the practical creation and re-creation of music; then formal teaching should help them to write down what they are doing or what they are hearing, put names to the different parts, and discuss them.[10]

Progression and experimentation: the systematic and the haphazard

Formal instrumental teaching, grade exams and many classroom music education practices from the primary school to the university involve the ordering of learning in a linear fashion. The learner begins with a variety of relatively simple – or simplified – tasks and rudimentary aspects of knowledge, then proceeds logically on to more complex ones. By contrast, the popular musicians in this study taught themselves in ways which were often geared more to experimentation than ordered learning, were more haphazard, and in some of their own words, sometimes seemed quite random. The older musicians tended to feel, on looking back, that 'things had fallen into place' only at a late stage. Whereas there are obvious disadvantages to this, there are also advantages. For example, from early on, learners can use and enjoy musical procedures which would have been denied them by formal education for years to come, such as Michael's relationship with the 'suspended fourth', as mentioned in Chapter 4 (p. 107):

Michael   [My Dad] said 'Well put in this, this F in the C chord here and then make it go down to the E and I thought 'Ooh that sounds nice'. I started doing it all the time after that.

And in a different part of the conversation:

Michael   I can recognize the 7ths and the suspended fourths and seconds which are quite commonly used.

As one reader of a draft of this book responded here, on the basis of his own teenage experience (using slightly different terminology to the classical):

You discover A-augmented–6 because you want to play a Stevie Wonder song; you discover A-augmented–9 because you want to play a Jimi Hendrix song; you discover A-major triad over a B bass-note because you want to play a Carole King song.

(Charlie Ford)

Campbell comments on young childrens' propensities for music learning:

Parents, teachers, and professional songwriters often establish that songs suited for children should be simple in rhythm, sparse in pitch information, and quaint in their texts about animals, friends, and modes of transportation (i.e., trains, boats, and planes). While many of the songs children sing – particularly those perpetuated by adults in their interactions with children – fit these criteria, many more do not. In fact, children's musical expressions do not always fit the adult conception of some universal progression of forms from simple to complex, either (Blacking, 1992). Songs, called 'childsongs', that children invent or refashion from earlier music materials and that they preserve in their transmission to other children (Campbell 1991a) may often consist of greater musical complexities and more diverse texts than those found in the numerous collections of songs that adults have prescribed for children.

(Campbell 1998, p. 191)

On the basis of studying community popular music projects for teenagers, Horn says:

One might argue that chaos activity could be more widely used for the development of creative skills, particularly in our educational institutions. Indeed, an encounter with what might be described as 'moments of not knowing' is a pre-requisite of creative action.

(Horn 1984, p. 116)

Spencer's research (1993) into university music students' opinions of the general music exam for ages 14 to 16 in England (the GCSE) strongly suggests that they found it an insufficient preparation for Advanced Level and university classical music courses, especially due to the lack of background in theory and technical matters which they thought it furnished. The students wanted a narrower focus with less choice and more teacher-directed exercises such as harmony and counterpoint, and aural tests. Meanwhile, evidence here suggests that pupils who take the GCSE music exam as a pathway towards either further participation or further study in *popular* music are likely to be supplementing the course with a high level of self-motivated, peer-directed and group-based informal learning, running alongside but separately from their formal education. Whereas further research is needed, it is reasonable to suggest that not only do such musicians demonstrate autonomy and responsibility for their own learning skills, but also sophisticated understandings of and aural abilities in harmony, form and other parameters, above and beyond those enjoyed by their colleagues who rely entirely on formal education. The field of jazz cannot go without mention here, in which players develop a particularly complex harmonic understanding, often initially in 'haphazard' ways such as those discussed above (see Berliner 1994); and another example is one of the most harmonically imaginative popular music composers of the early twentieth century, Noël Coward, who was self-taught and could not read notation (Castle 1974, pp. 56–7).

In Chapter 4 (pp. 94–104) I examined some of the tensions between viewing informal popular music learning as a disciplined or systematic approach on one hand, and as what Roger Scruton referred to as a process of 'osmosis', or a more natural, and in his terms, undisciplined way of absorbing skills and knowledge on the other hand. A deeper understanding of the apparently haphazard nature of some informal music learning processes and a recognition that there is perhaps 'method in madness' could give teachers and lecturers more confidence to allow learners to experiment, listen to what the learners enjoy and respect what they produce, without worrying too much if seemingly complex issues are then introduced before those that appear to be more primary or simple. This way, learning will be led, first and foremost, by music itself.[11]

Assessment and ability

The assessment of musical ability is perhaps one of the most difficult challenges facing music educators, and the introduction of a wide variety of musics into the curriculum, many of which call for new and distinct assessment procedures, has not made the task any easier. Popular music brings with it performance and composition practices and musical qualities that are relatively new to formal music educators, making it necessary to re-think some established assessment procedures. For example, the wide variety of styles now being assessed makes it difficult or even impertinent to set up standards of performance and composition that are equally relevant across the whole range; teachers and lecturers are unable to keep as up to date with musical developments as their students, making peer-assessment a major area for future growth; the assessment of improvisation brings with it new challenges, such as how to gauge originality as against stylistic suitability, or even how to tell whether an improvisation is a 'real' or a 'remembered' one (see pp. 41–3); and there are many other issues.[12] Furthermore, just as too much emphasis on linear progression might not always be in the best interests of learners, many music teachers, both in classrooms and instrumental settings, as well as teacher-educators and others, would agree that too much assessment can kill music and music learning.

Again some insights into this issue are offered by informal learning practices. Assessment is by no means missing from informal music learning practices. Rather, learners assess themselves throughout the learning process, in relation to their progression measured against their own past and projected performance, that of their peers and that of the models they are copying. Not only do they assess *themselves* in relation to such factors, but they also assess their peers, and they seek assessment *from* their peers. The decision to make their music public, on a stage at school, in a youth-club setting or in a more professional environment, is based on their own and their peers' assessment of how well their music sits in relation to its overall style and with this, the likely expectations of the audience; and of course when they do play in front of an audience, the latter will very soon let them know if the decision to make their work public was a mistake. However, as enjoyment is so much a part of popular music learning, the informal assessment that goes with learning is rarely punitive. In short, assessment is ongoing throughout the informal music learning process and is the total responsibility of the learners themselves.

Instrumental teaching, as mentioned in Chapters 5 and 6 (pp. 127–8 and 151) has developed in tandem with a variety of sophisticated grade exam systems which are in common use in many countries in the classical field, and increasing use in the popular field. In Britain it is the norm for instrumental students to take the exams at regular intervals during the period of tuition, although this is by no means universal. In schools, not only are pupils assessed as part of the monitoring of progress in the general music curriculum, but many school-based extra-curricular instrumental programmes are organized by selection: the most 'musically able' children are offered lessons in preference to other supposedly less able children. But a watertight musical ability test has never yet been invented; and how could one be? When so many variables, including the individual's experiences of musical enculturation, their delight in experimentation (which may go on for a long time before it sounds like music to anyone else), their personal identity and taste, the encouragement of their family and friends, the availability of instruments and of like-minded peers, the idolization of stars, a lust for fame perhaps, or just a desire to make music only *if* or only *because* it is fun, can all affect the ways in which latent musicality becomes manifest.

Voices are being raised higher and higher at the present time in calls for a reconsideration of musical ability, away from narrow definitions which tend to be associated with assessment models derived from formal music education and towards broader, more open definitions, often associated with traditional, vernacular, popular and other 'world' music learning practices.[13] The idea that only a few people are musically able is being challenged by a recognition that whilst some people do display greater propensity and ability in music than others, at the same time the vast majority of people are capable of making music to standards that are competent enough to meet the approval and engender the enjoyment of their communities. Cope's experience in introducing Scottish fiddle playing into schools was that 'parents do not want their children to be classical musicians – they want them to be able to play confidently and competently at social events' (Cope 1999, p. 71). Some of those youngsters who fail and drop out of formal music education – such as so many of the musicians in this study – are nonetheless able to develop acceptable levels and in some cases high levels of musical skill and knowledge through informal means. Formal music education, far from making this apparent, has tended to recognize and reward only certain aspects of musical ability, often in relation to certain styles of music, thus aiding the appearance that only a minority of human beings have musical ability.

Competitiveness and definitions of success

One result of too much emphasis on assessment and on measuring musical ability is the unintentional fostering of a competitive ethos where kudos is gained by being 'the best' or 'better than' most other people. Originally instrumental tuition in the West took place in the community, in convents and monasteries, and in the home, where during the eighteenth and nineteenth centuries it became part of a general, liberal education, especially for middle- and upper-class girls. During the nineteenth century such tuition became established within general and specialist educational institutions, where it has developed an increasing association with the production of professional classical musicians and music teachers. Meanwhile the majority of learners, of course, do not become professional musicians, and even those who become qualified music teachers are too often regarded as 'second class' when it comes to musicianship.[14] The vast majority of people who have received instrumental or vocal lessons as children and young people find themselves in the position of ultimately 'not succeeding'; and beginners can visualize themselves at the bottom of a very long ladder, the top of which they know will always be out of reach.

O'Neill (forthcoming a and b) shows how low the self-esteem of young classical musicians can drop when intense competitiveness is felt, and Lamont (forthcoming) suggests similar problems concerning children's identities as musicians within the primary school. Higher up the educational ladder, two ethnographic studies of music in higher education contexts in the United States, Kingsbury (1988) and Nettl (1995), although approaching their topic from different angles, present a worrying picture of the competitive ethos that tends to mark such courses, which will, I am sure, be recognized by lecturers in many other countries. Kingsbury suggests that the traditional conservatory model of classical instrumental and vocal training is based upon an anomaly: that talent is something which students must strive to attain, whilst at the same time being something that one can only be born with, and which therefore cannot be attained by striving. 'Thus we arrive at the paradoxical fact that musical talent is that which can't be taught to the few who can be taught it' (Kingsbury 1988, p. 82). Living with this contradiction is a source of stress for classical musicians, especially in environments where their skills are continually put to the test by formal assessment routines or the threat of losing one's job. Whilst he is uncomfortable about appearing to be critical, Nettl nears the end of his book with a description of university music departments as

...institutions that abound in conflict and inequality, in which population groups and their musical surrogates constantly jockey for position, in which little is said that does not make comparative evaluations and where everyone keeps score.

(1995, p. 144)

Other stresses concerning the norms of classical musical performance (a subject also discussed by Kingsbury and Nettl) can be illustrated by one example from a musician in the current study. In the world of classical music there is a postulated 'ideal sound' towards which all performance is geared, and against which it is measured. To re-quote Nanette from Chapter 5, p. 130:

Nanette   ... it's the actual sound, it's getting that sound, because either you've got that classical sound, either it is a real classical sound or it isn't anything, whereas in pop you've got a sound and it's not compared on those terms. After one term, what I've picked up is that the most important thing about classical music is not only the dexterity that you show, but it's the actual sound ...
        ... So it's, yeah, it's interesting. Ultimate challenge really: must be because if that's supposed to be a pure sound, if that's supposed to be, you know, the world recognises this sound as 'the' sound, it's quite a thing to actually try and achieve, do you know what I mean, it's quite a high goal.

Whereas the emphasis on achieving the 'right' tone quality or colour is in itself a beautiful aspect of classical music-making, it is also accompanied by some disadvantages: in particular, that in pursuing an ideal sound, idiosyncracy must be controlled and is nearly always considered to be 'wrong', there being only a few geniuses whose personal touch has ever been celebrated as such.

Several formal music education environments, from the youth orchestra to the conservatory, seem (without any ill intentions on the part of formal educators) to encourage attention to the relative skill or ineptitude of other students, rather than to any intrinsic enjoyment in making music. Even though some of the younger musicians in this study harboured dreams of stardom, they were quite clear that they became involved in popular music primarily for the sake of enjoyment. They were unwilling to appear critical of their friends and peers, and apparently quite prepared to admit their own defects. As Emily said:

Emily   ... it's quite frustrating when people don't get things which seem quite obvious to you but, because I'm not really that good I can't really stand there and judge them, their technique.

Informal practices are not only a window into alternative methods of learning and making music, but they increase the possibility of producing musical styles whose spoken and unspoken ideals and assumptions are more attainable, more vernacular, more celebratory of the performer's personal tone, more collaborative and which are primarily led by enjoyment and love of music and music-making.

Popular music in post-compulsory music courses

My main concerns in this book have been with instrumental tuition and classroom music education. Many of the points and suggestions raised in the present chapter would not be pertinent to post-compulsory popular music courses, where there is an integration of theory and practice, and higher levels of, for example, peer-interaction, group assessment, copying, aural and improvisatory work. But earlier in the book three issues arose concerning post-schooling popular music courses, as a result of topics covered in the lives of the musicians whom I interviewed, which are perhaps worth picking up at this point.[15]

First, three of the ten musicians over the age of 18 in my sample had negative experiences of applying to higher education music courses, even those which advertised themselves as involving popular music. If universities and other post-compulsory institutions aim to provide popular music courses or modules, they must surely develop admissions procedures that involve valid and reliable ways of assessing the suitability of applicants according to the knowledge and skills which popular musicians are likely to have gained through informal learning practices, rather than, as in the cases of Brent and Andy (p. 169–70), asking them to undertake tasks which they had already declared themselves unable to perform. Second, three others of the musicians had negative experiences, not of applying to but of taking further education courses. Should further and higher education music courses attract and cater for those students who are already set to benefit from formal music education, all well and good; but should they at the same time conspire to alienate those same individuals who are already responding negatively to formal music education, but whose response can by no rational means be taken to reflect any lack of personal musical ability and commitment, then this suggests that their approaches may negate or threaten, rather than develop and celebrate, the practices, attitudes and values which learners adopt in the informal sphere.

Third, many further and higher education courses are highly vocational in nature. Whilst vocationalism is clearly helpful for some students, too much emphasis on it will lead to a replication of the competitive ethos and the loss of enjoyment of music-making that tends to have characterized some classical music educational environments. There are also ethical considerations: as Jones (2000, pp. 14–15) observes, courses that are centrally geared to vocationalism can mislead students, who find the 'real world' of the music industry less available to them on finishing the course than they had expected when they began it. Most importantly perhaps, surely musicians and music teachers of all kinds are in a strong position to *resist* the music industry's power to dictate commercially driven notions of musical success and failure. The benefits of formal music education for young popular musicians must be measured in terms far beyond securing them a position inside the music industry. Nowadays, with the notion of 'key' and 'transferable' skills, as discussed in the section below, there is in any case far less need for courses to be explicitly vocational, and far more recognition that they provide a wide range of skills, many of which are intrinsically worthwhile.

Shared practices, attitudes and values

Many musical practices are generally accepted as worthwhile within formal music education circles. These include placing emphasis on 'feel' and musical sensitivity; encouraging *all* pupils not only to listen to music but to perform, and in many countries, also to compose, individually and in groups; integrating listening, performing and composing; listening attentively to a range of music, widening musical tastes and enhancing appreciation. Several claims concerning musically related attitudes and values are also agreed by a number of music educators, and are often put forward in support of instrumental programmes and classroom music in schools, particularly by writers and practitioners who aim to equip schoolteachers with justifications for their 'aesthetic' subject in an educational world that is increasingly obsessed with vocationalism. Such claims include the suggestion that music education enhances pupils' sense of pride and self-esteem; increases pupils' opportunities to gain pleasure and enjoyment from music and from the activity of learning; develops a number of 'key' and 'transferable skills', including communication skills, the ability to cooperate in a group, commitment, reliability, responsibility, punctuality, self-discipline, problem-solving skills, sensitivity to others and many more.[16] Such outcomes are considered especially helpful for children who cannot shine at more academic school subjects or who are disaffected. The entire life and morale of a school can be seen to be uplifted by a rich calendar of musical events, especially when pupils of all ages and abilities feel they are welcome to join in as active participants.

We have seen that, far from being foreign or running counter to informal popular music learning, such practices, attitudes and values are wholly shared by popular musicians, not only as ideals but in many cases as realities and necessities of their learning environment; and undoubtedly this has been the case in many vernacular music learning contexts for thousands of years. A wellspring of agreement already exists between the formal and the informal spheres of music teaching and learning; only the recognition of such agreement, and its articulation in teaching and learning contexts, are in their early stages.

What can teachers do?

There are many possibilities ahead, and much research to be done. But perhaps one of the most needed and most helpful ways to move forwards, for those teachers who believe in the potential of informal popular music learning practices, but who have *not* had personal experience of them, is to put themselves into the position of young popular musicians, and try out some informal learning practices for themselves.

In the case of teachers who are classically trained, this could involve, for example, purposive listening to a recording of music that they like, along with exact copying or looser imitation, either on an instrument that they can already play or one that is new to them. It could also involve attempts to reproduce music known through enculturation, in the absence of a recording to copy. During the time that I was working on the present book I occasionally undertook such tasks, not as a formal part of the research but for my own interest as a classically trained musician. In the process, I experienced a heightening of enjoyment and satisfaction in music-making, as well as significant improvements to my aural and improvisatory abilities. I think the main cause of the improvements was that, although such activities were not completely new to me, the research gave me greater confidence in what I was doing. I became less worried and put off by mistakes, more prepared to explore and less concerned to have a theoretical understanding of the harmonies, modes or other aspects of the music I was playing. With this new confidence and relative lack of inhibition, I found myself persisting with tasks, especially ones I was uncertain about, for longer than previously, and improvements soon began to occur above and beyond what I would have expected. Not only music-making itself, but also listening was enhanced, as such activities are tremendous ear-openers to a range of musical details and increase appreciation of the technique and 'feel' of the musicians being copied. They opened my ears far more than I had anticipated, to nuances, harmonies, voicings, timbre, mix and many subtleties on the original recordings. Björnberg, another classically trained musician and lecturer, made a similar point cited earlier (p. 201) when he wrote that the 'musicness' of even apparently 'poor' music may be discovered through playing the music oneself, adding 'as borne out by my own personal experience' (Björnberg 1993, p. 21).

Not only teachers who are trained musicians, but primary generalists who have little or no background in either informal music learning practices or formal music education, and who feel committed to music in their classrooms, may also benefit from trying out some informal learning practices for themselves. Such practices might include purposive listening, copying, and singing or playing along to records, even if at first this means little more than tapping a rhythm on the furniture. Again, further research is required to ascertain the feasibility and efficacy of this proposal, but it seems at least reasonable to suggest that such practices could enhance the confidence and enjoyment of many generalist teachers regarding music, help them to develop a more relaxed attitude towards music-making with children in their classes, and put them in touch with children's own music-making practices. For those music teachers who are popular musicians and who acquired their own skills and knowledge informally, noticing how they went about their own learning, respecting it and encouraging many aspects of it in their own pupils, alongside the added benefits of formal music education, should perhaps be regarded as a normal part of their teaching methods.

Formal music education and informal music learning have for centuries been sitting side by side, with little communication between them. On one hand, informal music learning practices have missed out on some of the skills and knowledge which formal music education can help learners to develop. As indicated by the musicians in this study, and as several others have told me, many popular musicians feel keenly their lack of formal education. They would like to be able to read music as well as improvise and play by ear; they would like to know a variety of technical terms. On the other hand, formal music education has not always enhanced either the music learning or the enjoyment of those who experience it and has often turned even highly motivated young popular musicians, and undoubtedly other potential musicians, away. By opening out our understanding that there are a multitude of ways in which to acquire musical skills and knowledge, surely we can reach out to more learners and reveal a much higher number of people with the capacity to make music for their own pleasure, a larger proportion of learners who would warrant being 'counted as musical' within formal settings, and a more open attitude towards music-making both on the part of those who specialize in it and on the part of amateur networks of families, friends and others in the community.

Playing music of one's own choice, with which one identifies personally, operating both as a performer and a composer with like-minded friends, and having fun doing it must be high priorities in the quest for increasing numbers of young people to benefit from a music education which makes music not merely available, but meaningful, worthwhile and participatory. Not only do identity, friendship and enjoyment go hand-in-hand with motivation, but they are also intrinsically and unavoidably connected to particular ways of learning: playing by ear, making both close copies and loose imitations of recordings by professional musicians who are respected and admired, transforming what is 'picked up' into a piece of music, improvising, jamming and composing with friends, attempting to create music that both fits in with and is distinct from the sounds one enjoys hearing around, eschewing any necessary concern with regular practice or with technique, and working with peers in the absence of a teacher, lecturer, curriculum, syllabus or system of assessment. The values that accompany such practices emphasize not only cooperation and teamwork, but 'feel', 'spirit' and idiosyncrasy, which are applauded at a level beyond the recognition of 'correct' technique or correspondence with formalized criteria; the development of passion for music; a broad knowledge, understanding and appreciation of a variety of music; commitment and the capacity to gain enjoyment and satisfaction from playing even the simplest music with friends. Surely formal music educators can create a teaching culture which recognizes and rewards such practices and such criteria of success, in the hope of some future day, restoring to people what is already ours: practical musical involvement for the majority.

Notes

1. The case of Rob's HE course is different here, in so far as the course went beyond instrumental tuition as such and was therefore able to incorporate such activities to a greater extent than is usually the case in one-to-one or small-group instrumental tuition. Post-compulsory popular music courses fall outside the sphere of interest in the present discussion but will be alluded to briefly later on.
2. As I mentioned in Chapter 1, a number of researchers are nonetheless taking different 'world music' learning practices into formal spheres, and formal education is benefiting from this work. An excellent example of the introduction of informal learning methods combined with formal music education, involving traditional Scottish fiddle playing rather than popular music, is available in Cope (1999); also see Cope (1998), Cope and Smith (1997), and for a not-dissimilar project in Brazil, Oliveira (2000). Also see Beale (2001) and the texts in Note 2, p. 176.
3. For some perspectives and beliefs that are in fundamental agreement with those put forward here, see Björnberg (1993), Byrne and Sheridan (2000), Campbell (1998, 1995), Cope (1999), Dunbar-Hall and Wemyss (2000), Glover (2000), Hargreaves (1994), Harwood (1998a and b), Herbert and Campbell (2000), Horn (1984), Lilliestam (1996), Marsh (1999), Newsom (1998), Small (1980, 1987), Stålhammer (2000), Vulliamy and Lee (1976, 1982), Wemyss (1999) and many others cited in this book and elsewhere.
4. Björnberg (1993) provides an illuminating discussion of a university-level course in Denmark in which lecturers were often learning alongside their students, with a number of beneficial effects; Horn (1984, p. 121f.) discusses the advantages of 'non-directive leadership' in community music education provision for teenagers in the UK; Byrne and Sheridan (2000) discuss and give examples of successful pupil-led projects in school classrooms; and many years ago Vulliamy and Lee (1976, pp. 2f., 50–5) and Nicholls (1976, pp. 123–32) put forward reasons why a dialogic approach in which teachers are willing to learn from pupils has benefits in classrooms.
5. Whilst this book was being printed I have carried out such a project with the Head of Music, Paul Newbury, in a London secondary school with, so far, positive and interesting results. See Byrne and Sheridan (2000, pp. 53–4) for some observations of classroom practices in Scotland, which are very much akin to the suggestions above, particularly one example where pupils in a small group were copying a recording by ear. Such practices are more common in post-compulsory settings; e.g. see Horn (1984).
6. For research and discussion on classical musicians' practice routines and their efficacy, mostly within the psychology of music and music education, see Hallam (1998) for a general introduction geared towards instrumental teachers and parents; Jorgensen and Lehman (1997) for a variety of perspectives; Sloboda and Davidson (1996), Sloboda *et al.* (1996), and the debate between Sloboda and Howe (1991), Gagné (1999) and Sloboda and Howe (1999). See Hallam (1997a) and Pitts *et al.* (2000) for discussion and advice on practice for young classical instrumentalists, some aspects of which accord with suggestions here that are derived from popular music informal learning practices.
7. Most of the relevant source texts by these authors are in the British national press: see Gammon (1999) and Shepherd and Vulliamy (1994) for quotes and discussion; also Scruton (1998) for a fully laid-out position. Some popular musicians such as Cole Porter and the Beatles meet with approval on the grounds that they adopt procedures recognizably similar to those one would expect to find in classical music. For an overview and response to similar debates in the USA see Herbert and Campbell (2000).

218HOW POPULAR MUSICIANS LEARN

8. The importance of practical participation in classroom music education has been argued by large numbers of researchers from Small (1980, 1987) to Elliott (1995), Campbell (1998, esp. p. 187), Swanwick (1979, 1988, 1994) and many others. Yet participation in popular music has been slow off the mark, and participation in popular music informal learning practices even slower.

9. See Morgan et al. (1997/8), Burnard (2000a and b) for some research on small-group composition in primary schools. See National Foundation for Educational Research (2000) and various articles in journals such as the *British Journal of Music Education, Music Educators' Journal, Music Education Research, Journal for Research in Music Education, International Journal of Music Education* for discussions and examples of primary and secondary children doing small-group composition work in classrooms.

10. See Downes (2000) and Lilliestam (1996, p. 14f.) for helpful discussions of the interface between theory and practice in higher education rock/popular music courses in Australia and Sweden respectively.

11. Calls for music educators to encourage experimentation and improvisation, and to allow students to be led by their imaginations are echoed in several texts already cited, including Bailey (1992 or 1996), Byrne and Sheridan (2000), Davidson and Smith (1997), Ford (1995), Glover (2000), Pitts *et al.* (2000) and Small (1980); also see Barrett (1996).

12. I consider some of the issues involved at secondary school level in Green (1990 and 2000). See Scott *et al.* (2000) for a discussion of findings from a research project on assessment in higher education popular music courses (there is also an accompanying CD-ROM of materials). Standard popular music analytic texts discuss or reveal many of the problems presented including Moore (1993), Brackett (1995), Walser (1993); and see especially Chapter 4 of Middleton (1990).

13. Blacking (1976) is one of the most renowned and passionately argued examples. Also see Small (1980, 1987), Campbell (1998, pp. 169–71), Cope and Smith (1997), Cope (1999, p. 71) and Sloboda (1985, pp. 11–23, and 1999); and see the provocative discussions between Sloboda and Howe (1991, 1999) and Gagné (1999); and also between Sloboda *et al.* (1994) and the responses by Davies (1994), Hargreaves (1994), Radford (1994) and Torff and Winner (1994). For considered studies of how talent and ability are constructed in higher education music settings in the USA see Kingsbury (1988) and Nettl (1995).

14. 'Those who can, do; those who cannot, teach' must be one of the most erroneous phrases ever coined about teachers. Not only does it suggest that teaching amounts to doing nothing and is devoid of skills, but the implication that teachers are in this case 'failed musicians' is often very far from the mark. Many students at the Institute of Education where I work, and I am sure at other similar institutions across the world, have decided to give up often high-flying performing careers to devote themselves to a vocation that they personally find more stimulating and worthwhile.

15. The following texts provide some excellent discussions of the problems and possibilities presented by the inclusion of popular music in further and higher education courses in a range of countries: Björnberg (1993) in relation to Denmark, Lilliestam (1996) in relation to Sweden, Tagg (1998) in relation to Sweden and the UK, Downes (2000) in relation to Australia, and Jones (2000), Scott *et al.* (2000), York (1992) and Horn (1984) in relation to the UK. Isherwood (2000) is proceedings from a conference on popular music in higher education, at which delegates from many countries were present.

16. See Merriam (1964) for a discussion of the breadth of skills and knowledge that can be developed by musical practices. In music education, see Hancox (1982, p. 239), Campbell (1998, pp. 175–8), Cope (1998, p. 240) and Horn (1984, p. 115).

Appendix: Summary profiles of the musicians

Table 1   Instruments and main music activities at the time of the interviews, 1998–9[1]

Name	Age	Main instrument(s)	Main musical activities
Bernie Holland	50	**Guitar** Bass, Drums Keyboards, Perc.	Session Composer/arranger
Terry Ollis	46	**Drums**	Originals band Covers bands
Rob Burns	45	**Bass** Guitar	Session Composer/arranger
Nanette Welmans	38	**Voice**	Session/covers/ originals bands/ composer
Brent Keefe	34	**Drums**	Freelance/session
Peter Williams	27	**Bass**	Covers/originals bands
Will Cragg	23	**Guitar** Drums, Bass Voice	Covers bands
Steve Popplewell	21	**Bass** Guitar	Originals band
Simon Bourke	19	**Drums** Guitar, Bass	Originals band
Andy Brooks	19	**Guitar** Sax	Originals band
Michael Whiteman	17	**Drums** Guitar, Keyboard	Covers/originals band
Emily Dicks	16	**Guitar**	Rehearsal band
Richard Dowdall	15	**Guitar** Bass, Drums	Rehearsal band
Leo Hardt	15	**Keyboard** Sax, Voice Guitar, Bass	Planning a band

1. The main instrument for each person is shown in bold. Many of them had also played other instruments which they had given up: these are not shown here but are discussed in the text.

Table 2   Instrumental lessons and grade exams taken at the time of the interviews, 1998–9[1]

	Classical lessons	Popular lessons	Practical grades	Theory grades
Bernie	–	Guitar	–	–
Terry	–	–	–	–
Rob	Trumpet Piano	–	Bass Guitar Grade VIII 1994, aged 41	Grade VII c. 1974, aged 21
Nanette	Voice Piano	–	–	–
Brent	Piano	Drums	Piano Grade III 1981, aged 18	Grade VI 1981, aged 18
Peter	–	Guitar	–	–
Will	–	Guitar	–	–
Steve	Trumpet	–	–	–
Simon	Percussion Piano	Drums	Percussion Grade IV 1994, aged 15	–
Andy	Guitar	–	–	–
Michael	Piano Percussion	Drums	Piano Grades I–IV 1988–90, aged 10–12	
Emily	Cello Piano	Guitar	Cello Grades I–IV 1993–8, aged 10–15	– –
Richard	–	Guitar	–	–
Leo	Violin	Saxophone	–	–

1. Not all the instruments played by each musician are shown here (for example, as well as the guitar, Bernie played the bass, drums, keyboards and percussion, all of them professionally on occasions) but only those instruments on which lessons were taken.

Bibliography

Alevisopolou, Antigoni (1999) 'Piano pedagogy in contemporary Greece', unpublished MA Dissertation, University of London Institute of Education.

Associated Board of the Royal Schools of Music (1994), (1997), (2000) *Making Music: The Associated Board Review of the Teaching, Learning and Playing of Musical Instruments in the United Kingdom*, London: The Associated Board of the Royal Schools of Music.

Bailey, Derek (1992) *Improvisation: Its Nature and Practice in Music*, 2nd edition, New York: Da Capo Press.

———— (1996) 'Classroom improvisation' (a reprint of part of Bailey 1992) in Gary Spruce (ed.) *Teaching Music*, London and New York: Routledge in association with the Open University.

Baily, John (1999) 'Ethnomusicological perspectives on Sawyer's ideas', *Psychology of Music*, vol. 27, no. 2.

Barrett, Margaret (1996) 'Music education and the natural learning model' in Gary Spruce (ed.) *Teaching Music*, London and New York: Routledge in association with the Open University.

Bayton, Mavis (1990) 'How women become musicians' in Simon Frith and Andrew Goodwin (eds) *On Record: Rock, Pop and the Written Word*, New York: Goodwin, Pantheon Books.

———— (1993) 'Feminist musical practice: problems and contradictions' in Tony Bennett, Simon Frith, Lawrence Grossberg, John Shepherd and Graeme Turner (eds) *Rock and Popular Music: Politics, Policies, Institutions*, London and New York: Routledge.

———— (1997) *Frock Rock: Women Performing Popular Music,* Oxford: Oxford University Press.

Beale, Charles (2001) 'From jazz to jazz in education: an investigation of differences between player and educator definitions of jazz', unpublished Ph.D. thesis, London University Institute of Education.

Becker, Howard (1963) *Outsiders,* New York: Free Press of Glencoe; MacMillans.

Bennett, Andrew (1997) '"Going down the pub!" The pub rock scene as a resource for the consumption of popular music', *Popular Music*, vol. 16, no. 1, pp. 97–108.

Bennett, H. Stith (1980) *On Becoming a Rock Musician,* Amherst: University of Massachusetts Press.

———— (1983) 'Notation and identity in contemporary popular music', *Popular Music Yearbook* 3, Cambridge: Cambridge University Press, pp. 215–34.

Berkaak, Odd Are (1999) 'Entangled dreams and twisted memories: order and disruption in local music making', *Young: Nordic Journal of Youth Research*, vol. 7, no. 2, pp. 25–42.

Berliner, Paul (1994) *Thinking in Jazz: The Infinite Art of Improvisation*, Chicago: Chicago University Press.

Björnberg, Alf (1993) '"Teach you to rock?" Popular music in the university music department', *Popular Music*, vol. 12, no. 1.

Blacking, John (1976) *How Musical is Man?*, London: Faber.
————— (1985) 'Versus Gradus Novos Ad Parnassum Musicum: Exemplum Africanum' in D. P. McAllester (ed.) *Becoming Human Through Music*, Reston: MENC: The Western Symposium 1984, Connecticut.
————— (1992) 'Theory and method: the biology of music-making' in Helen Myers (ed.), *Ethnomusicology: An Introduction*, New York: W. W. Norton, pp. 301–4.
Bowman, Rob (1995) 'The Stax sound: a musicological analysis', *Popular Music*, vol. 14, no. 3, pp. 285–320.
Brackett, David (1995) *Interpreting Popular Music*, Cambridge: Cambridge University Press.
Brewer, Roy (2000) 'String musicians in the recording studios of Memphis, Tennessee' in *Popular Music*, vol. 19, no. 2, pp. 201–17.
British Music Education Yearbook (2000), ed. Louise Head, London: Rhinegold.
British Phonographic Industries (1998) *BPI Statistical Handbook*, London: British Phonographic Industry.
Brooks, W. (1982) 'On being tasteless', *Popular Music Yearbook* 2, Cambridge: Cambridge University Press, pp. 9–18.
Bruce, Rosemary and Kemp, Anthony (1993) 'Sex-stereotyping in children's preference for musical instruments', *British Journal of Music Education*, vol. 10, no. 3.
Burnard, Pamela (2000a) 'Examining experiential differences between improvisation and composition in children's music-making, *British Journal of Music Education*, vol. 17, no. 3.
————— (2000b) 'How children ascribe meaning to improvisation and composition: rethinking pedagogy in music education', *Music Education Research*, vol. 2, no. 1, pp. 7–23.
Burnett, Michael (1972) 'Coming to terms with pop', articles 1–9, *Music Teacher*, vol. 51, no. 2 (Feb.) to vol. 51, no. 10 (Oct.).
Byrne, Charles and Sheridan, Mark (2000) 'The long and winding road: the story of rock music in Scottish schools', *International Journal of Music Education*, no. 36, pp. 46–58.
Campbell, Patricia Shehan (1991a) 'The child-song genre: a comparison of songs by and for children', *International Journal of Music Education*, vol. 17, no. 1, pp. 14–23.
————— (1991b) *Lessons from the World: A Cross-cultural Guide to Music Teaching and Learning*, New York: Schirmer Books.
————— (1995) 'Of garage bands and song-getting: the musical development of young rock musicians', *Research Studies in Music Education*, no. 4, June, pp. 12–20.
————— (1998) *Songs in Their Heads: Music and its Meaning in Children's Lives*, New York: Oxford University Press.
Castle, Charles (1974) *Noël*, London: Abacus.
Clawson, Mary Ann (1999a) 'Masculinity and skill acquisition in the adolescent rock band', *Popular Music*, vol. 18, no. 1, pp. 99–115.
————— (1999b) 'When women play the bass: instrumental specialisation and gender interpretation in alternative rock music', *Gender and Society*, vol. 13, no. 2, pp. 193–210.
Cohen, Sara (1991) *Rock Culture in Liverpool*, Oxford: Oxford University Press.

Cope, Peter (1998) 'Knowledge, meaning and ability in musical instrument playing', *British Journal of Music Education*, vol. 15, no. 3, pp. 263–70.

————— (1999) 'Community-based traditional fiddling as a basis for increasing participation in instrument play', *Music Education Research*, vol. 1, no. 1, pp. 61–73.

Cope, Peter and Smith, H. (1997) 'Cultural context in musical instrumental learning', *British Journal of Music Education*, vol. 14, no. 3, pp. 283–9.

Cutietta, Robert (1991), 'Popular music: an ongoing challenge', *Music Educators Journal*, vol. 77, no. 8, pp. 26–9.

Dane, Cliff and Laing, Dave (1998) 'The UK music industry: some recent developments', *Cultural Trends*, no. 31, pp. 3–23.

Davidson, Jane, Howe, Michael, Moore, D. G. and Sloboda, John (1996) 'The role of parental influences in the development of musical ability', *British Journal of Developmental Psychology*, no. 14, pp. 399–412.

Davidson, Jane, Sloboda, John, Moore, D. G. and Howe, Michael (1988) 'Characteristics of music teachers and the progress of young instrumentalists', *Journal of Research in Music Education*, no. 46.1, pp. 141–60.

Davidson, Jane and Smith, Jonathan (1997) 'A case study of "newer practices"' in music education at conservatoire level', *British Journal of Music Education*, vol. 14, no. 3, pp. 251–69.

Davies, John B. (1994) 'Seeds of a false consciousness', *The Psychologist*, vol. 7, no. 7, July.

Delzell, Judith K. (1994) 'Variables affecting the gender-role stereotyping of high school band teaching positions', *Quarterly Journal of Music Teaching and Learning*, vol. 4, no. 4/vol. 5, no. 1.

Dennis, Brian (1970) *Experimental Music in Schools*, Oxford: Oxford University Press.

Department of Education And Science (DES) (1986) *GCSE: The National Criteria*, DES.

————— (DES) (1992) *Music in the National Curriculum (England)*, London: HMSO, (April).

Department for Education (DFE) (1995) *Music in the National Curriculum (England)*, DFE.

Downes, Graham (2000) 'Technique vs. ideas in popular music curricula – letting the client decide' in Martin Isherwood (ed.) *Interactive 2000: Current Issues in Teaching Popular Music in Higher Education*, Proceedings of the conference, Liverpool Institute of Performing Arts, January, LIPA (www.lipa.ac.uk).

Drumbreck, Alan (2000) *Music Education Directory*, British Phonographic Industries: Ariadne Publications.

Dunbar-Hall, Peter (1996) 'Designing a teaching model for popular music' in Gary Spruce (ed.) *Teaching Music*, London and New York: Routledge in association with the Open University.

————— (2000) 'Concept or context? Teaching and learning Balinese Gamelan and the universalist-pluralist debate', *Music Education Research*, vol. 2, no. 2, pp. 127–39.

Dunbar-Hall, Peter and Wemyss, Kathryn (2000) 'The effects of the study of popular music on music education', *International Journal of Music Education*, no. 36, pp. 23–35.

Ehrlich, Cyril (1985) *The Music Profession in Britain Since the Eighteenth Century: A Social History*, Oxford: Clarendon Press.

Elliott, David (1989) 'Key concepts in multicultural music education', *International Journal of Music Education*, no. 13, pp. 11–18.

———— (1990) 'Music as culture: toward a multicultural concept of arts education', *Journal of Aesthetic Education*, vol. 24, no. 1, pp. 147–66.

———— (1995) *Music Matters: A New Philosophy of Music Education*, Oxford: Oxford University Press.

Epstein, Jonathon (ed.) (1995) *Adolescents and Their Music: If It's Too Loud, You're Too Old*, New York and London: Garland.

Everitt, Anthony (1997) *Joining In: An Investigation into Participatory Music*, London: Calouste Gulbenkian Foundation.

Farmer, Paul (1976) 'Pop music in the secondary school: a justification', *Music in Education*, vol. 40, no. 381.

Farrell, Gerry (1990) *Indian Music in Education*, Cambridge: Cambridge University Press.

Finnegan, Ruth (1989) *The Hidden Musicians: Music-Making in an English Town*, Cambridge: Cambridge University Press.

Finney, John (1987) 'An investigation into the learning process of a group of rock musicians', unpublished MA dissertation, University of Reading.

Floyd, M. (ed.) (1996) *World Musics in Education*, Aldershot: Scholar Press.

Ford, Charlie (1995) 'Free collective improvisation in higher education', *British Journal of Music Education*, vol. 12, no. 2, pp. 103–12.

Fornäs, Johan (1995) *Cultural Theory and Late Modernity*, London: Sage.

Frith, Simon (1983) *Sound Effects: Youth, Leisure, and the Politics of Rock'n'Roll*, London: Constable.

———— (1992) 'The study of popular music' in Lawrence Grossberg, Cary Nelson and Paula Treichler (eds) *Cultural Studies*, New York, London: Routledge, pp. 174–82.

———— (1996) *Performing Rites: On the Value of Popular Music*, Oxford: Oxford University Press.

Gaar, Gillian G. (1993) *She's a Rebel: The History of Women in Rock and Roll*, London: Blandford.

Gagné, François (1999) 'Nature or nurture? A re-examination of Sloboda and Howe's (1991) interview study on talent development in music', *Psychology of Music*, no. 27, pp. 38–51.

Gammon, Vic (1981) 'Babylonian performances' in Eileen Yeo and Stephen Yeo (eds) *Popular Culture and Class Conflict, 1540–1914*, Brighton: Harvester Press.

———— (1999) 'Cultural politics of the English National Curriculum for Music, 1991–1992', *Journal of Educational Administration and History*, vol. 31, no. 2, pp. 130–47.

Glover, Joanna (2000) *Children composing, 4–14*, Brighton: Falmer Press.

Gomes, Celson Henrique Sousa (2000) 'The street musicians of Porto Alegre – a study based on life stories', *International Journal of Music Education*, no. 35, pp. 24–8.

Green, Lucy (1984) 'The reproduction of musical ideology', unpublished D.Phil. thesis, University of Sussex.

———— (1988) *Music On Deaf Ears: Musical Meaning, Ideology and Education*, Manchester and New York: Manchester University Press.

———— (1990) 'The assessment of composition: style and experience', *British Journal of Music Education,* vol. 7, no. 3, pp. 191–6.

———— (1997) *Music, Gender, Education*, Cambridge: Cambridge University Press.

———— (2000) 'On the evaluation and assessment of music as a media art' in Rebecca Sinker and Julian Sefton-Green (eds) *Evaluation Issues in Media Arts Production*, London: Routledge.

———— (2002) 'From the Western classics to the world: secondary music teachers' changing attitudes in England, 1982 and 1998' in *British Journal of Music Education*, vol. 19, no. 2.

Hallam, Susan (1997a) 'Approaches to instrumental music practice of experts and novices: implications for education' in H. Jorgensen and A. Lehman (eds) *Does Practice make Perfect? Current Theory and Research on Instrumental Music Practice*, Oslo: NMH-publikasjoner.

———— (1997b) 'What do we know about practising?' in H. Jorgensen and A. Lehman (eds) *Does Practice make Perfect? Current Theory and Research on Instrumental Music Practice*, Oslo: NMH-publikasjoner.

———— (1998) *Instrumental Teaching: A Practical Guide to Better Teaching and Learning*, London: Heinemann.

Hancox, G (1982) 'Music education and industry' in John Paynter (ed.) *Music in the Secondary School Curriculum*, Cambridge: Cambridge University Press.

Hanley, Betty and Montgomery, Janet (forthcoming) 'Contemporary curriculum practices and their theoretical base' in Richard Colwell and C. P. Richardson (eds) *Second Handbook of Research on Music Teaching and Learning*, New York: Oxford University Press.

Hardy, Phil and Laing, Dave (1990) *The Faber Companion to 20th-Century Popular Music*, London, Boston: Faber and Faber.

Hargreaves David (1994) 'Musical education for all', *The Psychologist*, vol. 7, no. 7, July.

———— (1999) 'A psychologist's response to Sawyer', *Psychology of Music*, vol. 27 no. 2.

Harker, Dave (1985) *Fakesong: The Manufacture of British 'Folksong', 1700 to the Present Day*, Milton Keynes and Philadelphia: Open University Press.

Harvey, Eddie (1988) *Jazz in the Classroom*, London: Boosey and Hawkes.

Harwood, Eve (1998a) 'Learning in context: a playground tale', *Research Studies in Music Education*, no. 11, pp. 52–61.

———— (1998b) '"Go on girl!" Improvisation in African-American girls' singing games', in Bruno Nettl and Melinda Russell (eds) *In the Course of Performance: Studies in the World of Musical Improvisation*, Chicago: University of Chicago Press, pp. 113–26.

Hennessy, Sarah (2000) 'Overcoming the red-feeling: the development of confidence to teach music in primary schools amongst students teachers', *British Journal of Music Education*, vol. 17, no. 2, pp. 183–97.

Herbert, David G. and Campbell, Patricia Shehan (2000) 'Rock music in American schools: positions and practices since the 1960s', *International Journal of Music Education*, no. 36, pp. 14–23.

Her Majesty's Inspectorate (HMI) (1985) *Music 5–15*, London: HMSO.

Herskovitz, Melville (1948), *Man and His Works*, New York: Alfred A. Knopf.

Ho, Wai-chung (1996) 'Hong Kong secondary music education: a sociological enquiry', unpublished Ph.D. thesis, London University Institute of Education.

Horn, Kipps (1984) 'Rock music-making as a work model in community music workshops', *British Journal of Music Education*, vol. 1, no. 2, pp. 111–35.

International Federation of Phonographic Industries (2000) *The Recording Industry in Numbers*, IFPI.

Isherwood, Martin (ed.) (2000) *Interactive 2000: Current Issues in Teaching Popular Music in Higher Education*, Proceedings of the conference, Liverpool Institute of Performing Arts, January, LIPA (www.lipa.ac.uk).

Jorgensen H. and Lehmann, A. C. (eds) (1997) *Does Practice make Perfect? Current Theory and Research on Instrumental Music Practice*, Oslo: NMH-publikasjoner.

Jost, Ekkehard (1994) *Free jazz,* New York: Da Capo Press (a republication of the edition published in Graz, Austria in 1974).

Jones, Mike (2000) 'How can I go forward when I don't know which way I'm facing?' in Martin Isherwood (ed.) *Interactive 2000: Current Issues in Teaching Popular Music in Higher Education*, Proceedings of the conference, Liverpool Institute of Performing Arts, January, LIPA (www.lipa.ac.uk).

Kenyon, Nicholas (ed.) (1988) *Authenticity and Early Music: A Symposium*, Oxford: Oxford University Press.

Kingsbury, Henry (1988) *Music, Talent and Performance: A Conservatory Cultural System*, Philadelphia: Temple University Press.

Kirshner, Tony (1998) 'Studying rock: towards a materialist ethnography' in Thomas Swiss et al. (eds) *Mapping the Beat: Popular Music and Contemporary Theory*, Oxford: Basil Blackwell.

Koizumi, Kyoko (1998) 'Popular music as acquired capital: some problems in Japanese music education' in Toru Mitsui (ed.) *Popular Music: Intercultural Interpretations*, Proceedings of the International Association for the Study of Popular Music International Conference, Kanazawa 1998; published by the Graduate Program in Music, Kanazawa University.

———— (2002) 'Popular music, gender and high school pupils in Japan: personal music in school and leisure sites' in *Popular Music*, vol. 22, no. 1.

Kwami, Robert (1989) 'African music, education and the school curriculum', unpublished Ph.D. thesis, London University Institute of Education.

———— (1996) 'Music education in and for a multi-cultural society', in Charles Plummeridge (ed.) *Issues in Music Education II*, London University Institute of Education.

Lamont, Alexandra (forthcoming) 'Musical identities and the school environment' in Raymond MacDonald, David Hargreaves and Dorothy Miell (eds) *Musical Identities*, Oxford: Oxford University Press.

Lave, Jean and Wenger, Ettienne (1991) *Situated Learning: Legitimate Peripheral Participation*, Cambridge: Cambridge University Press.

Lennon, Mary (1996) 'Teacher thinking: a qualitative approach to the study of piano teaching', unpublished Ph.D. thesis, London University Institute of Education.

Lilliestam, Lars (1995) *Gehörsmusik. Blues, rock och muntlig tradering* (Playing by ear. Blues, rock and oral transmission), Göteborg: Akademiförlaget Corona AB.

————— (1996) 'On playing by ear', *Popular Music*, vol. 15 no. 2, pp. 195–216.

Lloyd, A. L. (1967) *Folk Song in England*, London: Lawrence and Wishart.

Losseff, Nicky (1999) 'Kathy's homecoming and the Other world: Kate Bush's "Wuthering Heights"', *Popular Music*, vol. 18, no. 2, pp. 227–40.

Lundquist, B. and Szego, C. K. (1998) *Music of the World's Cultures: A Source Book for Music Educators*, International Society for Music Education.

McCarthy, Cameron, Hudak, Glenn, Miklaucic, Shawn and Saukko, Paula (eds) (1999) *Sound Identities: Popular Music and the Cultural Politics of Education*, New York, Frankfurt, Brussels, Vienna, Canterbury: Peter Lang.

McCarthy, Maree (1997) 'Irish music education and Irish identity: a concept revisited', *Oideas,* no. 45, Autumn, pp. 5–22, Dublin: Department of Education and Science.

————— (1999) *Passing it On: The Transmission of Music in Irish Culture*, Cork: Cork University Press.

MacDonald, Raymond and Miell, Dorothy (2000) 'Creativity and music education: the impact of social variables', *International Journal of Music Education*, no. 36, pp. 58–68.

Manuel, Peter (1988) *Popular Musics of the Non-Western World*, New York and Oxford: Oxford University Press.

Marsh, Kathryn (1995) 'Children's singing games: composition in the playground?', *Research Studies in Music Education*, no. 4, pp. 2–11.

————— (1999) 'Mediated orality: the role of popular music in the changing traditions of children's musical play' *Research Studies in Music Education*, no. 13, December.

Martin, Peter (1996) 'Improvisation in jazz: towards a sociological model', University of Manchester, Department of Sociology, Occasional Paper no. 45.

Maryprasith, Primrose (1999) 'The effects of globalisation and localisation on the status of music in Thailand', unpublished Ph.D. thesis, London University Institute of Education.

Mellers, Wilfred (1976) *Twilight of the Gods: The Beatles in Retrospect*, 2nd impression; first printing, 1973, London: Faber and Faber.

Merriam, Alan (1964) *The Anthropology of Music*, Chicago: North Western University Press.

Messenger, J. (1958) 'Esthetic talent', *Basic College Quarterly*, no. 4, pp. 20–24.

Middleton, Richard (1990) *Studying Popular Music*, Milton Keynes: Open University Press.

————— (ed.) (2000) *Reading Pop: Approaches to Textual Analysis in Popular Music*, Oxford: Oxford Univeristy Press.

Monson, Ingrid (1996) *Saying Something: Jazz Improvisation and Interaction*, Chicago and London: Chicago University Press.

Morgan, Louise, Hargreaves, David and Joiner, Richard (1997/8) 'How do children make music? Composition in small groups', *Early Childhood Connections*, Winter, pp. 15–21.

Moore, Allan (1992) 'Patterns of harmony', *Popular Music*, vol,. 11, no. 1, pp. 73–106.

————— (1993) *Rock: The Primary Text*, Buckingham: Open University Press.

————— (1998) 'U2 and the myth of authenticity in rock', *Popular Musicology*, no. 3, pp. 5–33.

Music Educators' Journal (1969), vol. 55 and (1991), vol. 77: special issues on popular music and education.

National Foundation for Educational Research (2000), *Arts Education in Secondary Schools*, London: Royal Society for the Arts.

National Music Council (1996) *The Value of Music: A Report into the Value of the UK Music Industry*, London: NMC in association with the University of Westminster.

———— (1999a) *A Sound Performance: The Economic Value of Music to the United Kingdom*, London: NMC.

———— (1999b) *A Sound Performance: A Commentary,* London: NMC.

Negus, Keith (1999) *Music Genres and Corporate Cultures,* London and New York: Routledge.

Nettl, Bruno (1983) *The Study of Ethnomusicology: Twenty-nine Issues and Concepts*, Urbana and Chicago: University of Illinois Press.

———— (1995) *Heartland Excursions: Ethnomusicolgocial Reflections on Schools of Music*, Urbana: University of Illinois Press.

Nettl, Bruno and Russell, Melinda (eds) (1998) *In the Course of Performance: Studies in the World of Musical Improvisation*, Chicago: University of Chicago Press.

Newsom, Daniel (1998) 'Rock's quarrel with tradition: popular music's carnival comes to the classroom', *Popular Music and Society*, vol. 22, no. 3, pp. 1–20.

Nicholls, Malcolm (1976) 'Running an "open" music department' in Graham Vulliamy en Ed Lee (eds) *Pop Music in School*, Cambridge: Cambridge University Press.

Nketia, J. H. K. (1975) *The Music of Africa*, London: Gollancz.

Noble, Keith Allan (1995) *The International Education Quotations Encyclopaedia*, Buckingham, Philadelphia: Open University Press.

Nwezi, Meki (1999) 'Strategies for music education in Africa: towards a meaningful progression from traditional to modern', *International Journal of Music Education*, no. 33, pp. 72–87.

O'Brien, Karen (1995) *Hymn to Her: Women Musicians Talk*, London: Virago.

O'Brien, Lucy (1994) *She Bop: The Definitive History of Women in Rock, Pop and Soul*, London: Penguin.

Oehrle, Elizabeth (1991) 'An introduction to African views of music making', *Journal of Aesthetic Education*, vol. 25, no. 3, Fall, pp. 163–73.

Oliveira, Alda de (2000) 'Street kids in Brazil and the concept of teaching structures', *International Journal of Music Education*, no. 35, pp. 29–34.

O'Neill, Susan (1997a) 'The role of practice in children's early musical performance achievement' in H. Jorgensen and A. C. Lehmann (eds) *Does Practice make Perfect? Current Theory and Research on Instrumental Music Practice*, Oslo: NMH-publikasjoner, pp. 53–70.

———— (1997b) 'Gender and music' in D. J. Hargreaves and A. C. North (eds) *The Social Psychology of Music*, Oxford: Oxford Univeristy Press, pp. 46–63.

———— (forthcoming a) 'Self-identity of young performing musicians' in Raymond MacDonald, David Hargreaves and Dorothy Miell (eds) *Musical Identities*, Oxford: Oxford University Press.

———— (forthcoming b) 'Exploring the identity and subjectivity of "talented" adolescent female musicians', *Feminism and Psychology*.

Paynter, John and Aston, Peter (1970) *Sound and Silence: Classroom Projects in Creative Music,* Cambridge: Cambridge University Press.

Peters, R. S. (1978) *Ethics and Education*, 6th impression, London: Unwin.

Pitts, Stephanie, Davidson, Jane and McPherson, Gary (2000) 'Developing effective practise strategies: case studies of three young instrumentalists', *Music Education Research*, vol. 2, no. 1, pp. 45–56.

Polanyi, M. (1967) *The Tacit Dimension*, London: Routledge.

Radford, John (1994) 'Variations on a musical theme' in *The Psychologist*, vol. 7, no. 7, pp. 359–60.

Rainbow, Bernarr (1989) *Music in Educational Thought and Practice*, Aberystwyth: Boethius Press.

Research Studies in Music Education (1999), special issue on popular music in education, no. 13, December.

Research Surveys of Great Britain Ltd (1991) *RSGB Omnibus Arts Survey: Report on a Survey on Arts and Cultural Activities in GB*, London: Arts Council of Great Britain.

Russell, David (1997) *Popular Music in England, 1840–1914: A Social History*, 2nd edition, Manchester and New York: Manchester University Press.

Russell, Philip (1997) 'Musical tastes and society' in David Hargreaves and Adrian North (eds) *The Social Psychology of Music*, Oxford: Oxford University Press.

Sawyer, Keith (1999) 'Improvised conversations: music, collaboration and development', *Psychology of Music*, vol. 27 no. 2.

Schafer, R. Murray (1967) *Ear Cleaning: Notes for an Experimental Music Course*, New York: Associated Music Publishers.

School Curriculum And Assessment Authority (SCAA) (1995) GCSE Regulations and Criteria, SCAA Ref. KS4/95/269.

Scott, Derek, Dewhurst, Robin and Warner, Tim (2000) 'Project pop' in Martin Isherwood (ed.) *Interactive 2000: Current Issues in Teaching Popular Music in Higher Education*, Proceedings of the conference, Liverpool Institute of Performing Arts, January, LIPA (www.lipa.ac.uk).

Scruton, Roger (1996) 'Place of the sacred', review of Simon Frith, *Performing Rites: On the Value of Popular Music*, *The Times*, October.

———— (1998) *The Aesthetics of Music*, Oxford: Oxford University Press.

Self, George (1967) *New Sounds in Class*, London: Universal Edition.

Shepherd, John and Vulliamy, Graham (1994) 'The struggle for culture: a sociological case study of the development of a national music curriculum', *British Journal of the Sociology of Education*, 15/1.

Sloboda, John (1985) *The Musical Mind: The Cognitive Psychology of Music*, Oxford: Oxford University Press.

———— (1999) 'Music – where cognition and emotion meet', *The Psychologist*, vol. 12, no. 9, pp. 450–55.

Sloboda, John and Davidson, Jane (1996) 'The young performing musician' in F. Deliège and John Sloboda (eds) *Musical Beginnings: Origins and Development of Musical Competence*, Oxford: Oxford University Press.

Sloboda, John, Davidson, Jane and Howe, Michael (1994) 'Is everyone musical?', *The Psychologist*, August, pp. 349–54.

Sloboda, John, Davidson, Jane, Howe, Michael and Moore, D. G. (1996) 'The role of practice in the development of performing musicians, *British Journal of Psychology*, no. 87, pp. 287–309.

Sloboda, John and Howe, Michael (1991) 'Biographical precursors of musical excellence: an interview study', *Psychology of Music*, No. 19, pp. 3–21.

————— (1999) 'Musical talent and individual differences in musical achievement: a reply to Gagné, *Psychology of Music* no. 27, pp. 52–4.

Small, Christopher (1980) *Music – Society – Education*, London: John Calder.

————— (1983) 'The vernacular in music education', *Educational Analysis*, 5, pp. 65–75.

————— (1985) 'No meaning without rules' in Association of Improvising Musicians, *Improvisation: History, Directions, Practice*, London: Association of Improvising Musicians.

————— (1987) *Music of the Common Tongue*, London: John Calder.

Spencer, Piers (1993) 'GCSE Music: a survey of undergraduate opinion', *British Journal of Music Education*, vol. 10, no. 1, pp. 73–84.

Stålhammer, Börje (2000) 'The spaces of music and its foundation of values – music teaching and young people's own music experience', *International Journal of Music Education*, no. 36, pp. 35–46.

Stock, Jonathan (1991) 'A case for world music', *British Journal of Music Education*, vol. 8, no. 2, pp. 102–18.

————— (1996) 'Concepts of world music and their integration within western secondary music education' in Gary Spruce (ed.) *Teaching Music*, London and New York: Routledge in association with the Open University.

Stolzoff, Norman (2000) *Wake the Town and Tell the People: Dancehall Culture in Jamaica*, Durham, NC: Duke University Press.

Sudnow, David (1993) *Ways of the Hand: The Organization of Improvised Conduct*, Cambridge, Mass.: MIT Press.

Swanwick, Keith (1968) *Popular Music and the Teacher*, Oxford: Pergamon Press.

————— (1979) *A Basis for Music Education*, London: NFER Publishing Company.

————— (1984a), 'Problems of a sociological approach to pop music in schools', *British Journal of Sociology of Education*, vol. 5, no. 1.

————— (1984b) 'A further note on sociology of music education', *British Journal of Sociology of Education*, vol. 5, no. 3.

————— (1988) *Music, Mind and Education*, London: Routledge.

————— (1992) *Music Education and the National Curriculum*, The London File: Papers from the Institute of Education, London: The Tufnell Press.

————— (1994) *Musical Knowledge: Intuition, Analysis and Music Education*, London: Routledge.

Swiss, Thomas, Sloop, John and Herman, Andrew (1998) *Mapping the Beat: Popular Music and Contemporary Theory*, Oxford, Malden: Basil Blackwell.

Tagg, Philip (1998) 'The Göteborg connection: lessons in the history and politics of popular music education and research', *Popular Music*, vol. 17, no. 2.

Tate, Nicholas (1996) Speech, reported in *The Times* in an article entitled 'Schools must not blur culture boundary, says syllabus chief' by David Charter, 8 February, p. 18.

Thornton, Sarah (1995) *Club Cultures: Music, Media and Subcultural Capital*, London: Polity Press.

Torff, Bruce and Winner Ellen (1994) 'Don't throw out the baby with the bath water', *The Psychologist*, vol. 7, no. 7, July.

Toynbee, Jason (2000) *Making Popular Music. Musicians, Creativity and Institutions*, London: Arnold.

Volk, Therese (1998) *Music, Education, and Multiculturalism: Foundations and Principles*, New York: Oxford University Press.

Vulliamy, Graham (1977a) 'Music and the mass culture debate' in John Shepherd, Paul Virden, Trevor Wishart and Graham Vulliamy (eds) *Whose Music: A Sociology of Musical Language*, London: Latimer New Dimensions.

———— (1977b) 'Music as a case study in the "new sociology of education"', in John Shepherd, Paul Virden, Trevor Wishart and Graham Vulliamy (eds) *Whose Music: A Sociology of Musical Language*, London: Latimer New Dimensions.

Vulliamy, Graham and Lee, Ed (eds) (1976) *Pop Music in School*, Cambridge: Cambridge University Press.

———— (eds) (1982) *Pop, Rock and Ethnic Music in School*, Cambridge: Cambridge University Press.

Vulliamy, Graham and Shepherd, John (1984a) 'The application of a critical sociology to music education', *British Journal of Music Education*, vol. 1, no. 3.

———— (1984b) 'Sociology and music education: a response to Swanwick', *British Journal of Sociology of Education*, vol. 5., no. 1.

———— (1985) 'Sociology and music education: a further response to Swanwick', *British Journal of Sociology of Education*, vol. 6, no. 2.

Walser, Robert (1993) *Running with the Devil: Power, Gender and Madness in Heavy Metal Music*, Hanover and London: Wesleyan University Press.

Welch, Graham (1999) 'Education and musical improvisation: a response to Sawyer', *Psychology of Music*, vol. 27 no. 2.

Wemyss, Kathryn L. (1999) 'From T. I. to Tasmania: Australian indigenous popular music in the curriculum', *Research Studies in Music Education,* no. 13, December.

Westerlund, Heidi (1999) 'Universalism against contextual thinking in multicultural music education – Western colonialism or pluralism?', *International Journal of Music Education*, no. 33, pp. 94–103.

Wiggins, Trevor (1996) 'The world of music in education', *British Journal of Music Education*, vol. 13, no. 1, pp. 21–30.

Willis, Paul (1978) *Profane Culture*, London: Routledge and Kegan Paul.

Wulstan, David (1985) *Tudor Music*, Oxford: Oxford University Press.

York, Norton (1992) 'Pop music education in the '90s', *Music Teacher*, March.

———— (1993) 'Grand Union Orchestra receive prestigious award', *Music Teacher*, August.

York, Norton and Pitt, S. (1992) *Pop Goes to College: Pop Music Education in the UK*, London.

Zillman, D. and Gan, S. (1997) 'Musical taste in adolescence' in David Hargreaves and Adrian North (eds), *The Social Psychology of Music*, Oxford: Oxford University Press.

Index